Understanding
Abusive Families

Understanding Abusive Families

James Garbarino
Gwen Gilliam
Boys Town Center for the Study
of Youth Development

LexingtonBooks
D.C. Heath and Company
Lexington, Massachusetts
Toronto

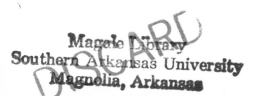

Library of Congress Cataloging in Publication Data

Garbarino, James.
    Understanding abusive families.

    1. Child Abuse—United States. 2. Child molesting—United States.
3. Youth—United States—Family relationships. 4. Youth—United
States—Crimes against. 5. Human ecology. I. Gilliam, Gwen, joint
author.
II. Title.
HV741.G37   362.8'2   79-47983
ISBN 0-669-03621-8

Third printing, December 1981

Published simultaneously in Canada.

Printed in the United States of America.

International Standard Book Number: 0-669-03621-8

Library of Congress Catalog Card Number: 79-47983

To Josh and Nate

Contents

List of Figures and Tables   xi

Preface   xiii

Part I   *The Human Ecology of Child Maltreatment*
                James Garbarino   1

Chapter 1   **Introduction**   3

                The Meaning of Mistreatment   3
                Problems with the Definition of Abuse   5
                Definition of Abuse   7
                Conclusion   14

Chapter 2   **A Look at the World of Abnormal Rearing**   19

                Origins of Child Maltreatment   19
                A Systems Approach to Sociocultural Risk   23
                The Human Ecology of Child Maltreatment   28
                Lives out of Control   30
                Necessary Conditions for Child Abuse   31

Chapter 3   **Social Isolation as the Price of Privacy**   41

                Stress and Social Support   42
                Privacy Sparks Maltreatment   45
                What Can Be Done?   47

Chapter 4   **Becoming a Parent and Creating a Family**   51

                Being Born   51
                The Psychology of Being Born   53
                Becoming Attached   56
                Birth as a Social Event   59

Chapter 5   **The Elusive Crime of Psychological Maltreatment** 67

                Emotional Abuse   67
                Emotional Abuse in the Lives of Children   70
                Toward an Actionable Definition   72
                Four Aspects of Psychological Abuse   74

Chapter 6   **The Community Context of Child Abuse and Neglect** 79

Chapter 7   **The Role of Schools in Child Maltreatment**   97

                 Issues for Schools as Part of the Human Ecology of
                     Child Maltreatment   98
                 Schools Can Help   101

Part II   *The Maltreatment of Youth*   James Garbarino and
                 Gwen Gilliam, in consultation with Michael Cohen,
                 Bruce Fisher, Robert Friedman, Peter Giannini,
                 Ira Lourie, and Norman Polansky   109

Chapter 8   **The Mistreatment of Youth**   111

                 Child Maltreatment as a Developmental Issue   111
                 Wives and Teenagers as Victims   113
                 An Empirical Introduction to Adolescent Abuse   116
                 Child- versus Adolescent-Abuse Cases   116

Chapter 9   **Patterns of Abuse**   125

                 Four Abusive Patterns   125
                 Two Contrasting Sets of Circumstances   127
                 Implications   132

Chapter 10   **Family Stress and Adolescent Abuse**   135

                 Adolescence   135
                 Parental Adaptation   141
                 The Adolescent Role in American Society   145
                 Families in Flotation   146

Chapter 11   **Sexual Abuse: A Special Case?**   151

                 Incidence   152
                 Domestic Sexual Abuse   153

Chapter 12   **Youth in Trouble Are Youth Who Have Been Hurt**   167

                 Different Effects   167
                 Adolescent Abuse as a Social Issue   184

Chapter 13   **The Teenager as Victim**   191

                 Images of Victims   191
                 The Family in Law and Custom   194
                 Inadequate Services   196

	Alternative Options	198
	Mistreatment and the Status Offense	202
	The Institutional End	203
	No Place to Turn	206
Chapter 14	**Conclusion**	213
	Meeting the Needs of Mistreated Children and Youth	213
	The Maze of Maltreatment	214
	Evidence of Progress	215
	Resources for Protecting Children and Youth	217
	Bringing the Developmental Perspective to Fruition	236
	Hope for the Future	242
Appendix A:	**Sources for Materials on Child and Adolescent Maltreatment**	249
Appendix B:	**Maltreatment of Youth Project Materials**	251
	Index	253
	About the Contributors	265
	About the Authors	267

List of Figures
and Tables

Figures

6–1	Actual and Predicted Rates of Total Child Maltreatment	87
8–1	Subjects Receiving AFDC, by Age	117
8–2	Parental Unemployment, by Age of Victim	118
8–3	Parental Marital Status, by Age of Victim	118
8–4	Source of Report, by Age of Victim	119
8–5	Severity of Maltreatment, by Age of Victim	120
8–6	Percentage Reporting Sexual Abuse, by Age	121
8–7	Out-of-Home Placement, by Age of Victim	122
9–1	Marital Status, by Percentage of Total Victims of Each Age Group	128
9–2	Percentage of Recent Relocation, by Age	128
9–3	Percentage of Services Provided to Different Types of Victims, by Age	129
9–4	Family Income, by Age of Victim	129
9–5	Percentage of Parental History of Abuse, by Age	130
9–6	Parent Alleged Perpetrator, by Age of Victim	131

Tables

6–1	Comparison of Two Discrepant Subareas Designated High and Low Risk for Child Maltreatment	88
6–2	Profiles of Social Life in Two Neighborhoods	90
6–3	The Child's Social Resources	92
6–4	Stresses: Demands for Social Readjustment	92
6–5	Maternal Ratings of Family Stresses and Supports	93

Preface

This book presents an ecological and developmental perspective on the mal-treatment of children and adolescents. As a perspective book, it seeks to develop and present a particular view of maltreatment, one that we believe will shed light on prevention, protection, and rehabilitation. Our goal is to tell the story of abusive families in a way that will humanize and normalize them. We seek to make them and the things that go on inside them more comprehensible. We believe that this is best accomplished by looking at them ecologically and developmentally, through their interactions with the social environment and through their changing character. The title of the book reflects both the per-spective approach and our goal.

Developmentalist Urie Bronfenbrenner, in *The Ecology of Human Develop-ment,* most fully developed the ecological perspective that is the root of our approach. This perspective sets the individual's development within a network of environmental systems, which "is conceived as a set of nested structures, each inside the next, like a set of Russian dolls." It takes seriously the implications for the development of scientific theory and empirical work of the commonly accepted assertion that "human development is a product of interaction between the growing human organism and its environment." This ecological perspective is outlined in chapter 2 and is the foundation for the ideas presented in the rest of the book.

Because of our developmental focus, we have explored the way the dynamics of abuse shift from infancy to childhood to adolescence. Causes, correlates, and effects vary as a function of developmental factors. The relevance of some social systems increases as the child grows into adolescence, while the relevance of others decreases. This shifting balance of forces reflects the social scope and competence of the individual child as well as the social history of the family. We think that understanding these shifting forces, both inside and outside the parent-child relationship, is an important but thus far underdeveloped enter-prise. We seek to fill this gap.

To understand the purpose of this book, it is important to know what the book is not, as well as what it is. It is not a discussion of clinical practice or the principles of psychotherapy as they apply to domestic violence. It is not a guide to the use of applied behavioral analysis (or behavior modification) in assessing and changing the patterns of interactions between abusive parents and their children. It is not a clinical treatment of child abuse and neglect as we ordinarily use the term *clinical.* Few clinical studies are cited, and there is little discussion of either the rationale or mechanics of counseling and therapy techniques. In-deed, there is little discussion of treatment, if by treatment one means the application of some sort of psychological medicine in the form of counseling or psychotherapy. The fact that many if not most readers would assume that such a book deals with the dynamics of personality highlights the need for this book.

This book looks at maltreatment across levels of social systems (from the microsystem to the macrosystem) and across ages (from infancy through adolescence). It is not a comprehensive review of research and theory dealing with abuse and neglect, however. There is very little objective weighing of the evidence in the form of "X reports this, but his results were not supported in a study by Y; however, their method differed, so we do not yet know if the difference is generalizable to all such groups." Excellent reviews of child-abuse and neglect research and theory already exist, and we have cited them in our discussion. This, however, is a perspective book.

We have worked out our perspective in the following manner. We begin with an introduction to the meaning of mistreatment that emphasizes the joint role of culture and science in defining norms for child care. We then consider the abuse and neglect of children (birth to age 11) in part I. Chapter 1 defines abuse. Chapter 2 presents our ecological perspective and uses it to explore the world of abnormal rearing. Chapter 3 examines the link between our individualistic culture and the problem of social isolation that underlies child maltreatment and cripples our efforts to help. Chapter 4 looks at the roots of social isolation in the alienating and alienated circumstances of modern childbirth. We highlight this connection by outlining the alternative, socially integrating family-centered childbirth. In chapter 5 we explore the elusive crime of psychological mistreatment and focus on threats to competence as the organizing principle. Chapter 6 presents our analysis of the community context of child maltreatment and relies heavily on Garbarino's research on high-risk neighborhoods as a factor in abuse and neglect. Finally, in chapter 7 we look at how schools' dealing with child maltreatment is a barometer of the overall effectiveness of the caring community.

We built part I on the very diverse and substantial body of research-based knowledge about child abuse and neglect. In part II, where we deal with adolescent victims, we have much less to go on. This relative lack of empirical documentation is a serious problem with any analysis of adolescent abuse and neglect. We have gone ahead anyway, using the limited data directly relevant, while drawing on a wide range of collateral research on adolescence.

Chapter 8 introduces the special issues facing us in dealing with the abuse and neglect of adolescents. In chapter 9 we report the results of our own study comparing adolescent- and child-abuse cases. Chapter 10 places the mistreatment of youth in social, cultural, and historical context. We concentrate on the human ecology of adolescence and the balance of stresses and supports affecting family life. In chapter 11 we consider the complex and difficult issue of sexual abuse. Chapter 12 explores the connections between antisocial and self-destructive behavior on the one hand, and adolescent abuse and neglect on the other. In chapter 13, we present what we believe are compelling reasons for a more sympathetic view of and response to the teenager as victim.

In chapter 14 we bring together our thinking about the maltreatment of children and youth into what we believe is a coherent strategy for helping. We think the fruit of our ecological perspective on maltreatment suggests some new tools and some new arenas for intervention. We conclude that we can make progress in understanding and helping abusive families if we see how they are a product of our society as well as of their own special dynamics.

A perspective book such as this·draws heavily on what has been absorbed from colleagues, students, mentors, and those who have firsthand experiences with the phenomena being studied. In this case, the list of contributors is long and varied. Urie Bronfenbrenner has already been mentioned. We owe him a great intellectual debt. We also owe an intellectual debt to the people who advised us in the thinking that went into part I. Glen Elder, Ann Crouter, Deborah Sherman, and Mary Davis played a special role in chapters 2, 3, 4, 6, and 7. Susan Collins made a major contribution to chapter 6. Add to these our colleagues in the human-service community in Omaha, Nebraska, and Garbarino's students at the University of Nebraska's School of Social Work, where he served as an adjunct professor while working on this book. One of these students, Mary Fran Flood, played a special role by working with us in the final discussions of the manuscript. She made a special contribution to the book's concluding chapter, in both substance and organization.

Part II has a special history. It grew directly out of our work with the Maltreatment of Youth Project at the Boys Town Center for the Study of Youth Development. We set out to do what we could to improve the quality and quantity of our knowledge about adolescent abuse and to develop materials to communicate what we learned. To this end, we conducted research, held conferences and consultations, started some pilot programs, and produced posters and brochures. Part II is the culmination of these efforts. We enlisted the aid of some expert consultants and some local advisors who agreed to let us pick their brains for a good cause. Our thanks to advisors Michael Cohen, Bruce Fisher, Peter Giannini, Ira Lourie, Norman Polansky, and especially Robert Friedman. We appreciate the advisory role played by Gay Angel, Karen Authier, Eldon Davis, Dennis Harding, Barbara Jessing, Maggie Mundy, Alfred Thomas, and John Weeks. Center colleagues who contributed to this work include Barbara Carson, Shelley Leavitt, Nancy Jacobson, Bob McCall, and Holly Stocking. Anne Garbarino contributed her own special blend of literary acumen and constructive criticism. For their work on final editing, proofreading, and indexing we thank Margaret Plantz and Don Wright. For preparing the manuscript we thank Betsy Penke, Vickie Kuehn, Marilyn Pittillo, Dorothy Runte, and Mary Pat Roy. James Sweetland, Donna Richardson, Betty Schnase, and Ann Potter of the Center's Library Services Division provided invaluable research. For supporting the project we thank the first two directors of the Center for the Study of Youth Development, Ronald Feldman and Morton Weir. Most of all, however, we thank Tom Gregory, director of the Center's Research Use and Public

Service Division. His wise counsel and support never wavered. Finally, we express our appreciation to the teenage victims who were willing to share their painful experiences with us to help others like themselves. Their words have been integrated to form the representative composite quotations that appear throughout part II. This composite approach has been used in the interest of protecting their identities.

Part I
The Human Ecology of Child Maltreatment

James Garbarino

1 Introduction

The Meaning of Mistreatment

Dick Brown is a caseworker for the Child Welfare Department in a medium-sized city. At any one time he is responsible for investigating and managing more than 30 cases of child abuse and neglect. This includes deciding just how dangerous a particular family situation is and what the prospects are for improving the situation. On any given day he may be called upon to judge whether or not a 6-month-old is in danger of being murdered, a teenaged mother is able to care for her two children currently in foster care, or a father known to have sexually molested his 10-year-old stepdaughter has progressed enough in a counseling program to return home without threatening the girl again. In the course of his work he may be threatened by an irate father, bullied by a defense attorney, and worn to a frazzle by the demands placed on him. Like his coworkers, Dick faces a burnout problem and may not last more than a year in his current position.

Joan Higgins is a 23-year-old mother of three children, aged 5, 3, and 1. Her life is a bleak procession of work (as a waitress) and children, which she must face alone. She no longer lives with the children's father. She has few friends, and none who are doing much better than she is in coping with day-to-day life. Her money goes for rent, cigarettes, beer, and whatever food she buys for her family. Each of her children shows signs of neglect. Often unattended, they have the dull eyes of children whose emotional and physical diet is inadequate. They do not see a doctor regularly and have little contact with anyone outside the family. Joan often feels like giving up, and she sometimes does. On one such occasion, a neighbor called the police when the three children were left alone overnight with no food in the house. Much of the time she is lonely and apathetic; sometimes she is very angry. This is nothing new. Her life has been this way as long as she can remember.

Melinda Sue Jones is a 15-year-old runaway. She left home two weeks ago when things got so bad that she could not take it anymore. Her mother remarried four years ago, and Melinda Sue does not get along with her stepfather. To make sure she did not get into trouble, he was very strict with her at first. That was bad enough. Then last year things changed and suddenly he was really nice to her. He began to act funny, telling her to sit on his lap and accidentally walking into the bathroom when she was taking a bath. A few months ago, while her mother was out shopping, he came into her room and had sex with her. She told him she did not want to but he threatened to kill her if she refused or if she told anyone about it. So she did what he told her. It happened three more times before Melinda Sue ran away. She now is out on the street and living with a guy she met hitchhiking.

Bob Thompson is 16. When he was a kid his father spanked him and Bob behaved pretty well. When Bob got to be a teenager he started hanging out with a bunch of guys from school who had a reputation for being a bit wild. His father forbade him to go around with those punks (as he called them), but Bob said he would do what he pleased. His father beat him with a belt and his fists to teach him a lesson about "mouthing off." No more was said about Bob's friends after that until a couple of weeks later when Bob was picked up by the police for breaking into the school one night with his friends and hitting the janitor when he caught them. The assault charge means Bob is facing a one-year sentence to the state's Training School.

Dick, Joan, Melinda Sue, and Bob all are involved in the social problem we call the maltreatment of children and youth. How can we help Dick provide adequate service to his case load and handle the deluge of new reports, each requiring thorough investigation and indicating a situation that may present an immediate threat of death or permanent injury to a child? How can we help Joan get her life into better shape and provide more responsible care for her children? How can we reach Melinda Sue before she falls victim to further victimization out on the street? How can we put a stop to the chain of events in Bob's life in which escalating violence is going to land him in jail for assault? Where can we find the resources to deal with the problem of abuse and neglect?

Until fairly recently, there was little public awareness of the plight of abused and neglected young children. This has been largely rectified through the efforts of crusading pediatricians, social workers, judges, psychologists, journalists, politicians, and concerned private citizens. However, the general public and even many professionals remain unaware of the abuse and neglect experienced by adolescents despite the fact that nearly one in three cases reported to protective-service agencies around the country involves a teenage victim. Adolescent abuse has only begun the long and complicated process by which a social phenomenon comes to be labeled a social problem. The research base is meager, the policy issues cloudy, and the service needs generally unmet. In the case of child abuse, more than a decade of professional and public discussion and debate has failed to state adequately, let alone resolve, some of the basic issues concerning causation, public policy, and professional practice. We really do not understand abusive families.

Our goal here is to look anew at the maltreatment of children and youth and to clarify the issues of prevention and treatment in their broadest sense. We hope that our perspective will help in dealing with the old issues of child abuse and neglect in a useful and scientifically sound way. We will view maltreatment both developmentally (from infancy to adolescence) and ecologically (from the microsystem of the family to macrosystems of culture and institutions).

The first step in this process of clarification is to examine the meaning of maltreatment while retaining our developmental and ecological perspectives.

We use the general term *maltreatment* (an ugly but evocative word) to include the more common terms *abuse* and *neglect*. There is so much social significance attached to these terms that we feel we must make some use of them. But while we recognize the need for fine distinctions in terms for some purposes, for a general discussion we do not need such fine distinctions.[1] In exploring the matter we refer to several sources that treat abuse as the central concept (and issue), and we can begin there, knowing that later we will wish to insert neglect into the discussion and eventually come round to maltreatment (in the tradition of Vincent Fontana).[2]

Problems with the Definition of Abuse

Defining abuse is difficult. This difficulty should not stop us from examining the problem, however. There are many things in life that we cannot define precisely and yet deal with nonetheless. Lack of a precise definition of time does not prevent us from using our watches. Nor does our inability to produce a conclusive definition of love stop us from loving. Neither time nor love has been defined satisfactorily, yet each exists and supports a body of scientific evidence. So it is with abuse.[3] As one of the best analyses of child abuse concludes, "a variety of definitions of child abuse have been offered and none is free of ambiguities."[4]

The basic problem in defining abuse is that the meaning of most actions is determined by the environment in which they occur, including (1) the intention of the actor, (2) the act's effect upon the recipient, (3) an observer's value judgment about the act, and (4) the source of the standard for that judgment. These four elements—intentionality, effect, evaluation, and standards—are the fundamental issues in defining abuse.

One's first thought might be to define abuse as any behavior by a parent that results in injury to a child. The proof of abuse, according to this definition, is found in the effect of parental behavior upon the child. But does the fact that a child who is beaten and has escaped injury negate the abusiveness of the beating he or she suffered? So-called invulnerable children who thrive despite deprived childhoods would be exempt, no matter how they were treated.[5] Conversely, children who were injured accidentally through innocent parental actions would be classified as abused nonetheless.

This brings us to the issue of intention. Two pioneers in the treatment of child abuse include intentionality in their definition. They define abuse as "*nonaccidental* physical injury that results from acts of omissions on the part of parents or guardians."[6] But this definition in turn has problems. It still relies upon injury, but only considers physical injury. However, it represents an advance by stating that the parent need only intend to do the thing that causes the injury, and does not seem to require that the parent intend to harm the child. Thus one can be abusive because one is ignorant about the possible effects of one's behavior.

One might argue that force itself is abusive, even without specific physical injury. The researcher-theoretician David Gil suggests that the use of any physical force to hurt a child is abusive. In this view, abuse is intentional, nonaccidental use of force aimed at hurting, injuring, or destroying the child.[7] If one reads "causing pain" for "hurting," one sees that this definition would call spanking abuse, and then the term *abusive* might apply to most parents. In other words, a parent need not intend to injure a child in order to abuse him or her. It leads naturally to saying that any use of force against a child is abusive. Many researchers reject this definition on the grounds that it is too broad (and also perhaps because they cannot envision a practicable, nonviolent style of child rearing).[8] Yet many scholars believe that cultural support for the use of force against children is at the heart of the child-abuse problem.[9]

The next issue is the judgment made by an observer. Some investigators rely on community standards as the criteria of child abuse.[10] They define abuse as "nonaccidental physical injury as a result of acts (or omissions) on the part of parents or guardians *that violate the community's standards concerning the treatment of children.* (emphasis added)"[11] According to this view, those within the community can best interpret its norms and identify acts that violate those norms. Empirical evidence exists to support the view that though such standards do vary, there is a surprising degree of consensus across ethnic groups in America.[12]

From an anthropological perspective, other scientists see abuse as a culturally-determined label that is applied to behavior and injuries.[13] For example, facial scarification as part of a tribal rite of passage is not the same as facial scars sustained from a violent argument. Specific events and behavior derive their meaning from the context in which they occur. This anthropological point is well-taken.

Although the environment determines the impact of such actions, there are limits to the power of culture to make things right. Some cultures support practices harmful to children. Infanticide in ancient Sparta is but one (albeit extreme) example. Our own culture contains elements (such as racism and sexism) that harm children. The point is that some cultural differences are just that, differences in style, while others represent actions that are intrinsically harmful to the children involved.

We constantly face the problem of knowing how to distinguish legitimate differences in style from practices based on cultural errors, that is, antichild values. One anthropologist recalls being questioned by native Hawaiian mothers about the "abusive" American practice of forcing infants to sleep in cribs and rooms apart from their parents.[14] Is this emotional abuse or cultural difference? We will return to this example as a vehicle for clarifying the issue of defining chid abuse.

In our definition of child abuse, there needs to be some authority beyond the opinions held by parents. At worst, those opinions may be modeled after abusive parental behavior or be based on incorrect assumptions about children. Therefore, our definition includes a second standard—our best scientific understanding of parent-child relations—in addition to the already established criterion of beliefs about child rearing based on custom. The evaluation must be made by both science and culture. Scientists know, for example, that rejection can be injurious to the psyche of a developing child. Some researchers are convinced that the evidence demonstrates a connection between the use of physical punishment and impaired psychological development and social competence. However, this culture so strongly supports the practice of physical punishment that only the most devoted child advocates would say that spanking in and of itself is abusive, and the empirical evidence is debatable. Reasonable people of good-will can and do differ. Abuse is a conclusion drawn about family life, and we think it must be based on a mixture of community standards and professional knowledge. Hawaiian mothers' concern cited earlier is a good example. As much as we may hate the ambiguity it implies, the process of defining abuse is, in practice, one of negotiation between culture and science, folk wisdom and professional expertise. It is not easy, but it is the way things work. Cultural differences are only that unless there is evidence to the contrary.

Definition of Abuse

Heretofore we have used the term *child* in our discussion. This is because nearly all the research has looked at abuse of young children without considering adolescents. We have used this material because it is all we have. However, one of our goals in this book is to work out the implications and applications of any definition of abuse for adolescents. Briefly mentioned here, these derivations are expanded in chapter 8. Our interest in adolescence takes us beyond the established child-abuse literature.

We define maltreatment as acts of omission or commission by a parent or guardian that are judged by a mixture of community values and professional expertise to be inappropriate and damaging. This definition covers the four issues discussed earlier. "Inappropriate" describes parental action; "damaging" covers its effect upon the development of the victim. Both are defined by a value judgment based upon community standards and professional expertise.

Inappropriate parental behavior may produce physical, emotional, or sexual damage. We cannot always accurately predict what effects abuse will have because victims most often suffer multiple damage and individual susceptibility to harm differs. Also while each type of maltreatment is distinct in principle, in practice there is so much overlapping that we rarely see only one type of abuse, at least when we observe a troubled family over a long period of time.

This overlapping and coincidence is one reason we are inclined to link abuse and neglect under the broader term *maltreatment.* Acts of commission (the typical distinguishing mark of abuse) often accompany acts of omission (the primary characteristic of neglect). In practice, neglect and abuse often are found in the same family, with some estimates indicating they occur together 50 percent of the time.[15] They may occur in sequence as well, as when neglect by one parent exposes the victim to abuse by the other. (This often seems to happen in cases of sexual abuse.) Whether we use the terms abuse and neglect, or maltreatment, the central issue remains one of protecting the child or teenager from damage and exploitation, of setting and enforcing high standards of care for children and youth. The whole point of the definition is to articulate both what parents and guardians must do and what they may not do. When we speak of guardians we include the state, certainly no paragon of virtue in these matters as we shall see.

The concept of inappropriateness is very important, particularly in adolescent abuse. Things that might be appropriate in the rearing of young children lose their meaning and appropriateness for teenagers. A fairly common problem parents face is difficulty in changing the habits formed while rearing young children when those children become adolescents. Teenagers are far more capable of abstract thought than are children, and can independently evaluate their own motives as well as those of others. This capability demands that parents reason and consult with their adolescent children when making family decisions and setting rules. This may be hard to do at a time when adolescents are first asserting their independence, and it produces disturbance even among otherwise smoothly functioning families.[16] Most parents eventually recognize the need for some adjustment to the new situation of having adolescent children. Some do not and are at special risk for abusing their teenagers.

We must direct our attention to those patterns of behavior that impose a high level of risk on their victims, that is, treatment that would cause most normal children and teenagers to suffer some social or psychological harm. The consequences of abuse and neglect are not well documented, and the resilience of the human being rules out any simple cause-effect relationship between maltreatment and impaired development. We must go beyond damage and focus on risk.

Many of us are drawn to the fever analogy in explaining the meaning of child abuse and neglect. Typically we speak of abuse and neglect as indicators of underlying problems with the family, just as a fever indicates infection in the body. We think the analogy is a good one, and can be pursued still further. Most fevers are not, in themselves, intrinsically dangerous. They are generally indicators, posing no direct threat to the organism. Very high fevers, on the other hand (particularly among very young children), are themselves dangerous. We would liken this to child abuse and neglect. It seems that most of the *physical* damage done by abusive and neglectful parents, while socially distressing, morally unconscionable, and requiring attention, is not itself a threat to the long-term health of the child.[17] Only the most extreme instances of abuse and neglect are life-threatening or produce substantial physical impairment. These injuries mainly affect very young children, and are relatively rare.

Statistics derived from the American Humane Association's compilation of report data from states around the country document this assertion. Despite the fact that petty domestic violence is widespread,[18] fatalities comprise a very small proportion of maltreatment cases, and relatively few cases (with the highest concentration being among infants) even require medical attention.[19] Figures like these give rise to the hardheaded assessment that child abuse and neglect are not major medical problems. Gil made this point when, after reviewing the data available, he concluded that the scope of the problem of child abuse that results in serious injury is minor, at least in comparison with other more widespread problems that undermine the developmental opportunities of many millions of children in American society, such as poverty, racial discrimination, malnutrition, and inadequate provisions for medical care and education.[20]

While the massive increase in reported cases since Gil's study was undertaken in the late 1960s would certainly enlarge the scope of the problem, the more recent figures presented in the American Humane Association data still indicate that serious physical harm is only a *relatively* small part of the child-maltreatment problem.[21] Does this mean that child maltreatment is a small problem? Clearly, this is untrue. Most professionals and members of the general public almost instinctively recognize that the problem of maltreatment goes well beyond serious physical harm to children.

Consider, for example, the problem of sexual abuse. While physical assault does accompany sexual misuse in numerous cases, the absence of such assault does little to diminish the seriousness of the incident.[22] Why? The coercive climate in which most sexual misuse takes place produces an emotional threat to the child. Although our formal statements about child maltreatment focus their attention on physical consequences, most of us recognize that the heart of the matter lies not in the physical but in the emotional domain. This recognition permits us to distinguish between normal domestic violence and abuse, while at the same time recognizing that normal domestic violence may be one of the principal underlying causes of abuse.[23]

We are concerned with physical damage, of course. No one with any moral sensibility can dismiss a battered child, or even a bruised one for that matter. What is more important, however, is "developmental damage." Garmezy argues that the effects of child abuse (defined primarily as physical assault) are neither so simple nor so absolute as many public pronouncements would have us believe.[24] Many victims of child abuse survive it and go on to avoid repeating the pattern in their own child rearing. The most important issue is therefore the threat to development, since we cannot know the outcome of most parent-child interactions. The real heart of the matter is not any specific action, but rather the overall pattern of parent-child relations and the *probable* impact of that pattern on the development of competence: social, intellectual, and moral. Thus the issues facing our efforts to define abuse practically will shift as the developmental agenda of the victim shifts; physical force may raise different issues for young children than it does for teenagers, and emotional abuse may take one form in childhood and another in adolescence. By focusing on inappropriateness and developmental damage, our definition draws the study of abuse and neglect back into the mainstream of issues in human development. This will benefit both mainstream child-development research and the study of maltreatment. Having defined maltreatment, we will now describe it.

Physical Abuse

> When we got there this baby was crying and we could see his leg was twisted kind of funny to one side. He had bruises on his face. He looked pretty bad.

> You can't say my dad didn't like me, but you can't say that he did, either. When he hit me he used anything from a belt to a beer bottle.

> And a beer bottle slightly smarts. You could go through a window very easy around him if he is mad. . . . I've gone through a window or two.

Physical abuse involves the inappropriate and developmentally damaging use of force. The actual injury is not as important as the way it came about. Youngsters who are injured in athletic pursuits typically bear none of the emotional scars that victims of abuse carry. A boy may be proud of the scar above his eye from a boxing match if he sees it as representing athletic prowess. But if the scar came as a result of a beating from his drunken father over a curfew violation, the boy probably would feel differently about it. Even here, however, there is variation. Some children and youth are proud of their ability to receive and withstand physical assault. We believe this represents a warped value system, however, and refuse to validate domestic violence in this form. Physical wounds, unless extremely severe, heal relatively quickly. Emotional injury lasts longer.

The use of physical force against children seems to reflect a mixture of positive belief in force as a tool for shaping behavior, lack of effective alternatives to force, and emotional tension in the parent: "A good swat on the rear lets him know I mean business"; "What else am I going to do when he runs into the street or breaks something?"; "I was so mad I could spit, but I felt better once I let him have it!" Straus, Gelles, and Steinmetz explored the meaning and significance of violence in the family, and concluded that violence is deeply rooted in some very basic aspects of the way our families work, particularly their focus on power assertion and authoritarian values.[25] We will talk more about the central role of the culture-of-violence hypothesis in producing abuse in chapter 2.

If the use of force against children is of dubious value, the use of force against adolescents is an outright disaster. Better than any other type of abuse, the use of physical force against adolescents illustrates the ill-effects of parental failure to adapt to adolescence. As children grow up, some parents who use spanking for discipline increase the level of force they use. The adolescent growth spurt significantly increases the child's size and parents who continue to rely on corporal punishment may feel they have no choice but to increase the amount of force they use. We think that the sheer amount of force necessary to subdue a teenager makes the practice abusive. Corporal punishment is a poor disciplinary tactic in childhood, but it is worse in adolescence.[26] This is reflected in the finding from a national survey that the overall use of force by most parents against their children decreases with the onset of adolescence.[27] Common sense dictates a shift away from physical discipline toward more mature, psychologically oriented discipline.

Because of their size, when adolescents (particularly males) are physically abused they usually sustain only minor injuries. The amount of force used to produce a concussion in an infant will probably cause only a black eye for a teenager. The adolescent body is better equipped to handle the shock. This understandably contributes to the fact that adolescents often are pushed aside by child protective service agencies in favor of younger children when excessive case loads force such a choice upon them. The teenager's tolerance for physical abuse may mask an equal or even greater susceptibility to emotional abuse, however.

Emotional Abuse

Emotional abuse is extremely difficult to define theoretically and practically, but it is at the heart of the social problem we call the maltreatment of children and youth. Chapter 5 deals with this issue in some detail, so we will only outline the matter here. For infants, emotional abuse typically involves parental refusal to be responsive. It may mean punishing normal behavior such as smiling and vocalization. It may mean rejecting the child and stunting the normal parent-infant attachment. For older children, it involves a pattern of behavior that punishes the child for normal social behavior and self-esteem. It means actively preventing the child from becoming socially and psychologically competent.

There are many inappropriate parental behaviors that can damage teenagers emotionally. One is overcontrol. Our interviews with young victims provided good illustrations.

> My dad started grounding me for finding dirty spots on the dishes. The last time he grounded me like that, it went on for six months and it got so bad that I had to start asking for everything: if I could get up, if I could go to the bathroom, if I could sit down and eat with him, if I could get ready to go to bed, if I could take a bath. You know, everything you take for granted. And his answer to me always was "do you deserve it, do you think you deserve it?" Well, of course, I deserved to eat. I have to eat to live, you know. And it just got really bad.

It is inappropriate to repeatedly force teenagers to do things that will disgrace them before their peers or to expect them to respect socially and psychologically suffocating restrictions. A parental need to control an adolescent's every action can make life unbearable for teenagers who are naturally programmed to become autonomous, to become more rather than less independent. Overcontrol can retard development by robbing youth of opportunities for making decisions and learning from normal mistakes. When an overcontrolling parent is faced with a resistant teenager, the result may be assault or rejection, and parental rejection is an extremely damaging form of emotional abuse.

> I think that I was always rejected. I think that often my parents would set me up. They would be very good to me until I was feeling [a] warm feelings type of thing, and then they would totally reject me. I never remembered doing anything good enough for them.

> I was 12 years old and I was pregnant and I was being very much rejected by my family and my mother would not allow anyone to know that I was pregnant and so I was very alone. I was dropped out of school and when people came to visit I was put in my room and stayed there, sometimes for up to a day and a half. But the last time I cried was when I was in the hospital. I was taken there by my mother and they had decided to do a cesarean section on me because she didn't want anybody to know or to have anybody around to take me to the hospital. I had really nobody to talk to and I wanted to see the baby and they wouldn't let me and so my mother had decided that my baby should be baptized before he was taken to where he was being adopted. And so after they had baptized the baby, she came strolling in my room and said "I got to hold the baby and we baptized it and they gave it a name." And she had left then because I couldn't go home until the next day. Then I did cry that night and it was the last time I cried, when I was 13.

Parental rejection is harmful. Its damaging effects are so well documented that it can justifiably be called psychologically "malignant."[28] Beyond the gross cases described above, a pattern of smaller assaults such as constant criticism, disdain for personal idiosyncrasies, and contempt for dress styles can have a seriously corrosive effect.

Rejection unquestionably meets our two criteria for abuse:It is inappropriate and it is damaging. It can produce low self-esteem. Children who are not loved and cherished by their parents tend to conclude that they must be unlovable. One researcher concludes that around the world, parental rejection leads to "hostility, aggression, passive aggression, or problems with the management of hostility and aggression; dependency; probably emotional unresponsiveness and negative self-evaluation (negative self-esteem and negative self-adequacy); and, probably, emotional instability as well as a negative world view."[29]

Parental rejection can take even more extreme forms.

> I ran because I didn't think they cared about me. The night before, my mom told me that they never liked me. She says, "Go live with your friend." And then she goes, "I don't give a damn about you. Just get the hell out of here. I never want to see your face in this house again."

Some parents reject their children so completely that they physically throw them out of the house, without making adequate provisions for their care. In twentieth-century America it is inappropriate to expect a teenager to be able to support or provide shelter for himself or herself without any assistance. Denial of a home endangers adolescents physically, emotionally, and sexually. Many of these teenagers are called runaways, but they are really "throwaways."

Sexual Abuse

> He told me to sit on his lap on the bed while we watched TV after my bath. Mom was out at the store and he was taking care of me like he always does. Then he told me to take off my pajamas and touch him there. I said I didn't want to but he made me and then he touched me all over. I felt real bad afterwards, and kinda scared.

Incest, of course, is inappropriate behavior in its most extreme form. Incest forces an inappropriate choice upon the youth, between obedience and integrity. It can cause many types of damage, the most predictable being sexual dysfunction, discussed in chapter 11 where we take a special look at sexual abuse.

Neglect

> I called the protective service people because those children never have enough to eat. They're left alone in that apartment, sometimes four

nights a week. The older one is only 9, and that's too young to be in charge of the baby like that. Then when I read in the paper about those children on the North Side who were killed in that fire 'cause they were all alone I decided I had to do something.

I just wanted my mom to tell me that she loved me. And she couldn't even do that, you know. Like, I fought with her so much. I just remember getting into fights with her. Just screaming at her, "why can't you tell me you love me? Why can't you just tell me that?" She never hugged me or nothing.

For children, neglect is probably a greater social threat than active abuse. Most estimates figure the rate of neglect at three to four times the rate for physical abuse, and it probably accounts for more deaths. A study by Downing looked at 30 children who had died after having been protective service cases but whose death certificates listed natural causes.[30] Downing found that half of these deaths were directly attributable to parental neglect, such as failure to give prescribed medication. Among infants, neglect can mean all kinds of damage and exposure to needless risk because the infant is so totally dependent on the parents for basic care. For older children, neglect can mean physical and psychological impoverishment when the basic necessities of life are denied. In both cases, we must look beyond the parents to the community that permits neglect.

Since adolescents are much more capable of handling their own daily living and personal hygiene needs than children, physical neglect per se is much less an issue once adolescence is reached. For teenagers, neglect usually means parental failure to sustain contact or to provide realistic supervision. Failure to care about the whereabouts of a 12-year-old at midnight is neglectful, as is an indefinite refusal to talk (even to a noncommunicative teenager). Neglect is distinct from other forms of abuse because it is passive. But many neglected adolescents seem to be harmed just as severely as victims of more active sorts of abuse. Indifference, forgotten promises, and withdrawal are all inappropriate parental behaviors, damaging to children and teenagers who may feel they are not worth their parents' concern and care. Neglect of this sort may lead to some very self-destructive behavior by its victims.

Conclusion

These examples give enough of a picture of the forms maltreatment may take. We have not tried to present an exhaustive list of abusive behaviors, nor have we tried to categorize their causes and effects; neither task is really feasible, nor is it necessary at this point. Our concern is the well-being of children. Our perspective tells us that the big issue is whether or not families are working well on behalf of children. When they are, the natural human capacity for adaptation and growth reassures us that the product will be a complete human being. When families are not working, children will suffer, as will their parents in their own way. Much abuse happens simultaneously (for example, sexual and emotional) or in sequence (emotional abuse followed by physically throwing the teenager out of the house; rejection followed by the child's rebellion that leads to a beating).

> They beat me. It hurts me real bad inside. It hurts right now. They yell at me about my hair and say I'd never amount to a hill of beans or something. Then they start to hit me with a belt or something, anything that was handy.

> My dad would get so pissed off if I didn't get dinner fixed on time. He would just throw me against the wall and say "you deserve this, you lazy slut." I never could go to games or go out with boys or anything. I could never make the house nice enough for him, so he'd always say I had more stuff to do. Finally, I just ran away.

Maltreatment is a many-faceted phenomenon. To understand its pieces and the whole we need to look at the human ecology of family life. To that task we turn next.

Notes

1. D. Walters, *Physical and Sexual Abuse of Children: Causes and Treatment* (Bloomington: Indiana University Press, 1975).

2. V.J. Fontana, "Further Reflections on Maltreatment of Children," *New York State Journal of Medicine* 68 (1968): 2214-2215.

3. R. Bourne and E. Newberger, eds., *Critical Perspectives on Child Abuse* (Lexington, Mass.: Lexington Books, D.C. Heath and Company, 1979).

4. R. Parke and C.W. Collmer, "Child Abuse: An Interdisciplinary Analysis," in *Review of Child Development Research,* vol. 5, ed. E.M. Hetherington (Chicago: University of Chicago Press, 1975).

5. M. Pines, "Invulnerability: Pioneer Studies." *Psychology Today* 12 (1979): 58-60.

6. C.H. Kempe and R.E. Helfer, *Helping the Battered Child and His Family* (New York: Lippincott, 1975), p. 1.

7. D.G. Gil, *Violence against Children: Physical Child Abuse in the United States* (Cambridge, Mass.: Harvard University Press, 1970), p. 6.

8. Parke and Collmer, "Child Abuse."

9. J. Garbarino, "The Human Ecology of Child Maltreatment: A Conceptual Model for Research," *Journal of Marriage and the Family* 39 (1977): 721-736; M. Straus, R. Gelles, and S. Steinmetz, *Behind Closed Doors* (New York: Doubleday, 1980).

10. Parke and Collmer, "Child Abuse."

11. Ibid.

12. J. Giovannoni and R. Becerra, *Defining Child Abuse* (New York: Free Press, 1979).

13. R. Walters and R. Parke, "Social Motivation, Dependency, and Susceptibility to Social Influence," in *Advances in Experimental Social Psychology*, ed., L. Berkowitz, (New York: Academic Press, 1964).

14. J. Korbin, personal communication.

15. J. Garbarino and A. Crouter, "Defining the Community Context of Parent-Child Relations: The Correlates of Child Maltreatment," *Child Development* 49 (1978): 604-616. J. Garbarino and B. Carson, "Mistreated Youth versus Abused Children" (Boys Town, Neb., 1979).

16. J. Hill, "The Family," in *Seventy-ninth Yearbook of the National Society for the Study of Education,* ed. M. Johnson (Chicago, Ill.: University of Chicago Press, 1980); L. Steinberg, "Research in the Ecology of Adolescent Development: A Longitudinal Study of the Impact of Physical Maturation on Changes in the Family System in Early Adolescence" (Paper presented at the Conference on Research Perspectives in the Ecology of Human Development, Cornell University, Ithaca, N.Y., August 17-20, 1977).

17. H. Martin, *The Abused Child* (Cambridge, Mass.: Ballinger, 1976).

18. R. Gelles, "Violence toward Children in the United States," *American Journal of Orthopsychiatry* 48 (1978): 580-592.

19. American Humane Association, *Annual Report of the National Clearinghouse on Child Abuse and Neglect* (Denver, Colo.: American Humane Association, 1977).

20. Gil, *Violence against Children.*

21. American Humane Association, *Annual Report.*

22. R. Summit and J. Kryso, "Sexual Abuse of Children: A Clinical Spectrum," *American Journal of Orthopsychiatry* 48 (1978): 237-251.

23. Gelles, "Violence toward Children."

24. N. Garmezy, "Observations on Research with Children at Risk for Child and Adult Psychopathology," in *Child Psychiatry Treatment and Research,* eds. M.F. McMillan and S. Henao (New York: Brunner/Mazel, 1977).

25. Straus, Gelles, and Steinmetz, *Behind Closed Doors.*

26. S. Coopersmith, *The Antecedents of Self-esteem* (San Francisco: Freeman, 1967); G. Homans, *The Human Group* (London: Routledge and Kegan Paul, 1975); M. Jeffrey, "Practical Ways to Change Parent-Child Interaction in Families of Children at Risk," in *Child Abuse and Neglect* ed. R. Helfer and H.C. Kempe, (Cambridge, Mass.: Ballinger, 1976); A. Bandura, *Social Learning Theory* (Englewood Cliffs, N.J.: Prentice Hall, 1977); B. Gilmartin, "The Case against Spanking," *Human Behavior* 7, no. 2, (February 1978): 18-23.

27. Gelles, "Violence toward Children."

28. R. Rohner, *They Love Me, They Love Me Not* (New Haven, Conn.: Human Relations Area Files Press, 1975).

29. Ibid.

30. D. Downing, "A Selective Study of Child Mortality," *Child Abuse and Neglect* 2 (1978): 101–108.

A Look at the World of Abnormal Rearing

Child maltreatment commonly is thought of as the product of three elements: a vulnerable adult, a special child, and a provoking situation. When these three elements come together their "psycho-logic" produces an incident of maltreatment. Typically, the experiences of the adult are emphasized: maltreatment breeds maltreatment. This view relies heavily on the proposition that we parent as we were parented.

There is much truth to this view. However, that truth is tempered by the fact that the potential for maltreatment lies within many if not most of us. What parent has never been negligent, or come close to some dangerous use of force against a child? Where does discipline end and abuse begin? When does carelessness become neglect? Assuredly some adults do have experiences, values, and attitudes that make them particularly prone to becoming involved in abuse and neglect. What often is overlooked is that the key to their behavior lies with the social conditions surrounding these parents. This combination produces a world of abnormal rearing (WAR), as it is called by Ray Helfer and C. Henry Kempe.

We believe that to understand abusive families we must understand their world. That world is partly of their own creation and partly foisted upon them by the way our society works. Our goal in this chapter is to look at the origins of child maltreatment in the hope that we can identify some of the basic issues for research, policy, and practice. This done, we will be able to look at how this world of abnormal rearing is created and maintained.

Origins of Child Maltreatment

Historical Perspective

The maltreatment of children is a phenomenon as old as mankind. Only recently has the standard treatment of children reached a point where maltreatment as a definable problem can even be meaningfully identified.[1] There can be little doubt that abuse and neglect are now significant issues for both policy and science. The enactment of legislation creating the National Center on Child Abuse and Neglect is testimony to this. The failure of that agency to exert clear and persuasive leadership is testimony to the scientific and political difficulty of the issues involved.

From its beginning as a field of inquiry, the study of child maltreatment has been dominated by a clinical aura of pathology.[2] David Gil[3] and others[4] noted that from the first public statements,[5] professionals and public alike defined child abuse as *qualitatively* deviant from normal caregiver-child relations—different in kind, not simply degree; sick rather than in error. The medical model reflects a kinds-of-people theory. In this emphasis on personality types it parallels the early history of efforts to understand and deal with juvenile delinquency[6] and cultural deprivation.[7] In many ways it represents our characteristic response to deviance. Thomas Kuhn demonstrated through historical analysis that, once they are established, such characteristic ways of thinking (paradigms) are resistant to change, and encourage piecemeal, ad hoc assimilation of new information as opposed to genuine revision of the basic idea.[8]

Initially, the clinical view held that only a crazy person would abuse a child. That is, abusive parents were thought to be definably psychopathological. More recently, as the definition of maltreatment has been broadened, this view has expanded to include the proposition that abuse is the result of a unique, discrete, and psychopathologically deviant pattern of parent-child relations.[9] This pattern has been variously called a sense of intense, pervasive, continuous demand;[10] emotionally crippled;[11] poor mothering imprint;[12] symbiosis;[13] and role reversal.[14]

The position that child abuse is best understood as a point along a more general continuum of caregiver-child relations, and is only *quantitatively* different from nonabusive relationships, has been and continues to be a minority view.[15] Seen this way, child abuse and neglect are only parts of a more general phenomenon: the maltreatment of children. The problem of child abuse can be understood only as part and parcel of the overall society's commitment to the welfare of children and families.[16]

We believe that child maltreatment is an indicator of the overall quality of life for families. It is concentrated among people who have the least going for them economically, socially, and psychologically, and who thus comprise high-risk families. The rationale for this view emerges from an ecological approach to the problem, one that systematically deals with the interaction of person and environment.

An Ecological Perspective

Nature and nurture can work together or in opposition. The level of risk and damage experienced by a specific individual depends upon the interplay of these two forces. In extreme cases, facts of nature can all but overwhelm environmental differences. Likewise, environmental conditions can be so extreme (either in a positive or negative way) as to override all but the most powerful and extreme conditions of biology. This is human nature; our nature is to be what conditions encourage.

Understanding the interaction between nature and nurture in producing social and personal risk is difficult. In fact, it is so difficult that most researchers do not even try to handle both parts of the equation at once. Rather, they tend to let one side vary while they hold the other constant—as in studying genetically identical twins reared apart to learn about the role of nature and nurture in intelligence, or in seeing how different newborns respond to a constant stimulus such as a smiling face. Another method is to vary one side systematically while letting the other vary randomly—as in presenting school-age children with three different teaching styles and seeing the overall effect of each. It is rare that a researcher is able really to look at the interplay of nature and nurture in development. Where risk is concerned, this is extremely unfortunate because the inevitable issues of policymaking and service delivery *need* a science of the costs and benefits of alternative experiences to the individual and to the society. In computing these costs and benefits we need to understand where history fits into individual and cultural development.

In a sense, our interest in development is really an interest in biography. We must discover how the lives of individuals, families, and societies are interdependent. Events taking place at the level of nations (the big picture) can reverberate down into the day-to-day life of the individual and the family (the little picture). One example is when the actions of an oil-producing cartel result in unemployment that affects domestic relationships and deprives a child of a nurturant relationship with his or her parents. Conversely, millions of individual decisions can add up to major social changes, as when millions of women decide to delay childbearing so that they can pursue careers. Understanding this interplay of biography and history is at the heart of understanding human development. One important aid in applying this concept practically is an emerging ecological perspective on development.

In using the word *ecological* here we mean to convey an interest in the way the organism and its immediate environment (the ecological niche) affect and respond to each other. This process of mutual adaptation and accommodation means that the terms of the equation that produce behavior are always shifting, sometimes subtly, sometimes drastically. It means that in the case of maltreatment the intimate relationships between the child and the parents cannot be accounted for or understood without understanding how the conditions surrounding the family affect interaction between child and parent.

The Great Depression as an Example

Economic deprivation is generally recognized as the principal source of risk to children. Within the space of two years (1976-1978), two major analyses of family life conducted by panels of experts concluded separately that poverty remains the principal threat to family life. The National Academy of Sciences[17] and the Carnegie Foundation[18] both cited inadequate economic resources as the central villain in undermining the adequacy of families as contexts for child development. Inadequate income is not the only source of troubles for families, of course. Rich people have family troubles, too. But anyone who looks at the data on the connection between poverty and disturbed family life must agree with the old aphorism, "I've been rich and I've been poor, and rich is better."

It is exciting, therefore, to see a well-conceived and well-executed study of the consequences of economic deprivation on human development. Conducted by sociologist Glen Elder, this study permits us to look at the impact of the Great Depression of the 1930s on the children of that era.[19] Two longitudinal studies of child development were launched by an earlier generation of investigators in the period 1929–1932 in northern California (one in Oakland, the other in Berkeley). The first dealt with children born in 1920–1921, the second with children born in 1928–1929. Both studies included middle-class and working-class families. A wide range of information was obtained about the children and their parents, and the data were collected for more than forty years. When Elder came to the project in 1962 he saw a unique opportunity to explore the impact of the Great Depression (an economic dislocation if ever there was one) on the life course of the children in these two studies. His findings demonstrate the complexity of family-economy interaction and the necessity for the organizing ecological perspective.

In families where the husband lost his job (or most of his income) and the marital relationship was weak, the mother often led the way in blaming the father for his economic failure. When this happened, girls were psychologically strengthened by the dominant performance of their mothers and boys were weakened by their father's failure. All these things were intensified if the sons and daughters were young children when the economic deprivation came because they were then more dependent upon their parents and were exposed to the new situation for a longer period of time in the home. The effects were greatest for middle-class families; the positive effects on teenagers from middle-class families with strong marital relationships were greatest, as were the negative effects on middle-class children from families with weak marital bonds.

These findings all refer to the long-term effects of economic deprivation. The short-term effects were different in some ways. Some of the groups showing the worst long-term prognosis showed little short-term problems, and vice versa. It should be noted that all these findings come from families with a predepression record of relative stability: married parents and an adequate work history. These were not the hard-core unemployed, nor were they single-parent households. For Elder's families, the experience of economic deprivation was an *event*, not a permanent condition. This is a significant part of the story and cautions against simple generalizations to other groups who experience lifelong, chronic economic deprivation.

To further the complexity, we must remember that Elder's Depression was followed by the economic boom of World War II and the 1950s. The teenage male victims were ready to benefit from that opportunity while the child victims were not. What is more, the Depression itself caused a whole social welfare system to be put into place: unemployment insurance, social security, and the like. Also these families were much more likely to see their economic deprivation as their own fault than people might today, with our greater appreciation for the role of impersonal economic forces. These things add to the already large number of variables that must be taken into account.

The impact of troubled economic times on a child—whether or not they will produce damage—depends on how those forces are experienced by the child's family and community and are transmitted to the child as well as on the child's own characteristics. Elder's study makes this clear. Families who were not hit directly with income loss did not show the effects that deprived families did, and some occupations were more affected than others. We also must keep in mind that the individual is not a passive participant. While Elder's account stresses the average effects of economic change on development, there was substantial individual variation. It is precisely this individual factor in concert with the social factors that makes the ecological approach a valid model of the real world. Rarely is risk absolute; rarely is it static.

Though it is clear from Elder's study that almost any risk can be overcome, the more impoverished the child's world, the more prone the child is to failure, particularly if his or her parents are part of the problem rather than part of the solution. Sociocultural risk refers to the impoverishing of a child's world in three ways: (1) depriving the child of important relationships (as happens when one parent is absent and no one is available to take his or her place); (2) depriving the child of the raw materials of self-esteem (as happens when the child is rejected by significant people or alienated from significant social settings such as the school); and (3) depriving the child of values and experiences that contribute to socialization and the development of competence (as happens when children do not learn how to be effective parents, productive workers, responsible citizens).

A Systems Approach to Sociocultural Risk

The framework proposed by Urie Bronfenbrenner is the most useful approach to the ecology of human development.[20] Like most frameworks, it relies on some special terms, which we now will define.

As stated previously, the ecology of human development is the scientific study of how the individual develops interactively with the social environment, defined as a network of interrelated systems. The child plays an active role in an ever-widening world. The newborn shapes the feeding behavior of its mother but is largely confined to a crib or a lap and has limited means of communicating its needs and wants. The 10-year-old, on the other hand, influences many adults and other children located in many different settings, and has many ways of communicating. The adolescent's world is still larger and more diverse, as is his or her ability to influence it. The child and the environment negotiate their relationship over time through a process of reciprocity. One cannot predict the future of either reliably without knowing something about the other. Does economic deprivation harm development? It depends on how old one is when it hits, what sex one is, what the future brings in the way of vocational opportunity, what the quality of family life was in the past, what one's economic expectations and assumptions are, and whether one looks at the short term or the long run. In short, it depends.

In asking and answering questions about developmental risk we can and always should be to ready to look at the next level of larger and smaller worlds to find the questions to ask and answer. If we see husbands and wives in conflict over lost income, we need to look to the economy that put the husbands out of work and now may welcome the wives into the labor force. We must also look to the culture that defines a person's personal worth in monetary terms and that blames the victims of economic dislocation for their own losses. But we also must look inward to the parent-child relationships that are affected by the changing roles and status of the parents. In addition, we must also look "across" to see how the several systems involved (family, workplace, and economy) adjust to new conditions over time.

Bronfenbrenner offers a terminology to express these concerns in a systematic way that permits scientific study and promises to increase our understanding.[21] Most immediate to the developing individual is the *microsystem*, the actual setting in which the individual experiences and creates reality. At first, for most children, the microsystem is quite small: it is the home, involving interaction with only one person at a time (dyadic interaction), doing relatively simple activities such as feeding, bathing, and cuddling. As the child develops, complexity normally increases: the child does more, with more people, in more places. In Bronfenbrenner's view, the expanding capacity to do more is the very essence of development. As we shall see in chapter 5, one characteristic of maltreatment is that it undermines the child's capacity for complexity and thus impoverishes development.

Play figures prominently in this process from the early months of life, and eventually is joined by work. Playing, working, and loving (what Freud called the essence of normal human existence) are the principal classes of activities that characterize the child's microsystem. However, the extent to which these activities take place, and their level of complexity are variable. Thus one source of sociocultural harm or risk is a narrowly-restricted range and level of activities, impoverished experience in playing, working, and loving, a stunted microsystem where reciprocity is limited; that is, where genuine *interaction* is lacking and where either party seeks to avoid or to be impervious to the other. One of the most important aspects of the microsystem as a force in development is the existence of relationships that go beyond simple dyads (two people). Where the child can observe and learn from being exposed to other dyads (such as his mother and father), development is enhanced. Where the child can observe differences in his own dyadic experience because a third party is present, development is enhanced. So long as increased numbers in a child's microsystem mean more enduring reciprocal relationships, larger and more complex microsystems as a function of the child's age mean enhanced development.[22] The social riches of a child are measured by enduring, reciprocal, multifaceted relationships that emphasize playing, working, and loving. This is crucial to understanding abusive families. First, however, we should examine the next level of systems, what Bronfenbrenner calls *mesosystems.*

Mesosystems are the relationships between contexts in which the developing person experiences reality. The richness of mesosystems for the child is measured by the size (number) and quality (depth) of connections. Bronfenbrenner uses the example of the child who goes to school on the first day unaccompanied. This means there is only a single link between the home and school microsystem, namely, the child's participation in both. Were this weak linkage to persist, it would place the child at risk, particularly if there is disagreement between home and school in terms of values, experiences, objects, and behavioral style. Homes that do not value schooling, do not have books or educated people, do not involve reading and other basic academic skills, and do not use the formal language used for instructional purposes jeopardize the child's academic development. Where all these links are strong, the odds favor the development of academic competence. Where the similarity of the two settings is bolstered by actual participation of people other than the child in both settings, academic success is still more likely. Thus it is important that the parents visit the school and even that the teachers visit the home.

The central principle here is that the stronger and more diverse the links between settings, the more powerful the resulting mesosystem will be. Such mesosystems are important in providing feedback to the parent and protection from maltreatment to the child. There can be much more to child care than the microsystem of the family. A rich range of mesosystems is both a product and a cause of development. A poor set of mesosystems both reflects and produces impaired development, particularly when home and school are involved. What governs the quality of the child's mesosystems? In large part it is events in systems where the child himself does not participate but where things happen that have a direct bearing on his parents and other adults who do interact with him. Bronfenbrenner calls these settings *exosystems.*

Exosystems are situations having a bearing on a child's development but in which the developing child does not actually play a direct role; he or she does not participate in those settings. They include the workplaces of the parents (for most children, since they are not participants there) and those centers of power (such as school boards and planning commissions) that make decisions affecting the child's day-to-day life.

In exosystem terms, risk comes about in two ways. The first is when the parents or other significant adults are affected in a way that impoverishes their behavior in the child's microsystem. For example, Melvin Kohn found that when parents work in settings that demand conformity rather than self-direction, they reflect this orientation in their child rearing, which stifles important aspects of the child's development.[23] Other examples include elements of the parent's working experience that result in an impoverishment of family life, such as long or inflexible hours, traveling, or stress. The second way risk flows from the exosystem is when decisions are made in those settings that adversely affect the child or treat him or her unfairly. For example, when the school board suspends extracurricular programs in the child's school or the planning commission runs a highway through the child's neighborhood, they jeopardize the child's development. Thus exosystem risk comes when the child lacks effective advocates in decision-making bodies. Psychologist George Albee identifies powerlessness as *the* primary factor leading to impaired development and psychopathology.[24] Powerlessness certainly plays a large role in determining the fate of groups of children, and may even be very important when considering individual cases, such as whether or not parents have the pull to get the youth a second chance when he or she gets into trouble at school or with the police. Risk at the exosystem level is largely a political matter.

Mesosystems and exosystems are set within the broad ideological and institutional patterns of a particular culture or subculture. These are *macrosystems.* Thus macrosystems are the blueprints for the ecology of human development. These blueprints reflect a people's shared assumptions about how things are done. To identify a macrosystem is to do more than simply name a group: Israeli, Arab, Swiss, American, Latino, black, Anglo, Indian. It more closely resembles the implications of linking a social system or group to the Judeo-Christian tradition, the Protestant ethic, communism, or fascism. We need variables rather than simply labels, however. We must compare these groups systematically on some common scales of measurement, such as collective versus individual orientation or schooled versus unschooled. But macrosystems are more than even these broad descriptive factors.

Macrosystem refers to the general organization of the world as it is and as it might be. The existence of historical change demonstrates that the *might be* is quite real. The *might be* occurs through evolution (many individual decisions guided by a common perception of reality) and through revolution introduced by a small cadre of decision makers. The suburbanization of America in the post-World War II era happened because of an intricate set of individual decisions, technological developments, and corporate initiatives. Together, they reshaped the experience of millions of children in families and schools.[25] The Iranian revolution of 1978-1979 overturned the government of a modernizing society and altered the institutional and ideological landscape. We can assume these changes have reverberated through that nation's schools and homes.

What is risk when it comes to macrosystems? It is an ideology alignment that threatens to impoverish children's microsystems and tems, and sets exosystems against them. It is a national economic p tolerates or even encourages economic dislocations and poverty for fam young children. It is institutionalized support for high levels of g̲ᵤₚₕᵢc mobility that disrupt neighborhood and school connections. It is a pattern nonsupportive of parents that tolerates or even condones intense conflicts between the roles of worker and parent. It is a pattern of racist or sexist values that demean some parents and thus raise the level of stress for their children. In general, it is any social pattern or societal event that impoverishes the ability and willingness of adults to care for children and children to learn from adults. Macrosystem risk is the world set against children.

As noted before, the microsystem is the immediate setting in which the child develops. Microsystems evolve and develop much as the child does—because of forces from within and from without. The setting "school" is very different in June than it was in September for the same children (who are themselves, of course, not the same). The setting of the family as experienced by the firstborn child is different from that experienced by subsequent children. We must remember that the microsystem has a life of its own; it develops, too.

It is also important to remember that Bronfenbrenner's definition speaks of the microsystem as a pattern *experienced* by the developing person. The cognitive maps we carry around in our heads are the reality we live by and act upon. One might consider who said it better: Shakespeare in *Hamlet* (II, ii, 249-250): "for there is nothing good or bad/but thinking makes it so . . . ," or sociologist W.I. Thomas, "If men define situations as real, they are real in their consequences."[26] The individual child constructs the microsystems much as he or she is shaped by it.

The child's microsystem becomes a source of developmental risk when it is socially impoverished. He or she suffers when it has too few participants, too little reciprocal interaction, or psychologically destructive patterns of interaction (or some combination of the three).

A microsystem should be a gateway to the world. Bronfenbrenner recognizes this when he offers the following proposition about microsystems and individual development: "The developmental status of the individual is reflected in the substantive variety and structural complexity of the . . . activities which he initiates and maintains in the absence of instigation or direction by others."[27]

The product of a healthy microsystem is a child whose capacity for understanding and dealing successfully with ever-wider spheres of reality increases. Such a child learns to have self-respect and self-confidence, to be socially and intellectually competent. Child maltreatment affects these developmental areas directly.

The Human Ecology of Child Maltreatment

The ecological perspective on human development is particularly well-suited to the task of understanding child maltreatment. As scholars and practitioners are increasingly recognizing, the maltreatment of children is the product of a multiplicity of factors, not of one influence acting alone.[28] There are multiple *sufficient* conditions for child abuse and neglect—that is, factors that by themselves are capable of causing maltreatment if the situation permits it. These sufficient conditions lie in the daily experiences of the child, principally in the family, since members of the immediate family were found to be the perpetrators in some 90 percent of the cases in Gil's national survey of case records.[29] While some of the story is told by the two-person system of the parent-child relationship, much of the problem can be understood only by looking beyond this dyad. This latter point is particularly important since there is growing agreement that a recurrent *pattern* of child maltreatment typically requires the compliance or acquiescence of persons other than the victim-perpetrator dyad. Moreover, some have concluded that the *instigation* of abuse generally comes from outside the victim-perpetrator dyad.[30] In this view, then, abuse is truly a system malfunction because individuals and groups other than the parent and child play pivotal roles.

A pattern of abuse is based on particular kinds of relationships between the victim-perpetrator dyad and others with whom they have or might have relationships. The processes involved in abusive behavior appear to be of two basic types. The first involves the psychopathological assault by the parent (be it physical, emotional, or sexual). This is the simplest form of abuse. It is linked to the parent's psychotic functioning. The second stems from the psychologically normal abuse implicit in our culture's support for the use of physical punishment and other forms of power assertion and authoritarianism within the family. This type of abuse is best understood as a process in which there is magnification of initial differences. Initially small asynchronies between child and caregiver, mild control problems, somewhat extreme forms of discipline, and slightly aversive interactions are multiplied over time until they become recognizable as deviant, dangerous patterns. In this way, the psychologically normal parent is set up for abuse by the combination of our culture and his own special circumstances.

As Friedman noted, we need better classification of abusive cases on the basis of their origins, characteristics, and consequences.[31] One important basis for such a classification scheme is the particular sufficient conditions leading to the abuse. It seems useful, for example, to distinguish between abuse caused by sadistic psychopathology (a small proportion of abuse in general but a high proportion of lethal abuse) and the behavior of psychiatrically normal adults. At this point it is possible to propose a set of hypotheses concerning such causes.

Abuse perpetrated by normal individuals may be described as a form of situationally determined incompetence in the role of caregiver.[32] It stems from the combination of social stress and a relatively low level of skill as a caregiver. These are the "process" variables that translate social structure into events directly shaping the interaction of family members.[33] The ability to care for a child adequately is, like all forms of competence, situationally determined.[34] As Green and others have shown, the key situational factor is the match of parent to child.[35] As experimental laboratory research and research in naturalistic settings have demonstrated, virtually anyone can be broken by some situation.[36] Almost no one is immune to the *role* of child abuser if the discrepancy between support and demands is great enough, though people vary in the degree to which they are prone to act in an abusive manner. The notion that the abusive parent has learned a role is an important point. As we shall see, many of the most important issues in understanding abusive families center around the cultural definition and social supports for the role of parent.

In contrast to psychiatrically oriented researchers who seek to understand maltreatment as a personality malfunction, a sociological approach focuses on maltreatment as a problem with roles. This is a social perspective on what is seen psychiatrically as a character disorder. As suggested by several investigators,[37] socialization and life-course development can best be understood as a process of role transitions and sequences that ". . . entail both entry and exit, some measure of rejection and acceptance, separation and integration. Their psychosocial effects are contingent on the nature of the change and the adaptive potential of the individual, as defined by resources, social preparation and support."[38]

The maltreatment of children comes from incompetence in the role of caregiver, and that incompetence is largely the responsibility of outside forces. Maltreatment is culturally defined inappropriate behavior, be it excessive use of force, sexual misuse, emotional rejection, or inadequate provision of essential nurturance. What are the origins of role incompetence, of the failure to make the transition to the role of caregiver successfully? Cottrell,[39] Burr,[40] and Elder[41] put forth a model of role transition including three major factors that facilitate effective adaptation: rehearsal of the role, clarity of expectations, and minimal normative change.[42] These factors are particularly important for the transition to the parental role. They go far in summarizing research findings concerning characteristics of people and institutions involved in mistreating children and youth, and societies that permit or even precipitate such maltreatment.

Parents who mistreat their children appear to have had little chance to rehearse the role of caregiver. They often were maltreated as children, did not have pets on which to practice being a parent, and have a history of social impoverishment. It is little wonder they have trouble learning the role of parent. There is repeated mention made in the research literature of their lack of knowledge and unrealistic expectations about children.[43] The role of caregiver requires substantial

.nge for most people. It requires a reordering of priorities, especially the ratification of needs. The child must come first. Parents who mistreat their children have been described as individuals who have trouble weighing their needs as against the child's, and receive little support in making appropriate choices.[44] Often they present an odd picture of both selfishness and impoverished self-image.

Incompetence in the role of caregiver is associated with stress, without mitigating personal and social resources. In terms of its psychosocial consequences stress without support is a pathogenic influence.[45] The work of sociologists Wilensky[46] and Pahl and Pahl[47] implies the relevance of a role-oriented as opposed to a character-disorder approach to the phenomena of maltreatment. In studying the relation between work life and social integration, Wilensky found that men with "orderly" careers, jobs that are related in a hierarchy of prestige, were more socially integrated than men with "disorderly" work lives. They were more involved in church and school functions, in friendship circles that were interconnected, and in wide-ranging social contacts both within and outside family and kin. Parallel findings are presented in Weissman and Paykel's study of depression among women.[48] They found that disorderly management of roles, often as a result of events beyond the woman's control, was a psychosocially disorganizing force related to the mistreatment of children (particularly neglect).

Lives out of Control

The more general problem revealed by these and other studies is that of lives out of control. This state of being out of control is manifest in many ways. Young found that neither parent took responsibility for decisions in 88 percent of abusive families.[49] Others noted that abusing parents often perceive themselves as impotent in the face of forces both internal and external to the family. Justice and Duncan found that abusive families are characterized by enormous demands for adjustment, by events that disrupt roles and relationships and require stressful psychosocial and behavioral accommodations.[50] Families involved in abuse seem caught up in a pattern of fundamental *asynchrony,* of chronic and acute mismatch between reality and the parents' ability to manage that reality effectively. This asynchrony is manifest in many ways among families suffering through child maltreatment. These include asynchronous mother-infant interactions in the early weeks of life,[51] an inconsistent use of discipline,[52] and lack of family coherence in general.[53]

The concept of "lives out of control" may best be thought of as a characteristic of family life-course development.[54] The inappropriate timing and sequencing of important events that require role transitions may be crucial. Unwanted or unplanned pregnancy, either at the beginning or end of a family's history, may interact with inadequate economic resources to produce a life crisis. Roles outside the immediate care-giving relationship, such as in the world of work, may be mismanaged or disrupted by social forces beyond the parent's control, such as happens during an economic depression. These events generate the kind of stresses that often result in attempts to assert control through violence or to surrender control through neglect. Linking such role malfunctions together to account for the maltreatment of children is a major and largely unexplored task for developmental research.

How do lives go awry? How do families get out of control? What is the weak link in the chain of events that normally supports families and protects children? We believe social isolation is the weak link that is responsible for abuse and neglect. Isolation from potent, prosocial support systems places even the strong and competent in jeopardy, and often sends the weak or incompetent over the edge when stresses from within and outside the family conspire.

Necessary Conditions for Child Abuse

Generally neglected in discussions of child abuse is the important distinction between sufficient and necessary conditions, a fundamental component in a scientifically sound analysis. Where this topic is treated it tends to be incidental to or implicit in another goal.[55] For any particular sufficient condition to cause a specific effect all relevant necessary conditions must be met.[56] The absence of any necessary conditions effectively disarms the sufficient conditions. This is a critical factor because there is reason to believe that approximately 25 percent of America's families are in danger of being prone to abusing because of sufficient conditions that include child-rearing ignorance, unrealistic expectations concerning children, propensity toward violence, psychopathology, or presence of a special child.

This 25 percent figure is drawn from several sources. Gil's survey found that over 22 percent of the adults sampled reported they thought they "could at some time injure a child" and nearly 16 percent actually had come very close to injuring a child in their care.[57] Results of a study designed to provide a perinatal assessment of mother-baby interaction concluded that 25 percent of the mothers are "at risk because they have child-rearing attitudes or experiences characteristic of abusers."[58] Work by Schneider and her colleagues in developing a predictive screening questionnaire for potential problems in mother-child interaction supports Gray's conclusion.[59]

Clearly the sufficient conditions for child abuse are in abundant supply. According to recent reports, increasing numbers of families are vulnerable to conditions that produce maltreatment of children.[60] This vulnerability derives from changing patterns of family structure as well as more general economic patterns and social conditions. More households with young children are headed by single parents who are likely to have low incomes and to be experiencing a variety of social stresses. We need to know the conditions that cause this vulnerability to be translated into abuse and neglect.

What are the necessary conditions for child abuse? There appear to be two. The first is twofold and involves the way a culture defines the rights of children. For a pattern of maltreatment to occur within families there must be cultural justification for the use of force against children and a generally held belief that children are the property of their parents to be cared for or disposed of as the parents see fit. This becomes apparent, of course, most clearly in social and historical comparisons.[61] A culturally defined concept of children as the property of caregivers and of caregivers as legitimate users of force against children and youth appears to be an essential component of child abuse and neglect: physical, sexual, and emotional.

As Albee has so persuasively argued, the central issue in mistreatment is the misuse of power. "... in primary prevention we attempt to prevent the arbitrary use of power in ways that damage others or reduce their opportunities."[62] Power and rights are the underlying ethical issues in child maltreatment.[63] Does the child have a right to its integrity and what powers are allied behind that right?

The validity of this proposition is supported by analyses of the history of child abuse,[64] the anthropological study of other cultures,[65] and analyses of the forces justifying violence in American society.[66] There can be little doubt that American society fulfills this necessary condition for child abuse.[67] In excess of 90 percent of parents reported employing physical force in the upbringing of their children in a survey conducted by Stark and McEvoy,[68] and this small study was supported by the results of the national survey of families conducted by Straus and his colleagues.[69] In a sample of Los Angeles mothers, it was found that one-quarter reported spanking infants before the age of 6 months and almost half were spanking by the time the children were 12 months of age.[70] Viano reported that two-thirds of the police, clergy, and educators polled condoned spanking.[71] There is clear legal sanction for the use of physical force against children. The Texas legislature, for example, in 1974 enacted legislation containing the following statement: "The use of force, but not deadly force, against a child younger than 18 years is justified: (1) if the actor is the child's parent or stepparent . . . (2) when and to the degree the actor believes the force is necessary to discipline the child."[72] This law reflects the historical role of violence in our civilization.

Nonviolent cultures tend to avoid child abuse. Cultures in which children are "citizens" do not permit neglect.[73] This is not to say that cultural support for violence or defining children as property is sufficient condition for child maltreatment. The existence of adults in American society who condone the use of physical force to discipline children or view children as property and yet are nonabusive and nonneglecting demonstrates this.

Of equal or greater importance on a day-to-day basis as a necessary condition is isolation of the parent-child relationship from potent prosocial support systems.[74] This factor pertains to the relation of the family system or victim-perpetrator dyad to the community. And it is amenable to change as much as or more so than the deeply rooted cultural patterns outlined above.

The concept of support system has been developed and elaborated by several investigators, among them Gerald Caplan.[75] In his terms, a support system performs several critical social functions relevant to the dynamics of child maltreatment by acting as:

> . . . continuing social aggregates that provide individuals with opportunities for feedback about themselves and for validations for their expectations about others, which may offset deficiencies in this communication within the larger community context. . . . People have a variety of specific needs that demand satisfaction through enduring interpersonal relationships, such as for love and affection, for intimacy that provides the freedom to express feelings easily and unself-consciously, for validation of personal identity and worth, for satisfaction of nurturance and dependency, for help with tasks, and for *support in handling emotion and controlling impulses.*[76] (emphasis added)

> They tell the individual what is expected and guide the individual in what to do. They watch what the individual does and they judge performance.[77]

The importance of such support systems increases, of course, as a function of the stressfulness of the family's external environment, the values of the individual, and the sources of stress emanating from within the family itself. It is the unmanageability of the stresses that is the most important factor. That unmanageability is the product of a mismatch between the level of stress and the availability and potency of personal and social resources, chief among which are support systems.

Support systems function through social networks.[78] While the concept of social network has been developed and utilized by sociologists and anthropologists to describe complex communication webs, it generally has not been applied to the study of development. Recently, ecologically oriented students of development have begun to adapt the concept for assessing the support systems for families.[79]

Cochran and Brassard defined four properties of social networks relevant to development: size and diversity of membership, interconnectedness among members, content of activities engaged in, and directionality of contacts.[80] Studying the social networks of families promises to operationalize systematically the concepts of social isolation and social integration. This is an important development because it describes the social isolation, the lack of support-system resources, of families involved in child maltreatment.

It would be misleading to assume that the fault for social isolation is entirely external to the individual. It is necessary to distinguish between lack of social supports and failure to use available supports. Elmer found parents who fail to use resources particularly high on anomie.[81] They distrust and retreat from society. Lenoski reported that 81 percent of the abusive families in his sample preferred not to seek help in resolving crises.[82] Young found abusive parents attempted to prevent their children from forming relationships outside the home.[83] Polansky and his colleagues found that neglecting parents had virtually no one to whom they felt they could turn confidently for assistance with day-to-day matters.[84] Social isolation, like virtually all important human phenomena, is determined by an interaction of the individual and the environment. We are dealing with the human ecology of family life.

Child maltreatment can occur only when a family is isolated from the community; when it is not being given proper feedback and support. This isolation may be structural (no social network) or cultural (a network that tolerates or even condones maltreatment). For the sufficient conditions noted previously to cause maltreatment they must occur in a context that permits the perpetrator-victim dyad to develop and be sustained.

Several citations may serve to illustrate this point, though caution must be exercised in generalizing from these studies which may contain sampling problems of undetermined direction and magnitude. Young found that 95 percent of severe abuse families had no continuing relationships with others outside the family.[85] This same study concluded that 85 percent of the abusve families did not belong to or participate in any organized groups. Lenoski found that 89 percent of the abusive parents having telephones had unlisted numbers, as opposed to 12 percent of the nonabusive parents.[86] More than 80 percent of the abusive families sought to resolve crises alone versus 43 percent of the nonabusive parents. Straus found that stress was linked to physical abuse when it occurred in the absence of participation in normal social groups (clubs, church, and so on).[87] Polansky and his colleagues found a history of estrangement from normal social experience among neglecting parents.[88] Giovannoni and Billingsley found that among a low-income group those who did not participate in the cooperative activities of the neighborhood (principally shared homemaking and child care) were more abusive and neglectful.[89] The unanimity of research findings on the issue of social isolation as we have defined it here is virtually complete.[90]

What is lacking in this body of research, however, is a firm grasp on the sequence of events. How does social isolation develop as a characteristic of families? There are, no doubt, at least two contrasting patterns. Type I includes families who form part of an "underclass" or deviant subculture. They may remain outside the normal support systems for generations. Pavenstedt called this group "the drifters."[91] These families become alienated from community structures through some event or series of events that has the effect of divorcing them from support systems. Such a pattern may arise from moving, illness, birth of a handicapped child, or severe income loss and the accompanying loss of social status.

There are numerous possible causes of isolation from support systems. They include the developmental history of parents, social stresses that cut families off from potential and actual supports, mobility patterns that disrupt social networks, and characteristics of the families that alienate people. Others are the lack of inclination and ability of neighborhoods to provide the observation and resources essential to the feedback function, and social-service systems inadequate to the task of identifying high-risk families. For prevention and treatment to work we need to find the worlds of abnormal rearing, get inside them, and open them up to the healing influences of the community. We need to establish a flow of information to and from these worlds so that parent-child relations can be normalized. While this may sound simple enough in the abstract, in practice it is very difficult.[92] American or Western thinking is so individualistically oriented that we find it difficult to grasp the many implications of the social-isolation thesis presented here. To understand the isolation of families from potent prosocial support systems we need to examine our cultural blueprint for social relations in which privacy and autonomy overshadow openness and connectedness. This is our next task.

Notes

1. S. Pfohl, "The 'Discovery' of Child Abuse," *Social Problems* 24 (1977): 310-323; S. Radbill, "A History of Child Abuse and Infanticide," in *The Battered Child,* ed. R. Helfer and C.H. Kempe (Chicago: University of Chicago Press, 1974).

2. R.J. Gelles, "Child Abuse as Psychopathology: A Sociological Critique and Reformulation," *American Journal of Orthopsychiatry* 43 (1973): 611-621; D.G. Gil, *Violence against Children: Physical Child Abuse in the United States* (Cambridge, Mass.: Harvard University Press, 1970).

3. Gil, *Violence against Children.*

4. Gelles, "Child Abuse as Psychopathology."

5. C.H. Kempe, F.N. Silverman, B.R. Steele, W. Droegamueller, and H.K. Silver, "The Battered-Child Syndrome," *Journal of the American Medical Association* 181 (1962): 17-24.

6. Gelles, "Child Abuse as Psychopathology."

7. S.R. Tulkin, "An Analysis of the Concept of Cultural Deprivation," *Developmental Psychology* 6 (1972): 326-339.

8. T. Kuhn, *The Structure of Scientific Revolutions* (Chicago: University of Chicago Press, 1971).

9. J.J. Spinetta and D. Rigler, "The Child-abusing Parent: A Psychological Review," *Psychological Bulletin* 77 (1972): 296-304.

10. B.F. Steele and D. Pollock, "A Psychiatric Study of Parents Who Abuse Infants and Small Children," in *The Battered Child,* ed. R.E. Helfer and C.H. Kempe.

11. V.J. Fontana, "Further Reflections on Maltreatment of Children," *New York State Journal of Medicine* 68 (1968): 2214-2215.

12. R. Helfer, J. McKinney, and R. Kempe, "Arresting or Freezing the Developmental Process," in *Child Abuse and Neglect: The Family and Community* ed. R. Helfer and C.H. Kempe (Cambridge, Mass.: Ballinger, 1976).

13. B. Justice and R. Justice, *The Abusing Family* (New York: Human Sciences Press, 1976).

14. M.G. Morris and R.W. Gould, "Role Reversal: A Necessary Concept in Dealing with the 'Battered Child Syndrome,'" in *The Neglected/Battered Child Syndrome* (New York: Child Welfare League of America, 1963).

15. Gil, *Violence against Children,* 2d ed., 1973.

16. E. Zigler, "Controlling Child Abuse in America: An Effort Doomed to Failure?" in *Critical Perspectives on Child Abuse* ed. R. Bourne and E. Newberger (Lexington, Mass.: Lexington Books, D.C. Heath and Company, 1979).

17. National Academy of Sciences, *Toward a National Policy for Children and Families* (Washington: U.S. Government Printing Office, 1976).

18. K. Kenniston, *All Our Children: The American Family under Pressure* (New York: Harcourt Brace Jovanovich, 1977).

19. G. Elder, *Children of the Great Depression* (Chicago: University of Chicago Press, 1974); G. Elder and R. Rockwell, "The Life Course and Human Development: An Ecological Perspective" (Boys Town, Neb.: Center for the Study of Youth Development, 1977).

20. U. Bronfenbrenner, *The Ecology of Human Development* (Cambridge, Mass.: Harvard University Press, 1979).

21. Ibid.

22. Ibid.

23. M. Kohn, *Class and Conformity: A Study in Values,* 2d ed. (Chicago: University of Chicago Press, 1977).

24. G. Albee, "Politics, Power, Prevention and Social Change" (Paper presented at the Vermont Conference on the Primary Prevention of Psychopathology, June 1979).

25. E. Wynne, *Growing up Suburban* (Austin, Tex.: University of Texas Press, 1977).

26. W.I. Thomas and D.S. Thomas, *The Child in America* (New York: Alfred P. Knopf, 1928).

27. Bronfenbrenner, *Ecology of Human Development.*

28. J. Belsky, "Child Maltreatment: An Ecological Integration," *American Psychologist,* 35 (1980): 320-335; R. Friedman, "Child Abuse: A Review of the Psychosocial Research," in *Four Perspectives on the Status of Child Abuse and Neglect Research,* ed. Herner and Company (Washington, D.C.: National Center on Child Abuse and Neglect, 1976); A. Green, "Self-destruction in Physically Abused Schizophrenic Children: Report of Cases," *Archives of General Psychiatry* 19 (1968): 171-197; R. Light, "Abuse and Neglected Children in America: A study of Alternative Policies," *Harvard Educational Review* 43 (1973): 556-598; R. Parke and C.W. Collmer, "Child Abuse: An Interdisciplinary Analysis," in

Review of Child Development Research, vol 5, ed. E.M. Hetherington (Chicago: University of Chicago Press, 1975); N. Polansky, "Analysis of Research on Child Neglect: The Social Work Viewpoint," in *Four perspectives,* ed. Herner and Company.

29. Gil, *Violence against Children.*

30. Justice and Justice, *The Abusing Family.*

31. Friedman, "Child Abuse."

32. D. McClelland, "Testing for Competence rather than Intelligence," *American Psychologist* 28 (1973): 1–14.

33. Tulkin, "Concept of Cultural Deprivation."

34. D. McClelland, "Testing for Competence."

35. A. Green, "Self-destruction."

36. B. Bettleheim, "Individual and Mass Behavior in Extreme Situations," *Journal of Abnormal and Social Psychology* 38 (1943): 417–452; S. Milgram, *Obedience to Authority* (New York: Harper and Row, 1974); P. Zimbardo and F. Ruch, *Psychology and Life* (Glenview, Ill.: Scott, Foresman and Company, 1975).

37. O.G. Brim, *Education for Child Rearing* (New York: Russell Sage Foundation, 1959); O.G. Brim, Jr., and S. Wheeler, *Socialization after Childhood: Two Essays* (New York: John Wiley and Sons, 1966); G. Elder, "Family History and the Life Course," *Journal of Family History* 1 (1977): 279–304.

38. Elder, "Family History."

39. L. Cottrell, "The Adjustment of the Individual to His Age and Sex Roles," *American Sociological Review* 7 (1942): 617–620.

40. W. Burr, *Theory Construction and the Sociology of the Family* (New York: John Wiley and Sons, 1973).

41. Elder, "Family History."

42. Ibid.

43. Parke and Collmer, "Child Abuse."

44. Justice and Justice, *The Abusing Family.*

45. E.S. Paykel, "Life Stress, Depression and Attempted Suicide," *Journal of Human Stress* September 1976: 3–12.

46. H. Wilensky, "Orderly Careers and Social Participation in the Middle Class," *American Sociological Review* 24 (1961): 836–845.

47. J.M. Pahl and R.E. Pahl, *Managers and Their Wives: A Study of Career and Family Relationships in the Middle Class* (London: Allen Lane, 1971).

48. M. Weissman and E. Paykel, *The Depressed Woman* (Chicago: University of Chicago Press, 1974).

49. L. Young, *Wednesday's Children* (New York: McGraw-Hill, 1964).

50. B. Justice and D.F. Duncan, "Life Crisis as a Precursor to Child Abuse," *Public Health Reports* 91 (1976): 110–115.

51. J. Kennell, D. Voos, and M. Klaus, "Parent-Infant Bonding," in *Child Abuse and Neglect,* ed. R. Helfer and C.H. Kempe.

52. Young, *Wednesday's Children.*

53. Parke and Collmer, "Child Abuse."

54. Elder, "Family History."

55. Polansky, "Research on Child Neglect."

56. U. Bronfenbrenner and M. Mahoney, "The Structure and Verification of Hypotheses," in *Influences on Human Development,* ed. U. Bronfenbrenner and M. Mahoney (Hinsdale, Ill.: Dryden Press, 1975).

57. Gil, *Violence against Children.*

58. J. Gray, C. Cutler, J. Dean, and C.H. Kempe, "Perinatal Assessment of Mother-Baby Interaction," in *Child Abuse and Neglect,* ed. R. Helfer and C.H. Kempe.

59. C. Schneider, J. Hoffmeister, and R. Helfer, "A Predictive Screening Questionnaire for Potential Problems in Mother-Child Interaction," in *Child Abuse and Neglect,* ed. R. Helfer and C.H. Kempe.

60. National Academy of Sciences, *National Policy for Children.*

61. Radbill, "History of Child Abuse."

62. Albee, "Politics, Power, Prevention."

63. J. Garbarino and J. Hershberger, "The Perspective of Evil in Understanding and Treating Child Abuse," *Journal of Religion and Health,* in press.

64. Radbill, "History of Child Abuse."

65. J. Korbin, "Very Few Cases: Child Abuse in the People's Republic of China" in *Child Abuse and Neglect,* ed. J. Korbin (Berkeley, Calif.: University of California Press, 1981). R.I. Levy, "On Getting Angry in the Society Islands," in *Mental Health Research in Asia and the Pacific* ed. W. Candill and T.Y. Lin (Honolulu, Hawaii: East-West Center Press, 1969); M. Mead, *Sex and Temperament in Three Savage Tribes* (New York: Morrow, 1935); R. Sidel, *Women and Child Care in China* (New York: Hill and Wang, 1972); H.W. Stevenson, "Society for Research," *Child Development Newsletter,* Fall 1974.

66. Gil, *Violence against Children;* C. Geis and J. Monahan, "The Social Ecology of Violence," in *Moral Development and Behavior,* ed. T. Lickona (New York: Holt, Rinehart and Winston, 1976); M.H. Lystad, "Violence at Home: A Review of the Literature," *American Journal of Orthopsychiatry* 45 (1975): 328-345; M. Straus, R. Gelles, and S. Steinmetz, *Behind Closed Doors* (New York: Doubleday, 1980).

67. Lystad, "Violence at Home."

68. R. Stark and J. McEvoy, "Middle Class Violence," *Psychology Today* 4 (1970): 52-65.

69. Straus, Gelles, and Steinmetz, *Behind Closed Doors.*

70. B. Korsch, J. Christian, E. Gozzi, and P. Carlson, "Infant Care and Punishment: A Pilot Study," *American Journal of Public Health* 55 (1965): 1880-1888.

71. E.C. Viano, "Attitudes toward Child Abuse among American Professionals" (Paper presented at the biennial meeting of the International Society for Research on Aggression, Toronto, 1974).

72. Justice and Justice, *The Abusing Family.*

73. A. Tietjen, "Formal and Informal Support Systems: A Cross-cultural Perspective," in *Protecting Children from Abuse and Neglect*, ed. J. Garbarino, S.H. Stocking, and Associates (San Francisco: Jossey-Bass, 1980).

74. Korbin, "Very Few Cases."

75. G. Caplan, *Support Systems and Community Mental Health* (New York: Behavioral Publications, 1974).

76. Ibid., pp. 4-5.

77. Ibid., pp. 5-6.

78. E. Bott, *Family and Social Network: Roles, Norms and External Relationships*, 2d ed. (New York: Free Press, 1972); M. Cochran and J. Brassard, "Social Networks and Child Development," *Child Development* 50 (1979): 601-616; Garbarino, Stocking, and Associates, *Protecting Children;* P. Craven and B. Wellman, "The Network City," in *The Community: Approaches and Applications*, ed. M.P. Effrot (New York: Free Press, 1974); J. Mitchell, *Social Networks in Urban Situations* (Atlantic Highland, N.J.: Humanities Press, 1969); C. Stack, *All Our Kin* (New York: Harper and Row, 1974).

79. J. Brassard, "The Nature and Utilization of Social Networks in Families Confronting Different Life Circumstances" (M.A. thesis, Cornell University, Ithaca, N.Y., 1976); U. Bronfenbrenner and M. Cochran, "The Comparative Ecology of Human Development: A Research Proposal" (Cornell University, mimeograph, 1976); Cochran and Brassard, "Social networks"; A. Collins and D. Pancoast, *Natural Helping Networks* (Washington, D.C.: National Association of Social Workers, 1976); J. Garbarino and D. Sherman, "Identifying High-risk Neighborhoods," in *Protecting Children*, ed. J. Garbarino, S.H. Stocking, and Associates (Boys Town, Neb.: Center for the Study of Youth Development, 1978); J. Garbarino, A. Crouter, and D. Sherman, "Screening Neighborhoods for Intervention: A Research Model for Child Protective Services," *Journal of Social Service Research* 1 (1978): 135-145; A. Tietjen, "Formal and Informal Support Systems: Service and Social Networks in Swedish Planned Communities" (Ph.D. diss., Cornell University, Ithaca, N.Y., 1977).

80. Cochran and Brassard, "Social Networks."

81. E. Elmer, *Children in Jeopardy* (Pittsburgh: University of Pittsburgh Press, 1967).

82. E.F. Lenoski, "Translating Injury Data into Preventive and Health Care Services—Physical Child Abuse" (University of Southern California School of Medicine, Los Angeles, 1974).

83. Young, *Wednesday's Children.*

84. N. Polansky, M. Chalmers, R. Buttenweiser, and D. Williams, "The Isolation of the Neglectful Family," *American Journal of Orthopsychiatry* 49 (1979): 149-152.

85. Young, *Wednesday's Children.*

86. Lenoski, "Translating Injury Data."

87. M. Straus, "Stress and Child Abuse," in *The Battered Child*, ed. R.E. Helfer and C.H. Kempe, 3d ed (Chicago, Ill.: University of Chicago Press, 1980).

88. Polansky, Chalmers, Buttenweiser, and Williams, "Isolation of the Neglectful Family."

89. J.M. Giovannoni and A. Billingsley, "Child Neglect among the Poor: A Study of Parental Adequacy in Families of Three Ethnic Groups," *Child Welfare* 49 (1970): 196-204.

90. D. Bakan, *Slaughter of the Innocents* (San Francisco: Jossey-Bass, 1971); H.D. Bryant, A. Billingsley, G.A. Kerry, M.U. Leafman, E.J. Merrill, C.R. Serrecal, and B. Walsh, "Physical Abuse of Children: An Agency Study," *Child Welfare* 52 (1963): 225-230; Elmer, *Children in Jeopardy;* Garbarino and Sherman, "Identifying High-risk Neighborhoods;" B. Lauer, E. Ten Brock, and M. Grossman, "Battered Child Syndrome: Review of 130 Patients with Controls," *Pediatrics* 54 (1974): 67-70; S.M. Smith, R. Hanson and S. Noble, "Social Aspects of the Battered Baby Syndrome," *British Journal of Psychiatry* 125 (1974): 568-582; I. Wollock and B. Horowitz, "Factors Relating to Levels of Child Care among Families Receiving Public Assistance in New Jersey" (Paper presented at the National Conference on Child Abuse and Neglect, New York, April 1978).

91. E. Pavenstedt, *The Drifters: Children of Disorganized Lower-class Families* (Boston: Little, Brown, 1967).

92. Garbarino, Stocking, and Associates, *Protecting Children.*

Social Isolation as ⲁ Price of Privacy

To most Americans, the value of privacy is unquestioned. To many, any invasion of privacy is a kind of "cultural treason." This orientation is reflected in our laws, in speeches made by politicians, in policies of both government and private agencies, and in opinions of citizens in public polls. Although privacy may be valuable, it does not come without costs to the individual and to the community; some are paid by children in the form of abuse and neglect. In this chapter we look at how social isolation is the price we pay for privacy in America. In chapter 2 we established the role of isolation from potent prosocial support systems in child maltreatment, and here we show how social isolation is built into the fabric of our society—its institutions, customs, and ideology.

While public attention is drawn to only the most lurid and dramatic cases of child maltreatment, we are surrounded daily with the more mundane incidents. An infant is dropped repeatedly. A toddler is whipped. A kindergartner is punched. A teenager is assaulted regularly by a parent for minor misbehavior. These events rarely reach the general public, but they are at the core of the problem. As Henry Kempe repeatedly has pointed out, our society tends to kiss newborns goodbye at the hospital door and not have any systematic and official contact with them until they enter school.[1] Even then children are treated as if they were the property of parents, not as the future citizens they are. By permitting this we encourage the conditions that spawn child maltreatment; we allow it by valuing privacy above the essential support-system functions of feedback and nurturance. Families need information from the outside world in order to do well by their children.

Information consists of both regular feedback on parent-child relations and general knowledge of appropriate norms, expectations, and techniques concerning child rearing. Adequate information depends upon three factors: regular observation and discussion of parent-child relations; informal folk wisdom based on extensive, historically validated firsthand experience; and formal, professional expertise, particularly in the areas of solving behavior problems. Third, the need for information is related directly to the situational demands of the parent-child relationship. As these demands increase, so does the need for information. Fourth, formal institutions can become effective sources of information if they are linked actively to the family's social network, either directly through the parent or indirectly through the parent's relationship with some other person.

Privacy can be hazardous to social health and development because it undermines these processes of information flow to and from the family. In analyzing the social experience of American youth, Edward Wynne reported on the value placed on being alone, being autonomous, and being removed from observation, monitoring, and evaluation.[2] Wynne makes a useful distinction between personal and impersonal observation. Youngsters seem to be receiving less and less personal observation (that is, behavior being evaluated in the context of enduring relationships with adults) and more impersonal observations characterized by disinterested bureaucratic contacts of short duration and narrow focus. Bronfenbrenner reinforced this interpretation in his analysis of the roots of alienation.[3] Impersonal observation has supplanted personal observation. Moreover, this pattern seems to apply to both adults and children. Families have become less and less dominated by kinship and neighborhood relationships, and more and more by individual privacy coupled with reliance on mass media and personal services.

American social history is pervaded with an ambivalence concerning individualism and collectivism, freedom and authority, privacy and social integration. This dynamic has been identified by a variety of authors. Webb called it "the parabola of individualism."[4] Philip Slater[5] more recently termed it "the pursuit of loneliness," and David Riesman labeled it "the lonely crowd."[6] The phenomenon is noted in Bronfenbrenner's *Two Worlds of Childhood*.[7] Americans place a high value on owning a single-family home, on the freedom a car brings, and on being independent of all regulations. It is as if we were trying to make every man (and woman) an island. Opportunities for privacy have increased markedly in recent decades. This provides a potentially dangerous context for parent-child relations. It is true particularly in stressful circumstances, such as when a single parent is struggling to make a living and raise a child. It makes it more disturbing to note, then, that in recent decades the likelihood that a single parent will maintain a separate household rather than moving in with another (typically with a household containing a close relative) has doubled.[8] This gives the parent-child relationship more freedom and privacy but less feedback and nurturance. In chapter 2 we identified the balance of stresses and supports as critical in the matter of child maltreatment. Here we are recognizing that our society has its finger on the scales, and may tip the balance over on the stress side through its insistence on autonomy, independence, and privacy. Rotenberg persuasively argued that because we define dependency as pathological and autonomy as healthy we doom ourselves to a pervasive sense of estrangement and alienation.[9] As always, children in general, and poor children in particular, pay the highest price.

Stress and Social Support

A growing body of literature identifies stress as a prime contributor to a wide range of personal and social problems, including illness,[10] suicide, and depression.[11]

But a more complete analysis has shown that it is the match of stress and social support that is most important.[12] A person with a large reservoir of social support and the skills to use it can cope with a lot of stress. An isolated and socially unskilled person is vulnerable to even low levels of stress.

Despite the great importance of economic factors in determining the quality of life, subjective well-being is not explained fully by socioeconomic and demographic conditions.[13] Rather, the felt quality of life is given its tone by the social exchanges and personal interactions one finds in the home, the neighborhood, and the workplace. Ironically, people recognize the contribution that social connectedness makes to their lives while at the same time they are pursuing privacy and thereby undermining that connectedness. We yearn to belong and yet seem to do everything we can to thwart the fulfillment of that longing. This is Slater's pursuit of loneliness.

Research on depression[14] and suicide[15] links overall psychological well-being to involvement in enduring supportive social relationships. Disrupting or terminating these relationships is highly stressful.[16] Where does privacy fit into this matrix of stress, psychological distress, and ultimately child maltreatment? It provides a fertile medium in which all three grow. What is more, privacy works against natural healing forces and makes it more difficult to deliver help as well as to ask for it.

As Elder noted, a condition of ascendancy to the middle class is the relinquishing of kinship and neighborhood bonds in return for the benefits of privacy.[17] Let us be clear in recognizing that traditional kinship and neighborhood relationships exact psychological costs. The sense of obligation, guilt, dependence, and intrusion weighs heavily on many. There is little privacy. One's time and resources are always on call to kin in need. Interpersonal relations and day-to-day activities are under the scrutiny of kin who have an investment in the nuclear family. Child-rearing practices are particularly subject to scrutiny by relatives, since the principal "currency" of kinship is children. Experiences that link the family into the social mainstream of the community, beyond the kinship circle, are essential. Children and parents both need this "protection." It appears that kinship lacking this community connection often reinforces rather than counteracts patterns of child maltreatment. A recent study by Straus reports that among people experiencing a high level of stress, if the only social network they have is kin, it is likely to mean higher rather than lower levels of domestic violence.[18] In this as in other matters, diversity and social pluralism are good for children.[19]

Many people have reacted to the potentially stifling atmosphere of intensive interaction with kin by rejecting intrusive social networks as a matter of both personal and professional policy.[20] They may trade in the intrusiveness of social integration for the privacy of social isolation. We recognize that when it comes to connectedness, too much can be a problem, but we believe the greater danger for most Americans at this point in our history is too little. The hypothesis emerging from this analysis is this: As the value and opportunity for privacy increase, the danger of isolation increases correspondingly. As isolation increases, so does the possibility of child maltreatment.

Involvement of families in extensive kin networks,[21] natural-helping networks,[22] or strong neighborhoods with positive values, organized to implement them,[23] can inhibit child maltreatment.[24] Such involvement provides both child-care resources and the right to call upon those resources. Both the time and expertise necessary for effective involvement are often lacking in high-risk homes.[25] Social connectedness provides access to social and economic resources that can aid the family in times of stress.[26] Such involvement provides personalized observation of the family. It combats family climates that induce depression, anger, helplessness, loss of control, and violence. Without privacy it is unlikely that a pattern of maltreatment can be established and maintained. Abuse or neglect generally will be inhibited or at least identified at an early stage when families are involved in an active exchange network with prosocial friends, neighbors, and relatives. In her study of domestic networks and kinship in a poor black community, Stack documented such an intimate and active network of mutual obligation and assistance that granted little privacy.[27] It is illuminating to note that the stresses imposed by racism and poverty seem to be deflected somewhat from children in such a setting. The active involvement of family friends tends to prevent stress from being translated into chronic maltreatment when those "outsiders" themselves are not abusive. We have been persuaded that children can survive maltreatment if they have someone in their social network who provides compensatory acceptance, nurturance, and a positive model for social experience. Studies of so-called invulnerable children and our own interviews with victims of maltreatment persuade us of this. Everyone needs someone. If, in the name of family privacy, we isolate the victims of child maltreatment, then we deprive them of a potentially important normalizing influence on their development. They are thus doubly victimized: By denying them prevention and denying them healing.

There are several problems facing traditional kinship networks and their nonfamilial surrogates. First, current levels of geographic mobility bend or break these networks. Mobility stretches the bonds of kinship over long distances. It makes effective feedback and nurturance difficult, and in many cases prevents the establishment and maintenance of effective surrogate systems. Strong neighborhoods may counter this, but even they are weakened by transience.[28] Second, there is a culturally sanctioned movement to escape the costs of kinship networks. Privacy is valued and social bonds are opposed as antithetical to individual development. The ascendancy of middle-class norms and practices offers the possibility of freedom, privacy, and individuation to unprecedented numbers of people. Fewer and fewer families contain adults other than the child's parents. As noted earlier, single parents increasingly maintain separate households.[29] Housing patterns encourage private residences, and where multifamily dwellings are available they increasingly create a ghetto of families with children. The overall development of our culture is downgrading intrusive kinship networks. We value independence and see dependence as being pathological.[30] These trends extend to and in some cases are led by professionals in the field of social services and psychology who often extol the virtues of autonomy and self-fulfillment without an appropriate regard for their costs.[31]

Privacy Sparks Maltreatment

Elder noted that middle-class observers often were dismayed by the way working-class families shared with kin during the Great Depression.[32] "How could they jeopardize their own marginal economic resources by committing themselves to help?" they asked. Stack's account of black kinship sharing points out that the typical professional evaluation of such behavior is that it is irrational and self-defeating.[33] In a study of Jewish social workers and clients, Leichter and Mitchell report some interesting differences in attitudes and values between caseworkers and clients. The more traditional clients, and their parents, expressed a belief in the rights, wisdom, and obligations of kinship. The more modern caseworkers downgraded kinship networks in favor of personal freedom, autonomy, and privacy.[34] Campbell noted the ideological commitment of most modern psychologists to liberation of the individual from collective bonds.[35] In Campbell's view, psychologists who counsel liberation are embarking on a socially dangerous course, a course in conflict with the human need for structure, obligations, and ties that bind. Although the liberation perspective may be strongest among psychologists, it has support from many social-work professionals and from segments of the general public.

The allure of privacy is great. It permits individualism to flourish and insulates the family against external meddling by persons who may have their own interests to advance. This protective function seems a major attraction to social workers.[36] Privacy provides the potential for a quiet atmosphere, whereas kinship intrusion is psychologically noisy. Despite this, privacy may be damaging or even lethal for children when combined with the factors that elicit abusive behavior.

Privacy alone is not, of course, sufficient to produce abuse and neglect. But then almost no factor uniformly produces the same effect in different human beings. Each of us is more vulnerable to some conditions than others. In an epidemic some are spared. In general, however, there are circumstances in which parent-child relations are placed in special jeopardy by privacy. Recent evidence on mothering by gorillas show that these conditions pertain to animals as well as humans. Young gorilla mothers have been separated from their peers by their human protectors to insulate the parent-child relationship from external interference. The result was a high rate of child abuse and neglect. When restored to the community of apes the abusive patterns were replaced with more healthy behavior.[37] Privacy (as isolation) went against the nature of the apes; they need social contact for healthy family relationships. People do too.

Privacy is a necessary condition that allows abuse to occur when sufficient conditions combine to create a socially critical mass. When families are exposed to loss of income, excessive work schedules (too much or too little), or other conditions that lead to frustration and tension, the probability of maltreatment is markedly increased. These social conditions interact with the parenting style of the child's caregivers. When the parent is deficient in the ability to empathize with the child, the potential for abuse is heightened. When the caregiver's style is inconsistent, the child is exposed to danger. When the caregiver approves of physical force as punishment, then too the danger is heightened. Caregivers who do not use lower-limit controls on behavior in an effective and consistent manner set the stage for uncontrolled behavior, from both themselves and their child. Caregivers even may violate their own values and rules of conduct when they cannot establish effective control. As Milgram's work[38] and Fischer's studies of arousal[39] imply, in a state of psychological stress many uncharacteristic behaviors by caregivers are possible. Thus one root of abuse is an unstable pattern of parenting, particularly when it includes the use of force in disciplining. A third factor contributing to abuse is the child as a stimulus. Some children are difficult to care for. This may be due to something intrinsic to the child, such as an overly active and nonresponsive temperament, or to something extrinsic to the child, such as its resemblance to a hated person, its position in the family, or its relationship to someone resented by the caregiver. The characteristics of the child can elicit abusive behavior when the caregiver is prone to abusive behavior because of stress or parenting style.

Many families can resolve unstable parenting patterns. Many families can overcome the problems of a difficult child. They can do all this. But to do it they generally require assistance from the outside, and some families do not seek or cannot get the help they need. Lenoski found that 81 percent of abusive families preferred to resolve their problems without outside involvement, whereas 43 percent of nonabusive families were so inclined.[40] This finding not only reveals the isolation of "abnormal" families, but points to the high value "normal" families place on freedom. For a child in a stable and psychologically healthy family, isolation is a limiting factor on development. For a child in a family plagued by stress and parental instability, isolation is dangerous and can be lethal. There is little to fear at this point in our history from too little privacy, at least in the sense we have been discussing the term here. The great outcry against Big Brother is really a product of the resentment that comes from impersonal observation and restrictions. Intimate "social smothering," though uncomfortable and even sometimes psychologically oppressive, seems less of a danger than social isolation.

What Can Be Done?

What can be done to resist our social excesses in the name of privacy? One way is to resist and even reverse the cultural sanction for privacy in its extreme form. We can recognize the value of kinship systems and their surrogates, and nurture their values of mutual obligation, authority, continuity, and accountability. We can encourage helping networks, particularly among populations prone to abuse, that is, those exposed to high stress, socially disintegrating communities, and difficult children.

Another way to do this is to encourage enduring relationships between families and professionals charged with the task of parent education and support. These relationships can begin prior to the birth of the child and can continue through childhood and adolescence. We can enlist the aid and support of the activities of natural-helping networks built around central neighbors.[41] Finally, we can promote the idea that a primary right of the child is access to the outside world, and a basic right of society is the opportunity to protect the child. Families do not own their children. They hold them in trust for society. Other societies have developed a clearer concept of what this implies for support systems for families.[42] This trust can be fulfilled best when families are not granted so much privacy that they can and do become isolated. Rather, they should be embedded in a web of social relationships that are personal, enduring, and reciprocal. Kinship and neighboring do this naturally. Where they are unavailable or ineffective, social action is needed to create and maintain surrogate networks to support and observe families. The price for privacy should not be paid by the thousands of American children who suffer maltreatment each year. Perhaps an extreme example reported in the mass media will serve to make this point, and establish the worst case as a basis for recognizing the danger of typical American social isolation.

> Police investigators said they could hardly remember a case worse than X's. Two- and three-inch strips of flesh had been torn from his face, arms, legs, back, buttocks, and stomach; a purple bruise covered his chest; blood soaked his shirt and pants by the time his stepfather brought him to the emergency room.
>
> Mr. X, 20, was charged with second-degree murder and is being held on $500,000 bond. He signed a statement saying he hit X with his hand and his belt because he had not learned his ABCs.
>
> Mrs. X, 22, was charged with manslaughter by culpable negligence for her son's death. Her bond was set at $250,000.
>
> Those who knew X often heard his cries and those of his 2-year-old half sister, Y, coming from the family's apartment. But they never thought, until too late, that he would die.

A string of "what if's" and "only if's" marred X's case. If neighbors had known about the twenty-four-hour toll-free answering service in the state capital for reporting child abuse.

If the children's grandmother, Z, had not been rebuffed by state welfare officials for three months while trying to gain custody of the two children.

If Mr. A, the postman, who lived above the family, had been more persistent when he told Mr. X not to beat the children. "He told me it was his kid and 'I'll do what I want.' I didn't bother him after that."

If the mother's sisters, who knew that she was being severely beaten by her husband, had not been afraid of stirring up trouble by checking on the children.

One further point must be made. This discussion has focused on the costs of privacy. This is not to say that the costs of protecting children are insignificant. Such control involves limitations on freedom and privacy. The Peoples' Republic of China has great concern for children and families.[43] It intrudes into every aspect of the life and mind of the Chinese people. It makes what most Americans see as staggering demands for self-sacrifice. It supports the development of children through totalitarian control of social relations. The costs to freedom and individual identity are unacceptably high. We in the United States are faced with the task of reducing the negative aspects of privacy without paying too high a price in the freedom and integrity of the individual. We need a positive concept of dependency.[44] Our heritage includes a theme of cooperation and collective identity that can provide a democratic-pluralist alternative to the totalitarian model of caring. We must tap that heritage on behalf of children through a process in which every family is woven into multiple networks of caring. This process begins with birth, as we shall see in the next chapter.

Notes

1. C.H. Kempe, "A Practical Approach to the Protection of the Abused Child and Rehabilitation of the Abusing Parent," *Pediatrics* 51 (1973): 804–812.

2 E. Wynne, "Privacy and Socialization to Adulthood" (Paper presented at the annual meeting of the American Educational Research Association, Washington, D.C., March 1975); idem, "Adolescent Alienation and Social Policy," *Teachers College Record* 78 (1976): 33-39.

3. U. Bronfenbrenner, "Reality and Research in the Ecology of Human Development," *Proceedings of the American Philosophical Society* 119 (1975): 439-469.

4. W. Webb, *The Great Frontier* (Austin, Tex.: University of Texas Press, 1952).

5. P.E. Slater, *The Pursuit of Loneliness: American Culture at the Breaking Point* (Boston: Beacon Press, 1970).

6. D. Riesman, *The Lonely Crowd* (New Haven, Conn.: Yale University Press, 1950).

7. U. Bronfenbrenner, *Two Worlds of Childhood* (New York: Russell Sage Foundation, 1970).

8. Bronfenbrenner, "Reality and Research."

9. M. Rotenberg, "Alienating Individualism and Reciprocal Individualism: A Cross-Cultural Conceptualization," *Journal of Humanistic Psychology* 17 (1977): 3-17.

10. R. Haggerty, "Statement to the American Public Health Association," Miami Beach, 1976; K.A. Fox, *Social Indicators and Social Theory* (New York: John Wiley and Sons, 1974).

11. E.S. Paykel, "Life Stress, Depression and Attempted Suicide," *Journal of Human Stress* (September 1976): 3-12.

12. B. Gottlieb, "The Role of Individual and Social Support in Preventing Child Maltreatment," in *Protecting Children from Abuse and Neglect,* J. Garbarino, S.H. Stocking and Associates (San Francisco: Jossey-Bass, 1980).

13. Haggerty, "Statement."

14. M. Weissman and E. Paykel, "Moving and Depression in Women," in *Loneliness* ed. Robert S. Weiss (Cambridge, Mass.: MIT Press, 1973), pp. 154-164; Paykel, "Life Stress."

15. Paykel, "Life Stress."

16. Fox, *Social Indicators and Social Theory.*

17. G. Elder, *Children of the Great Depression* (Chicago: University of Chicago Press, 1974).

18. M. Straus, "Stress and Child Abuse," in *The Battered Child,* R.E. Helfer and C.H. Kempe, 3d ed. (Chicago, Ill.: University of Chicago Press, 1980).

19. J. Garbarino and U. Bronfenbrenner, "The Socialization of Moral Judgment and Behavior in Cross-cultural Perspective," in *Moral Development and Behavior,* ed. T. Lickona (New York: Holt, Rinehart and Winston, 1976).

20. H.J. Leichter and W.E. Mitchell, *Kinship and Casework* (New York: Russell Sage Foundation, 1967).

21. C. Stack, *All Our Kin* (New York: Harper and Row, 1974).

22. A. Collins and D. Pancoast, *Natural Helping Networks* (Washington, D.C.: National Association of Social Workers, 1976).

23. P. Fellin and E. Litwak, "The Neighborhood in Urban American Society," *Social Work* 13 (1968): 72-80.

24. Garbarino, Stocking, and Associates, *Protecting Children;* J. Garbarino and D. Sherman, "High-risk Neighborhoods and High-risk Families: The Human Ecology of Child Maltreatment," *Child Development* 51 (1980): 188-198.

25. D.G. Gil, *Violence against Children: Physical Child Abuse in the United States* (Cambridge, Mass.: Harvard University Press, 1970).

26. J. Garbarino, "An Ecological Perspective on Child Maltreatment," in *The Social Context of Child Abuse and Neglect,* ed. L. Pelton (New York: Human Sciences Press, 1981).

27. Stack, *All Our Kin.*

28. Fellin and Litwak, "Neighborhood."

29. U. Bronfenbrenner, "The Origins of Alienation," in *Influences on Human Development;* ed. U. Bronfenbrenner and M. Mahony (Hinsdale, Ill.: Dryden Press, 1975).

30. Rotenberg, "Alienating Individualism."

31. A. Campbell, "Subjective Measures of Well-being," *American Psychologist* 31 (1976): 117–124.

32. Elder, *Children of the Great Depression.*

33. Stack, *All Our Kin.*

34. Leichter and Mitchell, *Kinship and Casework.*

35. Campbell, "Subjective Measures of Well-being."

36. Leichter and Mitchell, *Kinship and Casework;* Collins and Pancoast, *Natural Helping Networks.*

37. R. Nadler, "Child Abuse in Gorilla Mothers," *Caring* 5 (1979): 1–3; M. Rock, "Gorilla Mothers Need Some Help from Their Friends," *Smithsonian,* no. 4, 9 (1978): 58–63.

38. S. Milgram, *Obedience to Authority* (New York: Harper and Row, 1974).

39. R. Fischer, "Consciousness as Role and Knowledge," in *Readings in Abnormal Psychology: Contemporary Perspectives,* ed. L. Allman and D. Jaffe (New York: Harper and Row, 1976).

40. E.F. Lenoski, "Translating Injury Data into Preventive and Health Care Services—Physical Child Abuse." (University of Southern California School of Medicine, Los Angeles, 1974).

41. Collins and Pancoast, *Natural Helping Networks.*

42. U. Bronfenbrenner, *The Ecology of Human Development* (Cambridge, Mass.: Harvard University Press, 1979).

43. W. Kessen (Ed.), *Childhood in China* (New Haven, Conn.: Yale University Press, 1975).

44. Rotenberg, "Alienating Individualism."

4 Becoming a Parent and Creating a Family

How is a family created? How does the parent-infant relationship begin? How can we improve family functioning by strengthening the parent-child bond? As natural as families are, they are nonetheless a social creation. Most adults competently adopt the role of parent when they create and sustain adequate families. Some do not, however. In this chapter we seek to establish how some families go awry from their earliest hours and days, and how we can appreciate the significance of childbirth as a social event in shaping the course of early family development. In calling childbirth a social event we mean that the roles and statutes of the participants, and indeed who it is that participates, have an effect on the outcome. These social factors can play an important part in determining whether or not an infant born to a high-risk parent actually is exposed to a high-risk family and suffers maltreatment. Considering childbirth as a microsystem event is a starting point, but we need to view it in its full ecological complexity if we are to appreciate its role in understanding abusive families.

Being Born

Always one to cut to the heart of a matter, Charles Dickens titled chapter 1 of *David Copperfield* "I Am Born." What does it mean to be born? Does it matter *how* one is born? The human birth process is, of course, a physiological event, and recently we have begun to appreciate that it is a psychological one as well. Indeed, one recent book on the birth process is appropriately titled *The Psychology of Childbirth,*[1] and some psychodynamically oriented theorists believe people subconsciously remember their births. Biological and psychological influences are intertwined from beginning to end, from conception to delivery. The greatest challenges of pregnancy are typically psychological and social rather than biological in the modern world where bearing children has become a low-risk medical experience for most women.

The prenatal period is the beginning of psychological family creation. Both systematic and anecdotal evidence documents the potential development of a parent-child relationship prior to birth. Physicians have found that women report a perception of fetal activity patterns and even personality in the last trimester of pregnancy. Pediatrician Berry Brazelton speaks of parental "energizing" as birth approaches.[2] He notes a heightening of anxiety, role disruption, and fantasy, all serving to make the parent emotionally receptive to the newborn.

This phenomenon is supported naturally for women. But it can be encouraged for men by deliberate efforts on the part of physicians and others. Brazelton reports a marked increase in the emotional involvement of fathers with their children resulting from including fathers in prenatal visits. One manifestation of this involvement is a more active role in well-baby office visits. These positive forces stand in contrast, of course, to the negative experiences associated with an unwanted and unsupported pregnancy, where the process of rejecting the child and the role of parent may begin before birth. The legally illegitimate, socially repudiated, or personally unwanted can lead to a systematic negative relationship even prior to delivery. And this can be a serious contributor to subsequent maltreatment: Getting the relationship off on the wrong foot as it were. Simply to raise this issue is to highlight the importance of social factors in childbirth and the creation of a family. Public and professional concern about teenage childbearing reflects just how important the social context of childbirth and parenthood really is. The available research suggests that it is precisely the frequent lack of social supports for teenage parents rather than any physiological or psychological deficiency that makes teenage childbearing a social problem and threat to normal development.[3]

Consider two contrasting birth scenarios. We are all familiar, from our own experience or from the mass media, with the image of a nervous father-to-be pacing around the waiting room of a hospital. As he waits, the mother-to-be suffers in the labor room until she is wheeled into the delivery room. When her pain becomes unbearable she is given drugs to block the pain or even make her unconscious. The actual birth is thus a medical event actively witnessed only by doctors and nurses. The mother awakens afterward to be informed that she has delivered a boy or girl weighing X pounds. The father likewise is informed of the outcome, also secondhand. This scenario became the overwhelming American pattern during the twentieth century as powerful drugs were developed that enabled physicians to spare women the pain that many had suffered in childbirth.[4] What is more, this whole scenario is more bleak when the child is born via cesarean section; the whole affair is treated as an operation to remove the baby. The increase in cesarean-section deliveries symbolizes the best and the worst of modern obstetrics: the best because it saves lives; the worst because it psychologically impoverishes them. But it need not be that way.

Consider an alternative scenario. Some ten weeks before the baby is due to be born, the expectant mother and father begin attending prepared childbirth education classes. The course consists of exercises designed to prepare both partners to play an active role in the birth process. The physiology and psychology of childbirth are explained in detail. Exercises designed to prepare the woman to cope with the physical sensations of delivery (contractions and stretching) are demonstrated and the couple practices daily. The father-to-be plays a crucial role of monitoring and coaching. When labor begins, the couple starts the routine of relaxation and body-control techniques they have learned.

This continues through labor right into the delivery room. The birth is an active collaboration between medical personnel and the couple. When the baby is born it is greeted by the excited parents who are ready and able to start getting to know their child there in the delivery room. Even the more medically problematic cesarean can be included in this model of childbirth. Fathers and mothers can be active participants, and veterans of it report a heightened sense of attachment and commitment to the child and to each other.

This second scenario is becoming increasingly common in America (and it extends to the nursery where parents play a more active role and the family, rather than the hospital staff, is the star). One may ask, however, does it matter? Does it matter how you are born? The envy expressed by mothers and fathers denied the family-centered experience and the enthusiasm with which most of its veterans recommend it suggests strongly that it does. The available evidence tends to agree.

The medical circumstances of birth, of course, have important consequences. For example, lack of oxygen after separation from the mother (anoxia) can have a serious impact on development, including impaired motor development and even brain damage. There also are a variety of physical problems in delivery that can damage or kill the newborn. Along with the medical advances that relieve women of the pain of childbirth have been developments that decrease the mortality rate among both mothers and babies. This is progress. These medical gains mask some psychological losses, however, as growing numbers of researchers, physicians, nurses, and parents have come to recognize. These losses can jeopardize the early attachment between parent and infant by reducing opportunities for early bonding among family members. As Klaus and Kennell noted, "People who witness the birth process become strongly attached to the infant."[5]

The Psychology of Being Born

We must be aware of the newborn's potential for attachment-inducing behavior if we are to understand the impact of alternative delivery and nursery scenarios on human development. Newborns present a powerful combination of helplessness and responsiveness when they are healthy and their functions are not depressed by medications. Their helplessness draws parents in, while their responsiveness captures parents. Newborns are physiologically primed for social interaction. They can see, and prefer human faces to other objects. They can hear, and respond particularly well to voices. They can move their bodies, and actively do so in response to human stimulation. The more we allow the infant to demonstrate these capacities and the more we make parents aware of these abilities, the more we encourage strong, positive early attachment. In so doing, moreover, we improve the chances that a family will be a socially and psychologically healthy context for child development. This is the cornerstone for efforts to prevent child maltreatment.

Human infants are amazing creatures. They enter periodic alert states beginning in the first hour after birth (when medications do not inhibit this natural phenomenon).[6] Condon and Sander studied the "dance" between mother and infant.[7] The infant moves in rhythm to the mother's voice, a phenomenon that strains credulity but nonetheless is documented using slow-motion photography. MacFarlane's work shows that at six days the infant can reliably distinguish the scent of his own mother's breast milk from an array of pads used by nursing mothers.[8] Brazelton found that the neonate can turn its head to follow the mother visually for an arc over 180°.[9] Meltzoff and Moore produced evidence that as early as twelve days infants can imitate facial and manual gestures.[10] These are all capabilities that provide the modus operandi for developing early attachment.

There is accumulating evidence that the social conditions of the delivery and immediate postpartum setting themselves can have a significant impact on human development. Much of this work has been stimulated by two physician-investigators, Marshall Klaus and John Kennell.[11] One emphasis of their studies has been the effect of hospital policies and procedures upon the attachment bond. They are right on the mark for our purposes, pinpointing the modern trend toward isolating the birth experiences from its natural social context: kith and kin.

> . . . [I]t is necessary to note that crucial life events surrounding the development of . . . attachment . . . have been removed from the home and brought into the hospital over the past sixty years. The hospital now determines the procedures involved in birth and death. The experiences surrounding these two events in the life of an individual have been stripped of the long-established traditions and support systems built up over centuries to help families through these highly meaningful transitions.

All this is of special relevance to our concerns because it is precisely the richness of a family's resources that stands against maltreatment, while social impoverishment places the parent-child relationship in jeopardy. The quality of early parent-child contact can have an enduring impact on the child's development and the parent's behavior. When significant disruptions in early parent-child attachment occur, they increase the risk for child maltreatment. This is particularly true when the child is difficult to care for or the parent suffers from a high level of unsupported stress.

A major review by Kennell, Voos, and Klaus presents the case for this conclusion.[12] A number of circumstances, including a medically abnormal pregnancy, difficult labor or delivery, neonatal separation, other separations in the first six months, illnesses in the infant during the first year of life, and maternal illness during the infant's first year of life, all place a family at risk for child maltreatment. Threats to the parent-infant bond are particularly dangerous. In one study, 66 percent of the abused children were found to have experienced forty-eight-hour separations from their parents in the first week of life, while only 3 percent of those children's siblings had been separated.[13] Medically high-risk infants are particularly in danger. In a study of 146 infants who had been in an intensive-care nursery, it was found that a lack of parental visits was associated with the likelihood of later maltreatment.[14] Twenty-three percent of the infants receiving less than three visits during a two-week period subsequently experienced serious problems with their parents (abuse, abandonment, or failure to thrive). Only 2 percent of the infants receiving three or more visits per two-week period experienced such problems. While these results are not in and of themselves definitive, when combined with other research findings they persuade us that we can help protect children by doing all we can to help infants seduce their parents into becoming attached to them.

Interest in early contact as a basis for maternal-infant bonding represents a departure from the dominant twentieth-century medical attitude that sees child-birth as only a biological event. Emphasizing birth as a psychological event raises a whole new set of issues. These issues lead naturally into a fuller appreciation of birth as a social event, by which we mean an experience in which the roles and statuses of the participants have a significant effect on their behavior and on the outcomes.

The psychology of childbirth is particularly important today because of contemporary challenges to the maternal role. According to most expert ob-servers, the social and cultural supports for motherhood (and for fatherhood as well, for that matter) have been weakened. Therefore the psychological processes of attachment are more important than ever before. As a society, we need prac-tices that enhance bonding to get the attachment-formation process started. Rossi[15] addressed this historical problem by building on the observation that while a child's need for mothering is absolute, the need of an adult woman to mother is relative.[16] Thus we can predict that the needs of some infants will exceed the resources and motivation of some parents. Anyone familiar with babies and their parents will attest to this. The likelihood of this happening reflects both broad social forces such as our cultural blueprint for parenthood (a macrosystem issue) as well as the social psychology of childbirth (a micro-system issue).

First, as a society, we frequently offer inadequate support to mothers. Rossi noted that we tend to isolate mothers from natural-support systems, and ask them to assume total responsibility for infants.[17] Because infants have an almost insatiable need for mothering this tends to make motherhood extremely stressful. At the time when they need social support most, they are least likely to get it. Anthropologist Jill Korbin[18] reports a similar conclusion based on her cross-cultural review of child abuse, and Ronald Rohner[19] finds rejection is associated with these same isolating and alienating conditions. As we said in chapter 3, our culture's commitment to privacy and our increased ability to deliver on that value fuel the fires of autonomy over independence and self-fulfillment over collective responsibility. For women there is now more to life than mothering. The other side of historical changes liberating women from the narrow roles of the past is a greater sense of being imposed upon by the infant's great need for mothering. To quote Rossi: "It may be that the role requirements of maternity in the American family system extract too high a price of deprivation for young adult women reared with highly diversified interests and social expectations concerning adult life."[20]

These factors (social and cultural supports inadequate for motherhood) suggest that the process of psychological family formation has two social strikes against it in contemporary society. While fathers and substitute caregivers may help fill the gap, we think the experiences of other societies caution us against assuming that they inevitably will.[21] Research on the process of modernization in traditional societies supports this view. As modernization proceeds, the natural supports for family bonding, such as breast-feeding and family-centered delivery, tend to fade away and be replaced by technology-intensive approaches.[22] This trend is a threat to attachment, the most basic of forces at work to transform the human organism into the humane person.

Becoming Attached

The development of attachment has been one of the central concerns of modern developmental psychology. Until recently, however, the focus has been on events beginning in the third or fourth month of the infant's life. Emerging from work by Harry Harlow, John Bowlby, Harriet Rheingold, and others has been a view of attachment as "the infant's tendency during the first twenty-four months to approach particular people, to be maximally receptive to being cared for by these people, and to be least afraid when with these people."[23] This interest in attachment is part of a general trend toward recognizing competence in children at increasingly younger ages. The work stimulated by Kennell and Klaus posits important events related to attachment that *can* occur in the first hours of life and thereby give overall family strength a boost.

When they modified the conventional birthing procedure, Kennell and Klaus reportedly found important effects including richer maternal language in speaking to the child, more attention and affection and other developmentally beneficial outcomes. Other research suggests that the effects of early contact are present only when such contact begins *immediately* after birth. Thus in a study by Hales no effects were found when contact began twelve hours after birth, but only when it began in the first hour after delivery.[24] As research on this topic has proliferated, it naturally has become less unequivocal.[25] Trause suggests that the effects are clearest for firstborn males, and that some mothers do not take advantage of the opportunity presented by an early-contact arrangement.[26] Here we must note that those who need the most are often least likely (and able) to make use of opportunities when they are presented. The effect of early contact is not so powerful or so all-encompassing as to be the answer, but it certainly has much to offer because it costs little or nothing and can be part of a broader strategy to promote social integration, particularly among high-risk families. Moreover, it is a logical step toward family-centered childbirth, a more comprehensive and powerful social event.

The importance of enhancing parent-infant bonding as an intervention strategy is limited by several things. First, the demonstrated effects of early contact are relatively small when compared with socioeconomic and demographic factors, but paradoxically they can be biggest for those most in need.[27] This may appear to be a benign cycle, but in fact it is not. Under current policies and practices the families most in need are least likely to take advantage of early contact. Those who were attracted to early contact and family-centered childbirth first were able to break down institutional barriers. They used the principle of freedom of choice in their struggle. Now that hospitals are open, freedom of choice permits high-risk parents to avoid family-centered childbirth, and their experiences and attitudes predict they generally will. Hospitals need a positive policy favoring family-centered childbirth.

Second, a substantial proportion of families are deprived of the early-contact experience because of medical complications, including the rising rates of cesarean section and social arrangements such as adoption.[28] These families probably will be denied the experience of postpartum parent-neonate interaction, and it may be impossible for them to have any early contact whatsoever.[29] The existence of such families makes it imperative that we know where early interaction and bonding fit into the processes and outcomes of child development. The more we are able to demonstrate the importance of early bonding, the greater will be the urgency to minimize practices that inhibit it (such as inducing labor for purposes of convenience), and to provide compensatory experiences where it is not feasible.[30]

Third, human development tends to be congruent with environment. We cannot inoculate families against estrangement and disaffection any more than we can inoculate children against academic failure. The ongoing mutual accommodation of organism and environment permits beneficial modification, but only when we can introduce some permanent benevolent force into the family's social experience. We thus can encourage family development and help protect the child in its most physically vulnerable stages. However, we cannot ensure a tolerable upbringing and a reasonably stable family by a brief contact in the first few days of the child's life.

Is early contact a necessary condition for adequate family development? Clearly, the answer is no. By whatever criterion of adequate child care, whole generations grew up adequately cared for without the early-contact experience, and many children (including adopted children) still do.[31] As Lozoff and her colleagues remind us, current medical practices "are at the limits of human adaptability."[32] Flexible and creative as we human beings are, our ability to preserve our humanity is limited in the face of the depersonalizing technologies and efficiency-oriented social engineering that have dominated North American obstetrics in recent decades.[33] The current social scene may be contracting rather than expanding those limits. While attachment may well be a necessary condition for normal child development, early contact is not.[34] Attachment results from a long process of mutual investment; bonding, from a brief encounter. Indeed, one danger of the early-contact-bonding movement is that parents will emphasize bonding in place of attachment. The former can be done quickly and with a burst of enthusiasm. The latter requires a lengthy investment, patience, and a rich diversity of experiences. In the present epoch, when we suffer from a poverty of interpersonal relations[35] and a rising tide of expectations for freedom from constraining responsibilities,[36] there is a danger that parents who are resistant to giving of themselves may feel justified on the grounds that having bonded early they do not need to attach later. We should be especially wary of this in dealing with high-risk parents.

Early contact may have the effect of getting good family development started for some people, in some circumstances. It also can promote other aspects of family-centered childbirth. In this as in most human phenomena, the main effects are likely to be interactions.[37] The few experimental studies available make this inference all but inescapable.[38] What are the circumstances in which early contact can help family development? Our review of the research and theory on the matter suggests the hypothesis that the effect operates in direct proportion to the individual's and family's potential for dysfunction. Thus the effect is presumed to be stronger for poor than affluent families, stronger for fathers than mothers, stronger for sick than well children, stronger for socially-isolated than for socially-integrated families, and stronger for unwanted than wanted children. Studies conducted in developing countries are consistent with this hypothesis. For example, a study in Brazil found that the incidence of breast-feeding was tripled (from 27 to 77 percent) when early and extra contact and a supportive hospital staff were provided.[39] The results for affluent, modern families are much less marked.[40] The greater the need, the more successful is early interaction, if it is delivered effectively (no small feat).

Hospital-based interventions to enhance parent-infant bonding present two compelling rationales. First, enhanced parent-infant bonding is cheap and it is available.[41] The experience of hospitals around the country confirms that it can be done with little or no additional cost. Furthermore, the available evidence suggests it is medically safe.[42] Qualms about moving from a medical to a family model of childbirth have not been supported by research. The only real cost of a vigorous policy promoting early interaction is the disappointment or guilt that parents may feel if they are unable to have the experience.[43]

Second, in principle it applies to all families, and therefore does not require labeling or selecting families as being at risk or in need of special services. Recently this labeling problem has become a legal as well as social and an ethical problem.[44] In the case of child abuse, for example, where the incidence of serious harm is relatively low (on the order of 1 percent in the total population), any program that relies on screening people for special programs is likely to be overwhelmed by false positives no matter how good the instrument.[45] That is, most of the people identified as abusive actually will be nonabusive. They will be identified falsely because of the combination of measurement error and relatively low prevalence of abuse in the population. An experimental study by O'Connor, Vietze, Hopkins, and Altemeir confirms the dimensions of this problem.[46] Of 277 low-income primiparous mothers studied twelve to twenty-four months after delivery of the child, only ten displayed parenting disturbances requiring hospitalization of the infant. One of these came from a group of 134 randomly assigned to receive eight hours of rooming-in while 9 who came from a group of 143 receiving the routine hospital treatment, that is, contact every four hours for feeding. The experimental effect could be quite substantial, but the overall incidence is low.

The principal attraction of family-centered childbirth as an intervention strategy goes well beyond these points. Like cognitive enrichment programs, family-centered childbirth provides an occasion for improving the relationship of families to social-support systems. Early interventions to improve the cognitive functioning of children from economically and socially impoverished families testify to this. Successful programs often have the effect of increasing the parent's social competence, including money management, job performance, and citizenship activities.[47] By engaging in activities to enhance parent-infant bonding we reasonably can anticipate a positive effect on the social competence of the parent. Improved parent-infant bonding can lead to a more normal relationship between the parent and the social environment. It can improve family functioning directly, and thus enhance child development indirectly. The direct value to the child of improved bonding is of unknown importance. The value of efforts to enhance bonding is principally as a vehicle for increasing the social resources of both child and parent.

Birth as a Social Event

Brazelton noted that the dominant Western approach to childbirth is as a disease: "In most of the Western world there is a pervasive attitude on the part of the medical caretakers of mothers and infants which varies little. This attitude is that the birth of a baby must be treated as an illness or an operation—an attitude that creates an atmosphere of pathology, or of curing pathology at best."[48]

Chief among the correlates of this attitude is the degree to which birth is treated as a social event. This becomes apparent when we contrast the typical modern American pattern with that reported by Schreiber in a small agricultural community in Italy.

> When a woman is about to give birth in the hospital . . . the members of the family congregate outside the labor and delivery rooms. Within five minutes of the birth the parents, grandparents and, on the average, five other relatives will have kissed the baby. Within the first twenty minutes, the mother-in-law, who holds the baby first, returns him to his mother. The news of the birth is quickly dispatched to the parents' home and a pink or blue rosette, depending on the sex of the baby, is hung on the front door. The birth has been officially announced, and visits by all the near and distant relatives, acquaintances, and neighbors begin . . . Within six weeks, in a town of 1,500 people, 80 percent of the households had visited the home of a newborn with congratulations and usually a small gift for the mother or baby.[49]

The key insight, as Rossi showed, is to recognize that childbirth implies a social as much as a biological event. Thus attention to social conditions before and after, as well as during childbirth, is essential.[50] This is why the whole paraphernalia of family-centered childbirth must be taken as a package. Protecting children means, in part, systematically documenting the medical safety of humanizing policies and procedures.[51] For example, one needs to show that neonates are kept warm enough when placed in the mother's arms,[52] that family-centered policies do not increase infection,[53] and that prepared parents produce more healthy infants.[54] This is the technical side of the issue. But to appreciate childbirth fully as a social event we must see how it fits into the process of family-to-community attachment, and this is of overriding importance in evaluating enhanced parent-infant bonding as an intervention strategy for reducing child maltreatment. As shown in chapters 2 and 3, we need ways to promote social connectedness.

Contemporary concern with parenting can provide the energy needed to improve the social and psychological supports for becoming a parent and creating a family. We know that the human species can engineer itself into situations that impede the natural forces of attachment formation. That is clear from even the most cursory review of medical practice regarding childbirth. What remains to be seen is whether or not we can reengineer conditions to promote parent-infant attachment and thereby provide a sound emotional basis for parents and infants in the early period of family formation and child development. Attachment is the foundation for humane development.[55] We can save ourselves and our children a lot of grief by recognizing the importance of the conditions under which attachment begins through parent-infant bonding. The issues involved are as much political as scientific. Can the medical establishment plan an active role in promoting family-centered childbirth?

There is cause for hope. The medical establishment is recognizing the benefits of family-centered childbirth. A 1977 statement issued by the American

Medical Association (AMA) encouraged hospitals to do all they can to promote successful bonding between parents and infant. The AMA's statement recognizes that the birth of a child is a family affair. Joseph Butterfield put it this way: "This recognition of the importance of family-oriented childbirth is a major step. We have to constantly remind hospital personnel that the family is having the baby—not the physicians, or the nurses, or the hospital." The AMA statement was drafted by its committee on Maternal and Child Health. Committee Chairman Howard McQuarrie calls for hospitals to "examine their positions and work toward enhancing and sustaining this important nurturing event."

Again, enhanced parent-infant bonding and attachment cannot inoculate families against child maltreatment permanently. What it can do, however, is get the parent-child relationship going positively and help the family through the often stressful first year of the child's life. Of equal or greater importance is the role that early contact can play in the bonding of the family to the community. This point brings the discussion back to the general theme of social isolation. Family-centered childbirth can be a vehicle for building social as well as psychological resources.

This is a social analog to the psychological rationale for the importance of parent-infant bonding. The birth of a child is a time when families may be uniquely "ripe" for making social as well as psychological connections. While we have little systematic evidence on this matter, the extensive informal observations and what little systematic evidence we do have all point to the birth of a child, particularly a first child, as a time when the family is ready for socially integrating experiences despite a prior history of social isolation. Gray and her colleagues found that when they experimentally introduced a health visitor and a single permanent pediatrician into the lives of high-risk families through the birth of a child, these families formed an enduring attachment to the hospital-support system.[56] They maintained contact and used the hospital staff as a social resource. A control group randomly assigned to receive the normal delivery services did not form the same attachment. For example, after two years all the experimental group could be found for follow-up evaluation but half the control-group families had disappeared. Children in the experimental group experienced significantly less developmental damage than those in the control group.

The birth experience reportedly has the effect of drawing into the child's life those who participate. As noted earlier, people who witness the birth process become strongly attached to the infant.[57] To use bonding as an intervention strategy in the most effective manner possible we should capitalize on this experience. We should support family-centered childbirth as a way to spin a web of commitment around the infant (a strong family microsystem) and around the family as a whole (a strong mesosystem and exosystem network). We might, for example, use volunteer health visitors to introduce the family to child-care materials (such as the excellent *Pierre the Pelican* series). These volunteers thus could be a liaison between the formal-support systems and the individual family.

They thus provide a basis for continuing social involvement through the child's early years until school-based support systems can take over when the family reaches the next point at which professional contact and entree is likely, that is, when the child begins school.

If we appreciate this opportunity, we can proceed with our efforts aimed at using the first minutes, hours, and days of life as an opportunity to do two important jobs: one within the family, the other between the family and the community's support systems. If we are to deal with the principal socioeconomic and demographic sources of variation in child development, we must build social resources as much as psychological ones. In so doing we may shore up families that are jeopardized by the social isolation and alienation we discussed in chapters 2 and 3. Our success in building these resources will be measured in large part by our ability to improve the quality of parent-child relationships. We will be building a foundation for tackling the elusive crime of emotional abuse, our next topic.

Notes

1. A. MacFarlane, *The Psychology of Childbirth* (Cambridge, Mass.: Harvard University Press, 1977).

2. B. Brazelton, "How the Normal Newborn Shapes His Environment" (Address presented at a seminar on Treatment of the Abused and Neglected Child, Denver, Colo., October 1977).

3. F. Furstenburg, *Unplanned Parenthood: The Social Consequences of Teenage Childbearing* (New York: Free Press, 1976); L.G. Shelton and T. Gladstone, "Childbearing in Adolescence" (Paper presented at the American Orthopsychiatric Association, Washington, D.C., April 1979).

4. V. Elkins, *The Rights of the Pregnant Parent* (New York: Two Continents, 1976); M. Klaus and J. Kennell, *Maternal-Infant Bonding* (St. Louis, Mo.: C.V. Mosby Company, 1976).

5. Klaus and Kennell, *Maternal-Infant Bonding*.

6. M. Desmond, A. Rudolph, and P. Phitaksphraiwan, "The Transitional Care Nursery: A Mechanism of a Preventive Medicine," *Pediatric Clinics of North America* 13 (1966): 651-668.

7. W. Condon and L. Sander, "Neonate Movement is Synchronized with Adult Speech: Interactional Participation and Language Acquisition," *Science* 183 (1974): 99-101.

8. J. Macfarlane, "What the Newborn Can Do," in *Parent-Infant Interaction,* CIBA Foundation Symposium 33 (Amsterdam: Elsevier Publishing Company, 1975).

9. T. Brazelton, M. School, and J. Robery, "Visual Responses in the Newborn," *Pediatrics* 32 (1966): 513-531.

10. A.N. Meltzoff and M.K. Moore, "Imitation of Facial and Manual Gestures by Human Neonates," *Science* 198 (1977): 75-78.

11. Klaus and Kennell, *Maternal-Infant Bonding.*

12. J. Kennell, D. Voos, and M. Klaus, "Parent-Infant Bonding," in *Child Abuse and Neglect: The Family and the Community,* ed. R. Helfer and C.H. Kempe (Cambridge, Mass.: Ballinger, 1976).

13. M. Lynch, "Ill Health and Child Abuse," *Lancet* 2 (1975): 317-319.

14. Kennell, Voos, and Klaus, "Parent-Infant Bonding."

15. A. Rossi, "Transition to Parenthood," *Journal of Marriage and the Family* 30 (1968): 26-39; idem, "A Biosocial Perspective on Parenting," *Daedalus* 106 (1977): 1-31.

16. T. Benedek, "Parenthood: A Developmental Phase," *Journal of the American Psychoanalytic Association* 7 (1959): 389-417.

17. Rossi, "Transition to Parenthood."

18. J. Korbin, "Very Few Cases: Child Abuse in the People's Republic of China," in *Child Abuse and Neglect: Cross-Cultural Perspectives,* ed. J. Korbin (Berkeley, Calif.: University of California Press, 1981).

19. R. Rohner, *They Love Me, They Love Me Not* (New Haven, Conn.: Human Relations Area Files Press, 1975).

20. Rossi, "Transition to Parenthood."

21. U. Bronfenbrenner, *Two Worlds of Childhood* (New York: Russell Sage Foundation, 1970); idem, "Reality and Research in the Ecology of Human Development," *Proceedings of the American Philosophical Society* 119 (1975): 439-469.

22. V. Elkins, *The Rights of the Pregnant Parent* (New York: Two Continents, 1976); B. Lozoff, G. Brittenham, M. Trause, J. Kennell, and M. Klaus, "The Mother-Newborn Relationship: Limits of Adaptability," *The Journal of Pediatrics* 91 (1977): 1-12.

23. P.H. Mussen, J. Conger, J. Kagan, *Child Development and Personality* (New York: Harper and Row, 1974), p. 204.

24. U. Bronfenbrenner, "Toward an Experimental Ecology of Human Development," *American Psychologist* 32 (1977): 513-531.

25. Lozoff, Brittenham, Trause, Kennell, and Klaus, "Mother-Newborn Relationship."

26. M. Trause, "Defining the Limits of the Sensitive Period" (Paper presented at the biennial meeting of the Society for Research in Child Development, New Orleans, March 1977).

27. P.H. Leiderman and M. Seashore, "Mother-Infant Neonatal Separation: Some Delayed Consequences," *Parent-Infant Interaction,* Ciba Foundation Symposium 33, ASP (Elsevier, Excerptu Medica, North Holland, Amsterdam, 1975).

28. MacFarlane, *The Psychology of Childbirth.*

29. Elkins, *The Rights of the Pregnant Parent.*

30. MacFarlane, *The Psychology of Childbirth.*

31. S. Hersh and K. Levin, "How Love Begins between Parent and Child," *Children Today* 1 (1978): 2-6, 47.

32. Lozoff, Brittenham, Trause, Kennell, and Klaus, "Mother-Newborn Relationships."

33. Elkins, *The Rights of the Pregnant Parent.*

34. M. Ainsworth, "The Development of Mother-Infant Attachment," in *Review of Child Development Research,* vol. 3, ed. B. Caldwell and H. Riccutti, (Chicago: University of Chicago Press, 1973); J. Bowlby, *Attachment and Loss* (New York: Basic Books, 1969); J. Garbarino and U. Bronfenbrenner, "Research on Parent-Child Relations and Social Policy: Who Needs Whom?" (Paper presented at the Symposium on Parent-Child Relations: Theoretical, Methodological, and Practical Implications, University of Trier, West Germany, May 1976).

35. L. Sroufe, "The Coherence of Individual Development: Early Care, Attachment, and Subsequent Developmental Issues," *American Psychologist* 34 (1979): 834-841.

36. A. Campbell, "Subjective Measures of Well-being," *American Psychologist* 31 (1976): 117-124.

37. U. Bronfenbrenner, *The Ecology of Human Development* (Cambridge, Mass.: Harvard University Press, 1979).

38. Lozoff, Brittenham, Trause, Kennell, and Klaus, "Mother-Newborn Relationship."

39. P. Sousa, F. Barros, R. Gazalle, R. Begeres, G. Pinheiro, S. Menezes, and L. Arruda, *Attachment and Lactation* (XIV Congress Internacional de Pediatria, Buenos Aires, Argentina, 1974).

40. Lozoff, Brittenham, Trause, Kennell, and Klaus, "Mother-Newborn Relationship."

41. D.L. Gurry, "Child Abuse: Thoughts on Doctors, Nurses and Prevention," *Child Abuse and Neglect* 1 (1977): 435-443.

42. Elkins, *The Rights of the Pregnant Parent.*

43. Hersh and Levin, "How Love Begins."

44. V. Weitz, "A Legal Perspective on Instruments Designed to Prevent Primary Child Abuse and Neglect" (Paper presented at the Second National Conference on Needs Assessment in Health and Human Services, Louisville, Ky., March 1978).

45. R. Light, "Abuse and Neglected Children in America: A Study of Alternative Policies," *Harvard Educational Review* 43 (1973): 456-598.

46. S. O'Connor, P. Vietze, J. Hopkins, and W. Altemeir, "Postpartum Extended Maternal-Infant Contact: Subsequent Mothering and Child Health," *Sociological Pediatric Research,* 1977 (abstract).

47. Bronfenbrenner, "Reality and Research."

48. Klaus and Kennell, *Maternal-Infant Bonding,* pp. 38-39.

49. Ibid., p. 39.

50. J. Garbarino, "Changing Hospital Childbirth Practices: A Developmental Perspective of Child Maltreatment," *American Journal of Orthopsychiatry* 50 (1980): 588-597.

51. J. Garbarino, "Becoming a Family: A Review of Hospital Policies and Practices Affecting Parent-Child Relationships" (Omaha, Neb.: Center for the Study of Youth Development, 1978).

52. C. Phillips, "Neonatal Heat Loss in Heated Cribs vs. Mothers' Arms," *Child and Family* 13 (1974): 307-314.

53. Elkins, *The Rights of the Pregnant Parent.*

54. R. Caldeyro-Barcia, "Some Consequences of Obstetrical Interference," *Birth and the Family Journal* 2 (1975): 34-36.

55. J. Garbarino and U. Bronfenbrenner, "The Socialization of Moral Judgment and Behavior in Cross-cultural Perspective," in *Moral Development and Behavior,* ed. T. Likona (New York: Holt, Rinehart and Winston, 1976).

56. J. Gray, C. Cutler, J. Dean, and C.H. Kempe, "Prediction and Prevention of Child Abuse and Neglect," *Child Abuse and Neglect* 1 (1977): 45-58.

57. Klaus and Kennell, *Maternal-Infant Bonding.*

5

The Elusive Crime of Psychological Maltreatment

Psychological abuse and neglect is at the heart of the overall maltreatment problem. In chapter 2 we explored Bronfenbrenner's ecological perspective, an approach to human development that looks at both the ever-growing ability to comprehend the world and the content of that understanding. The child's development is measured by the richness and validity of his or her construction of the world. The real crime in abuse and neglect is that the child is taught a false reality, one dominated by negative feelings and self-defeating styles of relating with people. For our developmental understanding of maltreatment to proceed, we must tackle the very difficult problem of psychological abuse and neglect.

Psychological abuse has been discussed and debated, but there has been little success in operationally defining the phenomenon.[1] Nor have appropriate intervention strategies been designed. It is truly an elusive crime. Professionals in the fields of social work, psychology, psychiatry, and even law enforcement seem to believe that emotional–psychological abuse does exist, even if they have been unable to reach consensus in defining it.

Emotional abuse, or psychological abuse as it is often called, has been addressed in child-abuse legislation,[2] in formal discussions by students of child maltreatment,[3] and by child protective-services practitioners in the trenches.[4] Our goal here is to improve upon past efforts to define emotional abuse.

Emotional Abuse

The Meaning Is the Message

A recent panel on the topic of emotional abuse brought together a group of experts from several different disciplines for a serious attempt to make some progress in defining and alleviating this problem.[5] The results were disappointing. Very little that was substantive and virtually nothing conclusive emerged. To quote from the summary of this panel's report: "Although a precise definition of emotional abuse and a process by which the definition would be implemented were not formulated, it was generally agreed that emotional abuse and neglect have not been adequately defined in current law and regulations, but that they are definable."[6]

Other groups have been working toward defining psychological abuse. One such session, presumably typical of most others, provided a good illustration of the problem.[7] The following descriptions were supplied by participants in response to the leader's call for associations with the term *psychological or emotional abuse:*

Put-downs	Excessive responsibility
Labeling	Ignoring
Humiliation	Seductive behaviors
Scapegoating	Fear-inducing techniques
Name-calling	Extreme inconsistency
Rejection	Unrealistic expectations
Lying	

All these terms ring true intuitively. Each one evokes an image of psychological damage to the target child. The participating child protective-service workers were responding to the leader's request as best they could, from their experiences with psychologically unhealthy parent-child relations. Each of these behaviors has clear clinical relevance as a pathogenic influence.[8] These behaviors are among those discouraged in a variety of remedial parent-education programs. They clearly would be covered by Gordon's definition offered in the mid-1950s: "The parents' failure to encourage the child's normal development by assurance of love and acceptance."[9]

Though the list of behaviors is valid as a composite indicator of psychological abuse, it lacks conceptual organization and a clear developmental perspective. While Gordon's definition is broadly correct, it lacks specifics. The issue of emotional abuse is evident in these behaviors and this definition but it cannot be understood through them alone. Practitioners and researchers alike are stumbling on this issue. Emotional abuse is truly an elusive crime. It is definitely there in the lives of children, but it is very difficult to establish adequate conceptual and operational definitions that are linked to child development research.

What is the problem here? Whenever a problem does not yield to sustained interdisciplinary frontal assault it is time to stand back and rethink the issue. We need this to advance our understanding of what psychological or emotional maltreatment is, and deal with it in theory and practice. As a society, we need such an advance if we are to understand and help abusive families.

A Perspective for Viewing Psychological Abuse

Archimedes maintained that if given an appropriate place to set his fulcrum, he could move the world. In the intellectual realm we often lose sight of the power of a theoretical fulcrum to permit progress in solving social problems. Our characteristic orientation is, of course, the pragmatic, positivistic stance reflected in that most American of maxims, "don't just stand there, do something!" This approach has served us well in many ways and areas, but it has its limitations. Perhaps at this point, having been stymied in the positivist mode, we can profitably turn to another tradition. What is lacking in our attempts to understand emotional abuse, and thus define it in policy and practice, is a suitable theoretical perspective.

Early students of child abuse adopted a model dominant in clinical work that focused primarily on defective-person theories. Adopting this model may have impaired our understanding of maltreatment as a *developmental* and *social* problem.[10] This state of affairs has only recently begun to be rectified in theoretical and empirical work.[11] To understand the emotional aspects of abuse it is likewise necessary to move away from the limitations of a narrow clinical orientation. It is necessary to adopt a perspective emphasizing both developmental and social aspects of the issue. What does this mean in specific terms?

Much has been made of the need to consider cultural differences in child rearing as a basis for understanding and dealing with maltreatment. We noted this in chapter 1. Cultural relativism argues for the need to look at child-rearing practices on their own cultural terms as a starting point for complete understanding. When applied simplistically, the notion of cultural relativism in parent-child relations can lead to rationalization for practices that harm children, however. We need to have transcultural principles for evaluating child care. When applied with a more sophisticated understanding of where culture fits into family life, such a relativistic position can illuminate the meaning of behavior and thus can lead to a proper evaluation of it.

Is all behavior to be defined strictly by culturally relativistic criteria? Is all behavior developmentally equivalent? Are there any universals that can be applied across and within cultures? To ask these questions is to probe deeply into the meaning of maltreatment. Are there practices that are intrinsically harmful to children? We think there are, and our ecological perspective tells us these practices can be understood only by tackling them through the concept of emotional maltreatment.

One of the examinations of the notion of emotional maltreatment in cross-cultural (and transcultural) perspective is Rohner's study of parental rejection.[12] Using a variety of methods to relate cultural differences in family relationships to psychological development, Rohner concludes that parental rejection has a universal effect on children. His research leads to: ". . . the conclusion that parental rejection in children, as well as in adults who were rejected as children, leads to: hostility, aggression, passive aggression, or problems with the management of hostility and aggression; dependency; probably emotional unresponsiveness and negative self-evaluation (negative self-esteem and negative self-adequacy); and, probably, emotional instability as well as a negative world view."[13]

In Rohner's view, rejection has malignant effects on humans. The effects of severe psychological deprivation in infancy are well documented, of course. In humans and other mammalian species, early social deprivation leads to impaired cognitive and social development.[14] Rohner's work broadens the concept of deprivation (the focus of Mulford's essay on emotional neglect) to concentrate on rejection. The issue is rejection of the child and the child's developmentally necessary behaviors. For practical as well as theoretical reasons we must define the components of emotional maltreatment in terms of specific behavior.[15]

When placed in a broad developmental and social perspective, emotional abuse is the willful destruction or significant impairment of a child's competence. The idea of competence as a unifying theme in studying human development has emerged in recent decades.[16] It is to this tradition that we can turn for a developmental perspective on emotional abuse.

The general elements of human competence go beyond adaptivity, as intelligence is conceptualized by Caldwell,[17] Piaget,[18] Binet and Simon,[19] and others. McClelland argues that competence means successful performance in specific social contexts and typically consists of the following abilities:[20]

1. Communication skills: being able accurately to receive and transmit messages verbally and with gestures;
2. Patience: being able to delay one's response in a socially effective way;
3. Moderate goal setting: being able to recognize and commit oneself to realistic challenges;
4. Ego development: feeling basically confident and secure about one's ability to handle day-to-day challenges[21]

McClelland's definition of competence suggests a fulcrum with which to move the problem of emotional abuse. It permits us to evaluate parental behavior, or parent-child relations, or teacher-student relations, in light of a developmental criterion, namely, their contribution to the development of competence. It sets goals for the socialization process, as Inkeles and others argued is necessary.[22] To evaluate socialization practices we must know what will be demanded through the life course. This is the key to understanding emotional abuse. If we start with this conception of competence as the currency of development, we can proceed toward an understanding of emotional abuse as both a scientific issue and a problem for practical solution.

Emotional Abuse in the Lives of Children

The overall issue of child abuse pushes our scientific credibility to its extreme limits. Child abuse is not simply less than optimal child rearing. It is a pattern of behavior that drastically violates both moral and scientific norms concerning child care. In the United States a parent is free to engage in any and all forms of child care up to the point at which a clear and present danger to the child's welfare arises. In the opinion of many observers, this point is set far too high.[23]

Adults must be held accountable for behavior that is developmentally damaging if such behavior is conscious. Just as it is inexcusable for a parent to maintain that he or she was simply disciplining a child by burning him or her with cigarettes, it is no adequate defense to argue that one is only toughening the child when engaging in emotionally-destructive behavior. This highlights the responsibility of educational, health-care, and other service institutions to make sure that the acceptable lower limits of child-care activities are communicated clearly to everyone who cares for children. When this responsibility is not met these institutions become accomplices in the abusive pattern. In law and custom it is the task of society's institutions to guard against violations of the norms concerning minimal child care.

Whatever we may think of this lower-limit approach to parental autonomy, it does prevail in fact, in law, and in cultural practice. How can we set some lower limits as criteria to be used in acting against psychological abuse? How can we operationally define a clear and present danger to a child's developing competence? This is a pressing task for a policy science of child development.[24]

If we return to McClelland's suggested components of competence, the task becomes one of specifying dangers to communication skills, patience, moderate goal setting, and ego development. Whether scientists like it or not, the actual decision on whether or not the danger is real will be made on the level of family life by a variety of medical, child-care, police, social work, and legal personnel. Can we offer these helpers something that will stand up in court, the overarching criterion for people in the field?[25]

We certainly can direct their attention to specific outcomes, such as a child with a nonorganic communication disorder, an impatient youngster who cannot cope with everyday frustrations, a student who is wildly inappropriate in his goal setting, or a child with disablingly inadequate self-esteem. There are two problems with such an approach, of course. First, we must be able to specify when a parent is culpable for the psychologically-damaged child. This means there must be evidence that the parent is directly and willfully contributing to the maladaptive condition of the child. The problem with this is that there are many nonparental and nonculpable causes for failures to become competent. In fact, it is common for a child's aversive idiosyncratic behavior to act as a stimulus for abnormal parental behavior, as in the case of a colicky infant or a preschooler's oppositional tantrums.[26] Second, we need to be able to intervene *before* the damage is done, or at least before it is permanently debilitating. Here again, we face a problem of determining causation. These issues exactly parallel those faced in working with physical abuse, where both *unequivocal* diagnosis of risk and preventive intervention are often impossibly difficult tasks.[27]

As others have recognized, with respect to the issue of emotional abuse, there are always two interests to be served by the process of diagnosis in cases of child maltreatment.[28] First, ideally and in practice, diagnosis serves the function of identifying a need for service. Second, diagnosis provides a basis for invoking the coercive resources of the state when provision of service alone is not enough to meet the protective needs of the child or when the parent refuses to accept the services offered.

Both aspects of diagnosis are designed to produce evidence of maltreatment that serves to legitimate action by the state. Because of the adversary nature of legal proceedings required to invoke intervention by the state—such as court-ordered participation in parent-education programs or removal of the child-victim to foster care—the criteria for diagnostic proof in such cases are much more procedurally stringent and require more extensive documentation than do efforts to offer services on a voluntary basis. While prevention is always preferable to treatment in dealing with child maltreatment, we must make progress in defining actionable criteria for psychological abuse to ensure that families are restored to healthy functioning and children are protected.[29]

We need to recognize the importance of individual differences and the impact of the child's temperament in shaping the outcome of parent-child relations as a last qualifying condition before beginning the task of specifying actionable criteria for emotional abuse. While in the case of physical abuse there are at least some universals—a broken bone is a broken bone is a broken bone—in the matter of emotional abuse there are few. As developmental psychologists have recognized, the impact of any specific parental behavior is to some degree dependent upon the child toward whom it is directed. Temperament and experience produce a context in which parental behavior acts upon development, and some children seem to be almost invulnerable.[30]

Toward an Actionable Definition

Using competence as the criterion, we have seen that rejection of the child and his or her normal behavior stands at the heart of psychological maltreatment. Once we take this point of view many existing data are brought into focus. For example, the frequently reported finding that abusive families reject their children even during early days of life now can be seen not as a *predictor* of future physical abuse (which it may well be), but as an act itself of emotional maltreatment.[31] Polansky's extensive work on neglect focused on the apathy-futility syndrome.[32] Characteristic of this syndrome is a systematic rejection of the child as evidenced by failure to offer adequate care. Work on the child-rearing implications of maternal depression augments this view.[33]

The principal developmental threat of parental depression is the rejection that it implies. The observational studies conducted by Burgess and Conger further document this point.[34] The principal conclusion of these studies is that parents involved in maltreatment characteristically ignore positive behavior in their children, have a low overall level of interaction, and emphasize negative behavior. This is a "social engine" well suited to the task of producing psychologically damaged human beings. Burgess and Conger's results are quite consistent with Rohner's notions of rejection. Coopersmith's work on developing self-esteem in children suggests that a loving, involved, and actively contributing parent produces high self-esteem while a passive, neglecting, and uninvolved parent produces low self-esteem.[35] These findings also may be interpreted in light of the rejection hypothesis. They impinge on the development of competence.

In parents' relations with infants, broad concepts like rejection are translated into concrete and specific behavior. First, there is rejection of the child's natural prosocial actions, of the normal instinct to engage in social interaction. This rejection includes lack of parental or caregiver response to the infant's vocalizations, smiles, and attempts to initiate eye-to-eye and bodily contact. A recent study by Tronick and his colleagues involved an experimental manipulation in which the normal feedback that infants received from their mothers in face-to-face interaction was distorted.[36] Mothers faced their infants but remained facially unresponsive. The infants reacted with intense wariness and eventual withdrawal. This experimental treatment approximates maternal rejection by providing a demonstration of the operational meaning (and presumably the consequences) of emotional maltreatment. A related phenomenon is the rejection of an infant's intrinsic operant drive for mastery or motive for efficacy by rejecting the infant's exploration of the world.[37]

What are a child's rightful claims on a parent or other caregiver? As always, we must employ a mixture of culture and science, community standards and professional expertise, in answering this question. Briefly, we think we can establish that a child has a rightful claim to a parent (1) who recognizes and responds positively to socially desirable accomplishments; and (2) who does not inflict on the child his or her own needs at the expense of the child's. Thus an emotionally-abusive parent may reject the infant's smiling, the toddler's exploration, the schoolchild's efforts to make friends, and the adolescent's autonomy. An emotionally-abusive parent demands that the infant gratify the parent's needs ahead of the child's, that the child take care of the parent, and that the adolescent subjugate himself or herself to the parent's wishes in all matters (including perhaps sexual relations).

How can we hope to define actionable emotional abuse? We must specify some absolute standards for parental behavior. The idea of necessary information on and within parent-child relations presented in chapter 3 can be applied here.

To recapitulate, necessary information for parents consists of both general knowledge of appropriate norms, expectations, and techniques concerning child rearing and regular feedback on parent-child relations. Second, adequate information depends upon the three factors: day-to-day regularized observation and discussion of parent-child relations; informal folk wisdom based on extensive historically validated firsthand experience; and formal, professional expertise, particularly in the areas of solving behavior problems. Third, the need for information is a direct function of situational demands that are both internal and external to the parent-child relationship. As these demands increase, so does the need for information. Fourth, formal institutions can become effective sources of information insofar as they are linked actively to the family's social network, either directly through the parent or indirectly through the parent's relationship with some other person.

This conception leads directly to the conclusion that actionable evidence of emotional abuse is *necessarily* the result of applying general principles concerning the development of competence to specific family systems. This requires a source of information from as well as to the family. To advance our understanding of emotional abuse we need to study these mechanisms. Applying a set of general principles concerning child care to specific children requires observation and evaluation by both informal sources such as family, neighbors, and friends and by formal professional family-support systems. With reference to the model of competence noted earlier, four principles emerge. Each of them refers to a significant aspect of emotional abuse because it presents a clear and present danger to the child's developing competence. It thus represents actionable behavior, first, as a basis for initiating service and, second, as a basis for legal coercion.

Four Aspects of Psychological Abuse

Infancy

Principle I. Punishing positive, operant behaviors such as smiling, mobility, exploration, vocalization, and manipulation of objects is emotional abuse.

Research from a variety of contexts has demonstrated that caregiver behavior can have a direct impact on the performance of these building blocks of human development.[38] There is an operant drive to mastery or motive for effectance.[39] To punish this drive and its accompanying behaviors is a clear and present danger to the child's development of competence.

Principle II. Discouraging caregiver-infant attachment is emotional abuse.

Caregiver-infant attachment has emerged as one of the central issues in child development.[40] Disruptions in early attachment has been linked to physical abuse,[41] failure to thrive,[42] and a variety of deficits in competence.[43] Systematic efforts to discourage early attachment therefore pose a direct threat to adequate development and are actionable grounds for diagnosing emotional abuse.

Childhood and Adolescence

Principle III. Punishing self-esteem is emotional abuse.

Self-esteem is the positive valuing of one's characteristics, a positive iden-tity. Self-esteem rises and falls in response to the behaviors of others, and it is linked to a variety of prosocial characteristics.[44] To discourage self-esteem is to attack a fundamental component of competent development. It is emotion-ally abusive.

Principle IV. Punishing the interpersonal skills necessary for adequate perform-ance in nonfamilial contexts such as schools and peer groups is emotional abuse.

Burgess and Conger observed that families involved in child maltreatment do not provide positive reinforcement for important interpersonal behaviors.[45] Others noted that abusive parents typically discourage normal social relations for their children, including the formation of friendships outside the home.[46] In developing a set of actionable principles therefore, we can include system-atically discouraging behavior needed for competence in nonfamilial settings. This pattern corresponds to what has been called the world of abnormal rearing. To create such a world and force the child to live in it is emotionally abusive.

As a matter of primary prevention, parents should be steered away from each of these behavior patterns. They result in pervasive emotional deprivation, and the destruction of ego and self-esteem that leads to a variety of emotional deficits, among them inadequate empathy—a precursor to trouble with inter-personal relationships in general and parenthood in particular. Emotional mal-treatment conveys the developmentally dangerous message of rejection. When put this way, we can see that when it comes to defining emotional maltreatment, the message is the meaning.

When informed observation identifies grounds for suspecting that this message is being given, there is prima facie evidence that the child's competence is being undermined. These become actionable grounds for offering services, and ultimately for initiating coercive action if the offer of services is not successful. They key, of course, is having access to the family and thus being able to provide the necessary data. The pressing need is for development of appropriate pro-cedures for gaining valid lay and professional testimony concerning the character of parent-child interaction. Once again, social isolation emerges as the villain. When families are cut off from the caring support and observation of and by others, the necessary flow of information to and from the family dries up. A healthy family is a well-connected one. The elusive crime of emotional abuse can be grasped, both conceptually and practically, only if this is understood. We see this best when we look at the community context of child maltreatment, in the neighborhood where concepts like social impoverishment are defined in daily experience.

Notes

1. R. Mulford, "Emotional Neglect of Children," *Child Welfare* 37 (1958): 19–24.

2. S. Katz, L. Ambrosino, M. McGrath, and K. Sawitslsy, "The Laws on Child Abuse and Neglect: A Review of the Research," in *Four Perspectives on the Status of Child Abuse and Neglect Research,* ed. Herner and Company (Washington, D.C.: U.S. Department of Commerce, National Technical Information Service, 1976).

3. National Conference on Child Abuse and Neglect Program (Houston, Tex.: Resource Center on Child Abuse and Neglect, 1977).

4. National Association of Social Workers Child Abuse and Neglect Resource Project, 2 Park Avenue, New York.

5. I. Lourie and J. Kent, "Defining Emotional Abuse" (Symposium presented at the Second Annual National Conference on Child Abuse and Neglect, Houston, Tex., April 17–20, 1977).

6. Ibid.

7. Nebraska Association of Social Workers Conference on Child Abuse and Neglect, Lincoln, Neb., May 1977.

8. T. Millon, *Modern Psychopathology* (Philadelphia: Saunders, 1969).

9. H. Gordon, *Casework Services for Children: Principles and Practices* (Boston: Houghton-Mifflin Co., 1956).

10. R. Friedman, "Child Abuse: A Review of the Psychosocial Research," in *Four Perspectives,* ed. Herner and Company.

11. Ibid.; J. Garbarino, A. Crouter, and D. Sherman, "Screening Neighborhoods for Intervention: A Research Model for Child Protective Services," *Journal of Social Service Research* 1 (1978): 135–145; R. Parke and C.W. Collmer, "Child Abuse: An Interdisciplinary Analysis," in *Review of Child Development Research,* vol. 5, ed. E.M. Hetherington (Chicago: University of Chicago Press, 1975).

12. R. Rohner, *They Love Me, They Love Me Not* (New Haven, Conn.: HRAF Press, 1975).

13. Ibid., p. 168.

14. U. Bronfenbrenner, "Early Deprivation: A Cross-species Analysis," in *Early Experience and Behavior,* ed. S. Levine and G. Newton (Springfield, Ill.: Charles C. Thomas, 1968).

15. I. Lourie and L. Stefano, "On Defining Emotional Abuse. Child Abuse and Neglect: Issues in Innovation and Implementation," *Proceedings of the Second Annual National Conference on Child Abuse and Neglect* (Washington: D.C.: U.S. Government Printing Office, 1978).

16. S. Goldberg, "Social Competence in Infancy: A Model of Parent-Infant Interaction," *Merrill-Palmer Quarterly* 23 (1977): 164–177; R. White, "Motivation Reconsidered: The Concept of Competence," *Psychological Review* 66 (1959): 297–333.

17. B. Caldwell, "What Is the Optimal Learning Environment for the Young Child?" *American Journal of Orthopsychiatry* 37 (1967): 8-21.

18. J. Piaget, *The Origins of Intelligence in Children,* trans. M. Cook, (New York: International Universities Press, 1952).

19. A. Binet and T. Simon, *The Development of Intelligence in Children,* trans. E.S. Kite, (Baltimore, Md.: Williams and Wilkins, 1916).

20. D. McClelland, "Testing for Competence Rather Than Intelligence," *American Psychologist* 28 (1973): 1-14.

21. Ibid., p. 10.

22. A. Inkeles, "Social Structure and the Socialization of Competence," *Harvard Education Review* 36 (1966): 279-285.

23. D.G. Gil, *Violence against Children: Physical Child Abuse in the United States* (Cambridge, Mass.: Harvard University Press, 1970); E. Zigler, "Controlling Child Abuse in America: An Effort Doomed to Failure?" in *Critical Perspectives on Child Abuse,* ed. R. Bourne and E. Newberger (Lexington, Mass.: Lexington Books, D.C. Heath and Company, 1979).

24. M. Wald, "Legal Policies Affecting Children: A Lawyer's Request for Aid," *Child Development* 47 (1976): 1-5.

25. Ibid.

26. G.R. Patterson and J.B. Reid, "Reciprocity and Coercion: Two Facets of Social Systems," in *Behavior Modification in Clinical Psychology,* ed. C. Neuringer and J. Michael (New York: Appleton-Century Crofts, 1970), pp. 133-177.

27. Friedman, "Child Abuse."

28. Lourie and Kent, "Defining Emotional Abuse."

29. J. Gray, C. Cutler, J. Dean, and C.H. Kempe, "Prediction and Prevention of Child Abuse and Neglect," *Child Abuse and Neglect* 1 (1977): 45-58.

30. U. Bronfenbrenner, "The Experimental Ecology of Education," *Teachers College Record* 78 (1976): 157-204; W.C. Bronson, "The Role of Enduring Orientations to the Environment in Personality Development," *Genetic Psychology Monographs* 86 (1972): 3-80; J. Kagan, *Change and Continuity in Infancy* (New York: Wiley, 1971); A. Thomas, S. Chess, and H.G. Birch, "The Origin of Personality," *Scientific American* 223 (1970): 102-109.

31. J. Kennell, D. Voos, and M. Klaus, "Parent-Infant Bonding," in *Child Abuse and Neglect: The Family and the Community,* ed. R. Helfer and C.H. Kempe (Cambridge, Mass.: Ballinger, 1976).

32. N. Polansky, "Analysis of Research on Child Neglect: The Social Work Viewpoint," in *Four Perspectives,* ed. Herner and Company.

33. M. Weissman and E. Paykel, *The Depressed Woman* (Chicago: University of Chicago Press, 1974).

34. R. Burgess and R. Conger, "Family Interaction Patterns in Abusive, Neglectful and Normal Families," *Child Development* 49 (1978): 163-173.

35. S. Coopersmith, *The Antecedents of Self-esteem* (San Francisco: Freeman, 1967).

36. E. Tronick, H. Als, L. Adamson, S. Wise, and B. Brazelton, "The Infant's Response to Entrapment between Contradictory Messages in Face-to-Face Interaction," *Child Psychiatry* 17 (1978): 1-13.

37. Goldberg, "Social Competence in Infancy"; White, "Motivation Reconsidered."

38. Y. Brackbill, "Extinction of the Smiling Response in Infants as a Function of Reinforcement Schedule," *Child Development* 86 (1958): 3-80; B.M. Foss, ed., *Determinants of Infant Behavior* (London: Methuon, 1965).

39. Goldberg, "Social Competence in Infancy"; White, "Motivation Reconsidered."

40. M. Klaus and J. Kennell, *Maternal-Infant Bonding* (St. Louis, Mo.: C.V. Mosby Company, 1976).

41. Kennell, Voos and Klaus, "Parent-Infant Bonding."

42. R.A. Spitz, "Hospitalism: An Inquiry into the Genesis of Psychiatric Conditions in Early Childhood," in *The Psychoanalytic Study of the Child*, vol. 1, ed. A. Freud et al., (New York: International Universities Press, 1945).

43. U. Bronfenbrenner, "Is 80% of Intelligence Genetically Determined?" in *Influences on Human Development*, ed. U. Bronfenbrenner and M. Mahoney (Hinsdale, Ill.: Dryden Press, 1975).

44. Coopersmith, *The Antecedents of Self-esteem.*

45. Burgess and Conger, "Family Interaction Patterns."

46. Friedman, "Child Abuse."

The Community Context of Child Abuse and Neglect

As stated in chapter 2, human ecology is based on the proposition that behavior and development arise out of a mutual adaptation of person and environment occurring within an ecological niche, defined in large part by politics and economics.[1] An individual's environment, particularly a child's environment, can be understood as a series of settings, each nested within the next broader level, from the microenvironment of the family to the macroenvironment of the society.[2] One of the implications of this approach for child development is that as children grow and mature socially and biologically, the size of their environment increases. More and more social systems are directly experienced by them; more and more are immediately relevant to them. Concepts like rejection and acceptance do not exist apart from social contexts. Rather, they operate in concrete settings. The great value of the ecological perspective derives in part from its ability to help us systematically explore this aspect of human development. The nature of the phenomenon makes for an approach in which we move back and forth between process and context. Chapters 2 and 3 probed social isolation, while chapter 4 examined this and other phenomena in the hospital setting. Chapter 5 explored psychological mistreatment, and we now look at the neighborhood context of abuse and neglect in general.

People for the most part and families in particular do not really live in countries or states. They live in communities to some extent, but mainly in neighborhoods (using that term at this point only in a descriptive sense). The neighborhood is a primary context for the family with a young child.

In developing this ecological perspective on child maltreatment we have been drawn to work from diverse sources. A patchwork quilt of evidence results, that roots parent-child relations in context. A few examples will suffice to give the flavor of this evidence and provide a basis for stating our principal ideas concerning the neighborhood ecology of child maltreatment.

In an essay on "Space: An Ecological Variable in Social Work Practice," Germain concluded that: "Where the environment is supportive, creative adaptation and growth occur. Where the environment is nonprotective or depriving, stress is created and growth and adaptive functioning may be impeded."[3]

The evidence mounts that while there is substantial variation in what forms the Good Life may take, the Bad Life is revealed clearly in the welfare of children. When life is bad for children it means that life is bad for adults, whether they realize it or not.[4] Research linking social indicators to family survey data makes the same point.[5] It is for this reason that we think we are justified in using child maltreatment as a social indicator.

Economic deprivation is the principal deleterious influence, of course, but it is the social impoverishment it produces that concerns us most. Social impoverishment is denuding the child's life of supportive relationships and protective behaviors.[6] It stands in contrast to social enrichment, in which the child is enmeshed in an elaborate web of caring that can compensate for individual failings. Jane Howard describes this social enrichment when she says of her strong family: "But we are numerous enough and connected enough not to let anyone's worst prevail for long. For any given poison, our pooled resources can come up with an antidote."[7]

One need only recall the radically different fate of children in two collectivist situations (China and the U.S. military) to appreciate the importance of social impoverishment. In China, by all accounts, even being economically poor does not result in social impoverishment and child mistreatment because there is an ideological basis for protecting children and supporting parents.[8] Indeed, most antisocial impulses are suppressed.[9] In the American military, on the other hand, children often live in compounds,[10] with high-risk parents unable to cope with high levels of stress in the midst of an ideological system that tolerates domestic violence.[11] When the military does use its capacity for social control to protect children and support families, the results can be impressive, as one demonstration project in El Paso showed.[12] The goal of our analysis is to identify situations in which the conditions of life conspire to compound rather than counteract the deficiencies and vulnerabilities of parents. As implied in chapter 3, in this respect our approach moves beyond the individualistic orientation that dominates social theory and policy, and focuses jointly on social support and social control.[13] We are most interested in the circumstances of life as families experience them.

Our principal interest is with those circumstances that can be subsumed under the term *neighborhood*. Neighborhood is typically the ecological niche in which families operate, and neighborhoods are one of the principal places where one finds the conditions of life that can conspire either to compound or to counteract the deficiencies and vulnerabilities of parents. Defining a neighborhood is the first problem we face in working out the practical implications of this idea for understanding and dealing with child maltreatment.

There is no neat and airtight solution to the problem of defining neighborhood. Both geographical and social concerns must be reflected in whatever definition is used. We think Kromkowski does a good job of highlighting the essential features of a neighborhood, however. In so doing, he presents the criteria with which to evaluate the quality of the neighborhood as a social environment and this is the central concern of our work in this area. Kromkowski notes:

The organic life of a neighborhood, created by the persons who live in a particular geographic area, is always a fragile reality. A neighborhood's character is determined by a host of factors, but most significantly by the kinds of relationships that neighbors have with each other. A neighborhood is not a sovereign power—it can rarely write its own agenda. Although neighborhoods differ in a host of ways, a healthy neighborhood has pride in the neighborhood, care of homes, security for children, and respect for each other.[14]

These themes are reflected in Donald Warren's research[15] and in other studies of how neighborhoods work for or against families.[16] A neighborhood can be rich economically but poor socially and vice versa. The consequences of a poor (or weak) neighborhood differ for rich and poor families, however. At the heart of our analysis is the kind of socioeconomic concern contained in Gil's analysis of child abuse: low income increases vulnerability.[17]

Here then is our thesis: economic factors affect the adequacy of personal resources and, therefore, the compensatory importance of social resources for successful parenthood. Poor people generally have fewer personal resources, and thus their need for social resources is greater if they are to succeed as parents. Rich people generally have more personal resources, and therefore are less dependent upon social resources. For this reason, the importance of neighborhood is different for people with different levels of economic resources. Rich people can afford a weak neighborhood better than poor people, who therefore must rely much more heavily on the social resources of their ecological niche for support, encouragement, and feedback. As always in human behavior, the important outcomes (in this case, adequate child care) are the product of interacting factors (in this case, the personal and social resources of the parent). It is in this sense that an ecological perspective sheds light on child maltreatment. It directs our attention to personally impoverished families clustered in socially impoverished places: High-risk families and high-risk neighborhoods.

We have a lot of information about high-risk individuals and families, even if we do not really know much that is definitive. We have much less information about high-risk environments. In our work we have sought to discover the meaning of "high risk" when it is applied to the immediate social environment of the family, particularly in the neighborhood.[18] What we have learned has strengthened our belief that an ecological approach to child maltreatment can complement anthropological and psychological perspective, thereby enhancing our understanding of etiology and improving the delivery of services.

We use four working assumptions to guide our efforts.

1. Economic forces are significant but not exclusive determinants of neighborhood character. Within given economic levels there can be considerable variation in the quality of life for families. Thus poverty is as much a social concept as it is an economic one.

2. Residential segregation based on socioeconomic factors presents a serious threat to family well-being because it produces concentrations of high-need, low-resource families. The resulting neighborhoods lack people who are free from drain (that is, who have surplus personal and social resources) and can thus afford (materially and psychically) to offer help to others. Just as diversity in the gene pool is a hedge against biological disaster, so social diversity is a bulwark against psychological disaster.

3. The process by which socially impoverished neighborhood character affects child maltreatment is threefold. The high level of neediness inhibits sharing; the lack of positive models reinforces inappropriate and inadequate behavior; and the lack of intimate and confident interaction inhibits nurturance and feedback. All three contribute to a vicious cycle of social impoverishment in which the (socially) rich get richer while the (socially) poor get poorer. Outside intervention is typically necessary to reverse the trend in socially impoverished areas.

4. Values and attitudes of a family that place it at risk for maltreatment are accentuated by the stresses of social impoverishment. Stress is a challenge. It tends to exaggerate characteristics. Thus people who are prone to violence, apathy, depression, or inadequate child care will become worse when faced with socially harsh circumstances.

What does an ecological approach to child maltreatment look like in practice? We think it begins with a geographic orientation to cases. This means plotting cases on a map in much the same way public health officials plot a variety of health-related phenomena. We like to recall one particular example of such mapping because it reveals how the process can stimulate creative scientific thinking. The example comes from a discussion of scientific method by Bronfenbrenner and Mahoney.[19]

Some years ago, Dr. Louis DiCarlo, then the director of a speech clinic in Syracuse, New York, was surprised by the unexpectedly high proportion of cases of cleft palate coming from certain sparsely populated counties in upstate New York. He was so struck by the phenomenon that he reported it to the district office of the U.S. Public Health Service directed by Dr. John Gentry. Gentry responded by doing what public health physicians have done for decades; he started putting up pins on a map, in this instance a map of New York State, one pin for each case, not only of cleft palate, but of all reported congenital malformations (which are deformities present at birth). When all the pins were in place, they made a pattern that Gentry found familiar. Where had he seen it before? After some effort, he remembered. It was in a geology course, on a map of igneous rock formations in New York State. Igneous rocks are those that were originally extracted from within the earth's surface. They are found in mountainous areas and glacial deposits. What is more, some of these rocks emit natural radiation, and, as Gentry knew, radiation had been suspected as a possible source of cleft palate and other deformities present at birth.[20]

Odd though it may seem, this story has much to tell us about identifying neighborhoods that are at risk for child maltreatment, for just as cases of cleft palate can be mapped and their underlying geological causes exposed, so cases of child abuse and neglect can be understood by exposing the ecological conditions associated with them.

Because counties typically are the unit for providing service in child protective-service work [21] and because report data are most likely to be systematic when analyzed using counties as units, [22] they are usually the appropriate context for studying the human ecology of child maltreatment. Counties typically contain subunits that correspond more or less to neighborhoods, as we are using the term in light of our previous discussion. In the county where we worked, for example, there are some twenty neighborhood areas. These areas have historical significance, are used for public-planning purposes, and exist (to a greater or lesser extent) in people's ideas about neighborhood identity. These areas include anywhere from two to six census tracts, and therefore socioeconomic and demographic data are available from published U.S. census sources. Recent decisions by the federal government to conduct the census every five rather than ten years may make these data even more useful. Furthermore, the U.S. Census Bureau has made a commitment to organize and report census data on the basis of neighborhoods as defined by local authorities if those authorities will work with the Census Bureau in defining the neighborhood units.

Mapping can identify clusters of reported child-maltreatment cases. It should be remembered that child maltreatment is being used as a social indicator here, an indicator of the quality of life for families. Its relation to other social indicators (such as measures of economic adequacy, family composition, and population dynamics) is a matter of interest on both theoretical and practical grounds. As such, it lends itself to research from a variety of perspectives, employing a range of methods from the simplest to the most complex.

In our work we limited ourselves to relatively simple (and thus gross) indicators readily available from existing census data. Naturally, where the researcher possesses the necessary expertise and resources, more methodologically sophisticated variables can be employed and analyses undertaken. The possibilities range from a simple comparison of child-maltreatment rates with the proportion of an area's population having low incomes [23] to complex multivariate analyses.[24] Various treatments of income adequacy are possible, as are alternative computations of the child-maltreatment rate, for example, for different age groups and by type of mistreatment. The levels of sophistication and resources combine with the scientific and service obligations of the investigator to shape the questions asked.

Computing a child-maltreatment rate in cases per hundred families requires up-to-date population figures, of course. For this reason we can eagerly look forward to using the results of the latest U.S. census rather than relying on the vagaries of local enumerations and interim census updates. These data permit us

to compute the relationship between socioeconomic and demographic characteristics on the one hand, and rates of child maltreatment on the other. We thus
obtain a correlation between economic resources and the treatment of children.
(Naturally, this approach lends itself to identifying the neighborhood correlates
of other child welfare phenomena besides child abuse and neglect.) Based on this
analysis we know the strength of the relationship between the character of the
social environment and the likelihood that children will experience reportable
(or rather reported) maltreatment. By applying this information to the demographic and socioeconomic characteristics of any given area, we can figure out
how much maltreatment to expect (predict) in that area. We then can see if that
area's *actual* reported rate conforms to its *expected* rate.

This approach can identify areas that have more or less than their share
of cases. That is, some neighborhoods will have a much higher rate of child
maltreatment than would be expected on the basis of their economic and
demographic character, while others will have a much lower rate than expected.
Both situations are important for researchers, and the first particularly so for
those charged with planning, administering, and providing protective and other
social services. The following material is drawn from our studies to illustrate
the process of mapping and screening, and to highlight the service implications
of these efforts.

We used state and local child-maltreatment reports from a metropolitan
county to generate a map of reported child maltreatment (abuse or neglect).
Previous work suggested that reporting in the county had become reliable
enough to use the data for purposes of statistical analysis.[26] Neighborhood rates
of maltreatment ranged from 2.4 to 89.9 cases per 1,000 families.

To find out more about the rates, we looked at the source of the report.
Our interest was in whether the report came to the child protective services
agency from an institutional (distant) source such as a doctor, hospital, or
social-service worker, or if it came from a private citizen, such as a relative,
friend, or neighbor (close).

At the outset, it should be made clear that this issue is not simply some
arcane detail of bureaucratic practice. In examining the reporting system
we are dealing with an important line of defense (sometimes the last line of
defense) for protecting the well-being of children. Informed experts agree
that early attention to maltreatment (and even the precursors of maltreatment)
is essential for protecting children.[27] Since reporting usually initiates some
action (both protective and supportive) it is an important component of the
community's network of family-support systems. Knowing whether or not it
works across neighborhoods is an important substantive issue.

If reporting by distant (institutional) sources is biased along socioeconomic
lines, it presumably discriminates against less affluent groups and areas. But
what of bias in reporting by close sources? Although Gil found that there was
no class difference in expressed willingness to take some action when they

suspected abuse (only 7 percent of those surveyed indicated that they would not take any action), there is reason to doubt that this means they would report the case.[28] Suspicion and resentment of officials is substantially greater in low-income areas than in more affluent ones. Moreover, Gil's own data revealed that persons from ethnic minorities and those with less than a high school education said they would speak directly to the parents when they suspected abuse, rather than report to a social service agency.

Discussions with law-enforcement and child protective-services workers in our study's target county revealed a widespread belief that people in low-income areas are less likely to report (rat on) their neighbors and family. Moreover, it appears that community standards used in defining inadequate and unacceptable child care are either not as high or are not enforced as tightly in the most socioeconomically distressed areas. Put most directly (and bluntly), in the informed opinion of fieldworkers, patterns of behavior that would be judged abusive or neglectful in more affluent areas are more likely to be tolerated in less affluent areas. It would be misleading, in our opinion, to attempt to justify discrepancies as cultural or ethnic differences. What is more, the racial composition of an area does not play a statistically significant role in any of the analyses reported. We concluded that if there was overreporting by institutional sources in low-income areas, there was likely to be underreporting by non-institutional sources. The net effect, we hypothesized, was that the overall validity of the report data was good.

When we looked at the reports from the two different sources, we found that reports from more affluent areas characteristically came from private citizens, whereas reports from less affluent areas were more likely to come from institutional representatives. This finding squares with Gil's national survey which found that people from minority groups and those with little formal education were not inclined to report child abuse to the authorities.[29] Rather, they would involve themselves personally. Clearly, one can map the source of the reports when screening neighborhoods. This may reveal needs for different types of public awareness campaigns, depending upon the area in which one is working.

We wanted to know if reporting by institutional sources was biased along socioeconomic lines. We reasoned that if only the report data from distant sources were biased, our correlations of socioeconomic and demographic factors with child-maltreatment rates would reveal a substantially different pattern when computed separately for maltreatment rates based on distant- and close-reporting sources. If, on the other hand, the two sources of data are equivalent, we would expect to find similar patterns. What we found was that while both sources appear somewhat biased (with 30 percent of the variance in rate of maltreatment accounted for by differences in reporting sources), the bias is not systematic. The maltreatment rates reported from the two sources *do* behave in a similar fashion. The correlational relationships *are* the same for the two sets of data. We took this as evidence that the reporting system was sufficiently non-biased to justify our use of the resulting data for the substantive analyses.

Based on our previous work, we selected five variables on which to focus in developing a map of neighborhood characteristics: Two to indicate the level of economic resources and three to indicate important social factors.[30] Our two economic variables were percentage of households with incomes less than $8,000 a year (in 1975 dollars), and percentage of households with incomes greater than $15,000 a year (in 1975 dollars).

Our assumption was that these two measures would provide a good indication of the economic character of the neighborhood as an ecological niche for families. Other analyses suggested that income differences affect families by placing them in different economic life-styles.[31] The U.S. Department of Labor prepares model budgets that illustrate this idea with each budget indicating the income needed to achieve a particular style of living. We find it useful to go beyond the commonly used category of poverty to focus on struggling and comfortable families.[32] In the former, life is a struggle because the necessities of life are barely available. In the latter, one can be comfortable with prudent management. We chose the dividing lines of $8,000 and $15,000 per year in 1975 dollars to designate struggling (below $8,000) and comfortable (above $15,000) families. Naturally, inflation has changed the specific amounts and presumably will continue to do so.

We chose three social variables as an indication of the social resources in the neighborhood: percentage of female-headed households, percentage of families with children under age 18 where both parents are in the labor force, and percentage resident less than one year.

Single-parent families, families where both parents of dependent children work outside the home, and transients all are drains on the neighborhood as a support system for families (even if they are strengthened individually by being single, by working, or by moving). When people are in these categories, they tend to be concerned with meeting their own pressing needs. When a neighborhood consists mainly of families in these categories it has few people who are "free from drain."[33] This is important because it is such established people who usually provide the focal point for natural-helping networks, and such networks are important to families coping with stress.[34]

In our statistical comparison of the two maps, we found that the five indicators of social conditions were related strongly to the child-maltreatment rates for the twenty neighborhoods in the study.[35] The economic character of the neighborhood was very important, but the information about social drain was important in its own right. When put together, a neighborhood's economic and social character provided a very good account of neighborhood differences in child maltreatment.

The economic and social factors were themselves related, of course. When we looked just at economic factors while holding constant neighborhood differences in social factors, we found a stronger relationship with child maltreatment than if we reversed the process and looked at social factors while holding constant neighborhood economic differences. In this statistical sense, economic factors were more powerful than social factors. However, the two are powerfully intertwined in the daily lives of families. While economic factors have some direct effect on families, it seems most of their influence occurs *through* social factors.

Figure 6-1 plots the reported maltreatment rates against what would be expected (predicted) on the basis of the combined economic and social variables for the twenty neighborhood areas. This provides a way to visualize the statistical relationships involved.

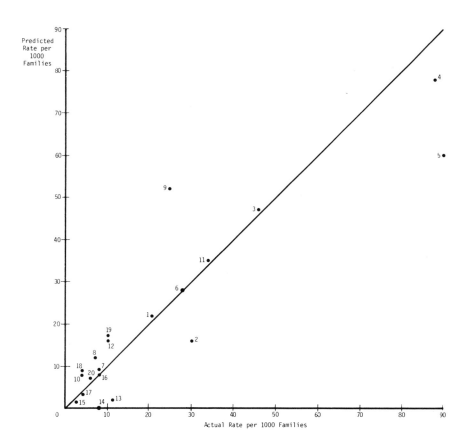

Source: J. Garbarino and A. Crouter, "Defining the Community Context of Child Maltreatment," *Child Development* 49 (1978): 604–616.

Note: Based on Multiple Regression Analysis Containing Economic and Social Resource Factors for Twenty Douglas County, Nebraska, Subareas (1976 Report Data)

Figure 6-1. Actual and Predicted Rates of Total Child Maltreatment

Of the twenty areas, ten show a nearly one-to-one correspondence of actual and expected rates (using the combination of economic and social factors). Eight areas reveal discrepancies between the expected and the actual rates of 25 percent or more (that is, the actual rate is at least 25 percent more or less than the expected rate). Two areas reveal the very large discrepancies of −27 and +30, respectively (in the first case a 100 percent discrepancy and in the second case, 45 percent). These areas are very interesting. The screening process shows that their child-maltreatment rates are least predictable using the economic and social indicators. Why? What is going on in these areas to make one better and the other worse than would be expected? The two areas have very similar expected rates (52 and 59 cases per 1,000 families). Their actual rates differ markedly, however (26 versus 89). Table 6–1 compares these areas in a variety of economic conditions, social characteristics, and attitudes (drawn from another investigation of factors ranging from housing conditions to attitudes about neighbors), based on the assumption that the first neighborhood is a more supportive environment for families than the second—above and beyond gross economic and social factors.[36]

As can readily be seen, areas 5 and 9 are similar economically and socially. The survey data reveal less positive attitudes and feelings about life in area 5 as

Table 6–1
Comparison of Two Discrepant Subareas Designated High and Low Risk for Child Maltreatment

Comparison Variable	Area 9 (Low Risk)	Area 5 (High Risk)
Factors in regression		
1. Percentage of households with incomes less than $8,000	56	60
2. Percentage of households with incomes greater than $15,000	7	4
3. Percentage of female-headed households	16	21
4. Percentage of families (with children under age 18) where both parents are in labor force	39	36
5. Percentage of population resident less than 1 year	52	43
Other factors		
1. Percentage of single-family housing	31	11
2. Composite assessment of housing market (1 = growing, 5 = badly deteriorated)	3	4
3. Percentage dissatisfied with housing	14	26
4. Percentage rating neighborhood conditions as poor or fair	42	67
5. Percentage strongly desiring to move	22	32
6. Percentage indicating good neighbors are essential neighborhood feature	95	85
7. Percentage of persons describing their neighborhood as least desirable area in which to live	2	9

compared with area 9. This difference exists despite the similarity of economic and social resources. It is consistent with the designation of high versus low risk because it suggests a nonsupportive neighborhood environment in area 5.

These results were reinforced by another study designed to discover how people perceive high-risk versus low-risk neighborhoods, and by interviews with matched samples of parents in a high-risk versus a low-risk area. The high-risk neighborhood is seen as an unsupportive environment for family life both by observers (parish priests, visiting nurses, educators, and police officers) and by participants (parents living in the area). We found that in well-matched samples of parents randomly selected from the two neighborhoods, those in the high-risk area had more stresses, less support, less adequate child care, and a less positive view of family and neighborhood life.[37] Tables 6-2 through 6-5 summarize these data. These conditions are, of course, the stuff of which child maltreatment is made: high-risk families in high-risk environments.

It has been noted repeatedly by students of child abuse that abuse-prone parents seem adept at finding mates who also are prone to abuse. There is certainly truth in this assertion. Mating patterns in America reveal a great deal of likes attracting likes. What is more, a recent study on domestic violence among a representative sample of married Americans reinforces this view.[38] The explicit or implicit collusion of spouses in child maltreatment is a significant aspect of the problem. For our purposes, the likes-attract-likes hypothesis can be applied to neighborhoods. Socially-impoverished families tend to be clustered together. This geographic clustering influences not only the incidence of mental-health problems[39] but also successful coping with those problems.[40] We find this in our neighborhood analyses, which go beyond earlier efforts of this sort that involved case studies.[41]

Using a statistical technique called nearest-neighbor analysis, Lewis[42] provided an illustration of the general hypothesis noted earlier that neighborhood is a more important force for low-income than high-income families, thus adding to the evidence gathered by Stack and others.[43] This finding is of special interest for training, because professionals tend to come from middle-class settings where neighborhood may be less important than it is for their lower-class clients.

Given that child maltreatment is a more serious issue for low-income populations, the ecological approach can make its greatest contribution in understanding and helping these families. Indeed, fragmentary evidence from our own pilot studies suggests that high-risk families may be more influenced by neighborhood social climate than are low-risk families.[44] Our results reveal stronger correlations between neighborhood characteristics and relevant behavior (use of social services, for example) among high-risk than low-risk families. (These results are based on a self-selected group of high-risk parents who may be presumed to be more oriented toward community participation than their peers, due to the fact that they did agree to participate in the study.) Thus just as some high-risk individuals marry low-risk individuals (and are in effect saved from

Table 6-2
Profiles of Social Life in Two Neighborhoods

Neighborhood public image
Low risk   "That's one of the most sedate areas." (police officer)
            "That's a good quick area." (postman)
High risk   "That's a little less tranquil. The bars are just pits. The crowd is hoodlums, Hell's
            Angels, and cowboys." (police officer)
            "There's a lot of 'night activity' there." (visiting nurse)

Neighborhood appearances, housing, public notices
Low risk   "The housing, mainly single-family homes, is kept up well. Home-improvement
            activities apparent. Empty lots are usually mowed, cared for, and look as though
            they are used as play areas." (D. Sherman's observation)
High risk   "It's low rent there. They don't have good locks. There are no screens on the
            windows. Cockroaches are all over. We're concerned about the children's safety
            since the second-floor windows are without screens." (visiting nurse)

Social characteristics
Low risk   "This is a solidly middle-income area, and upwardly mobile. There is a tendency
            to change to private doctors and to see our organization as for low-income
            groups only." (visiting nurse)
High risk   "There is a dichotomy in the neighborhood. There is a significant number of
            rather stable, well-put-together families that live in their own homes. Then there
            is the other group of people (and they comprise about half of the students) who
            are living in apartments or who rent broken-down homes. They kind of move in
            and out of the neighborhood. There are a number of families where we'll have
            the kids for three or four months, they will leave, and then we'll have them
            again." (principal of an elementary school)

Neighborhood change or stability
Low risk   "I see it as a stable neighborhood. People have roots in the neighborhood. It's
            not a very mobile place." (visiting nurse)
High risk   "The parents cling to this school as a sign of hope. The neighborhood is facing
            a lot of change and deterioration. . . . They probably felt threatened by the con-
            struction of the Interstate through the neighborhood. . . . Just this year we've
            had several new cases of loiterers, and some families report burglaries where
            they have never happened before. . . . The parish bought up a building opposite
            the school which had been recently turned into a rough place." (principal of a
            parochial school)

Neighborhood lifestyle and quality
Low risk   "We have very few cases there, only six families with children." (visiting nurse)
High risk   "That's an area that needs plenty of scrutiny as far as quality of life." (director
            of a neighborhood community center)
            "There's stealing from each other." (visiting nurse)
            "That's one of our heaviest case loads, both as number of families and as prob-
            lems within each family. Alcoholism is quite a big problem. . . . There are
            mental-health problems, a very high death rate, a high birthrate to unmarried
            mothers, poor nutrition . . . medical knowledge is only of emergency care . . .
            many of the girls are early school dropouts." (visiting nurse)

Child abuse and neglect
Low risk   "There used to be a number of cases there, but now it will be real hard to find
            one." (Child Protective Services worker)
            "I would say that child abuse and neglect is not as much a problem in the area as
            in others. Most of the referrals are for neglect, about 80 percent." (visiting nurse)
High risk   "There are probably a significant number of 5-to 8-year-olds at school who got
            themselves up this morning. They may or may not have been at their own
            homes, but they got themselves to school and took care of their needs." (ele-
            mentary school principal)

Table 6-2 *continued*

"There were probably about six to eight suspected cases of physical abuse last year. We see neglect cases maybe twenty-five to thirty times a year at X school, and as high as fifty times in Y school." (elementary school principal)

Neighborhood involvement of families

Low risk   "Z school has an active, ongoing Girl Scout troop." (Girl Scout leader)

High risk "X and Y schools are just beginning to be organized by our fieldworkers." (Girl Scout leader)

"About 35 percent of the parents are active with the school. On a scale from +3 to −3 I'd rate the level of activism as 0." (principal of parochial school)

"We have the least amount of input from them compared to other centers . . . we're not as close to that neighborhood. Nobody is." (director of community center)

Social relations–informal supports

Low risk   "These women often rely on the help available to them through their families. One client of mine lives next door to her mother-in-law whom she turns to for help." (visiting nurse)

High risk "The family unit is not real strong here." (parochial school principal)

"The women sometimes form a buddy system, but there is not a lot of interlinking between them . . . they don't know very many people. They don't associate very much. They don't have a lot of family supports. They may be on bad terms with the family. This area is sometimes a hideout for them . . . there are a lot of teenage girls with their babies who want to get away from their families downtown." (visiting nurse)

Note: Based on expert informants; selected comments and observations.

their backgrounds), so some high-risk families find themselves in low-risk settings that can help them overcome their special vulnerabilities. There is no substitute for a socially-competent friend when it comes to child rearing. It is worth recalling Jane Howard's conclusion about healthy families and social networks: "For any given poison, our pooled resources can come up with an antidote."[45]

Many of the issues here directly parallel (and even incorporate) efforts to counteract the effects of racial segregation. That is, stereotypes and exploitive real estate policies play a major role. It is encouraging to note in this regard that public opinion polls have shown a substantial decrease in opposition to residential integration along racial lines.[46] If done on a small scale, integration along social lines may be possible as well. Residential segregation of personally impoverished people tends to produce social impoverishment unless there are countervailing forces at work. We need to recognize those countervailing forces where they exist naturally (and then not tinker with them) and to learn how to generate and sustain them where they do not already exist. This theme is echoed in the recent report of the National Neighborhood Commission. Community organizing is inseparable from child protection in this sense.[47] It is not necessary that we move people so much as that we alter the nature and structure of the high-risk neighborhood as a social entity. Technologies for doing this exist.[48] Basically, they involve teaching community organization and helping skills.

Table 6-3
The Child's Social Resources

	High Risk	Low Risk
Latchkey—caregivers present when child returns home		
from school	n = 16	n = 21
No one	13%	0%
Parents	25	86[a]
Other	62	14
Number of people in the child's social network (people who take an interest in the child's welfare	4.1	5.3[a]

Note: These data come from the parental interviews we conducted. Among many such items, they show that children in the low-risk area have both more caregiving by their parents (less latchkey and babysitting arrangements) and more people taking an interest in their welfare. These findings obtained despite the fact that the two samples of families contained an equal number of working and single parents.

[a]$p < .05$.

Table 6-4
Stresses: Demands for Social Readjustment

	Neighborhoods	
	High Risk	Low Risk
Distribution	258.42	165.62[a]
0–149: no crisis	37%	74%
150–199: mild crisis	5	5
200–299: moderate crisis	21	9
300+: major crisis	37	12

Note: These data are based on the Holmes-Rahe scale, a checklist of events requiring social readjustment. While subject to a number of limitations, the scale does provide a gross indication of the uproar and stress in a family's life. What is more, other investigators found an association between this score and child abuse. Parents in the low-risk area neighborhood are 2.5 times more likely to be in the no-crisis range than are parents in the high-risk neighborhood.

[a]$p < .05$.

We think the goal of these efforts is to achieve a neighborhood where each family is participating in informal-support systems, where the level of need matches the level of resources, where there is good morale, where there are effective links between formal- and informal-helping services, and where children are enmeshed in a web of caring and protective relationships. This ideal is simply that, a description of what we should be seeking in our efforts at social policy and practice. But as an ideal, it can make an important contribution to our understanding of child maltreatment, for, as what Bronfenbrenner calls Dearborn's Dictum remind us: "If you want to understand something, try to change it."[49]

Table 6-5
Maternal Ratings of Family Stresses and Supports

	Neighborhoods	
	High Risk	Low Risk
	(ratings)[a]	
Finances	.09	.21
Family health	2.00	1.66
Work situation	2.23	1.91
Chances to enjoy recreation	.96	1.66
Child care: availability	2.19	3.04[b]
Child care: quality	3.00	2.86
Neighbors-friendliness	2.90	3.25
Neighborhood as place to raise children	.09	1.66[b]
Help as parent		
Family	.89	1.83
Friends	1.55	1.47
Neighbors	.437	1.14[b]
Professionals	1.32	2.09
Ease/difficulty raising child	2.43	1.29[b]
(note: +5 = difficult, − 5 = easy)		
Self-rating as parent	1.45	1.83

Note: These data come from the parental interview. Each rating concludes a section in which the parent has responded to several open-ended questions about family life. Note that the items with the biggest (and statistically significant) differences include two focusing on the neighborhood as it directly affects child rearing.

[a] − 5 = very negative to +5 = very positive

[b] $p < .05$.

We can expand our understanding of child maltreatment by including a better appreciation of how a family's ecological niche accounts for some of the variation in parental behavior. Without denying the importance of psychological factors, we can profit from incorporating the role of economic and social impoverishment into our calculations. This will help us see that we have several fronts on which to combat the problem of child maltreatment, and that child maltreatment is woven into the fabric of our society. One of the fronts for these efforts is the school, the natural institution to serve as the focal point for community efforts to build an environment that supports parents and protects children. That is the topic of chapter 7.

Notes

1. A. Hawley, *Human Ecology: A Theory of Community Structure* (New York: Ronald Press, 1950).
2. U. Bronfenbrenner, *The Ecology of Human Development* (Cambridge, Mass.: Harvard University Press, 1979).

3. C. Germain, "Space: An Ecological Variable in Social Work Practice," *Social Casework* 59 (1978): 522.

4. A. Emlen, "If You Care about Children, then Care about Parents" (Address to the Tennessee Association for Young Children, Nashville, November 1977).

5. L. Kogan, J. Smith, and S. Jenkins, "Ecological Validity of Indicator Data as Predictors of Survey Findings," *Journal of Social Service Research* 1 (1977): 117–132.

6. Emlen, "If You Care about Children."

7. J. Howard, *Families* (New York: Simon and Schuster, 1978).

8. J. Korbin, "Very Few Cases: Child Abuse in the People's Republic of China," in *Child Abuse and Neglect: Cross-Cultural Perspectives,* ed. J. Korbin (Berkeley, Calif.: University of California Press, 1981).

9. A. Messer, "Curing the Urge in Red China," *Human Behavior* (April 1979): 18–23.

10. D. Sattin and J. Miller, "The Ecology of Child Abuse," *American Journal of Orthopsychiatry* 41 (1971): 675–678.

11. C.H. Kempe, "Recent Developments in the Field of Child Abuse," *Child Abuse and Neglect* 2 (1978): 261–267.

12. R. Miller, "Child Abuse in the Military," in *Child Abuse and Neglect: The Family and the Community,* ed. R. Helfer and C.H. Kempe (Cambridge, Mass.: Ballinger, 1976).

13. J. Garbarino, "The Price of Privacy: An Analysis of the Social Dynamics of Child Abuse," *Child Welfare* 56 (1977): 565–575; R.J. Gelles, "Community Agencies and Child Abuse: Labeling and Gatekeeping" (Paper presented to the Study Group on Research and the Family, October 1975); P.E. Slater, *The Pursuit of Loneliness: American Culture at the Breaking Point* (Boston: Beacon Press, 1970).

14. J. Kromkowski, *Neighborhood Deterioration and Juvenile Crime* (South Bend, Ind.: South Bend Urban Observatory, 1976).

15. D. Warren, "Support Systems in Different Types of Neighborhoods," in *Protecting Children from Abuse and Neglect,* ed. J. Garbarino, S.H. Stocking, and Associates (San Francisco: Jossey-Bass, 1980).

16. A. Tietjen, "Formal and Informal Support Systems: A Cross-cultural Perspective," in *Protecting Children from Abuse and Neglect,* ed. J. Garbarino and S.H. Stocking (San Francisco: Jossey-Bass, 1980).

17. D.G. Gil, *Violence against Children: Physical Child Abuse in the United States* (Cambridge, Mass.: Harvard University Press, 1970).

18. J. Garbarino and A. Crouter, "Defining the Community Context of Parent-Child Relations: The Correlates of Child Maltreatment," *Child Development* 49 (1978): 604–616; J. Garbarino, A. Crouter, and D. Sherman, "Screening Neighborhoods for Intervention: A Research Model for Child Protective Services," *Journal of Social Service Research* 1 (1978): 135–145; J. Garbarino and D. Sherman, "High-risk Neighborhoods and High-risk Families: The Human Ecology of Child Maltreatment," *Child Development* 51 (1981): 188–198.

19. U. Bronfenbrenner and M. Mahoney, "The Structure and Verification of Hypotheses," in *Influences on Human Development,* ed. U. Bronfenbrenner and M. Mahoney (Hinsdale, Ill.: Dryden Press, 1975).

20. Ibid., p. 2.

21. R. Helfer and R. Schmidt, "The Community-based Child Abuse and Neglect Program," in *Child Abuse and Neglect,* ed. R. Helfer and C.H. Kempe, pp. 229–265.

22. J. Garbarino and A. Crouter, "A Note on Assessing the Construct Validity of Child Maltreatment Report Data," *American Journal of Public Health* 68 (1978): 598–599.

23. J. Garbarino S.H. Stocking, and Associates, *Protecting Children.*

24. Garbarino and Crouter, "Defining the Community Context."

25. Garbarino and Sherman, "High-risk Neighborhoods."

26. R. Banagale and M. McIntire, "Child Abuse and Neglect: A Study of Cases Reported to Douglas County Child Protective Service from 1967–1973," *Nebraska Medical Journal* (October 1975): 393–396; J. Benjamin, "Breaking the Child Mistreatment Cycle: A Study of Child Abuse and Neglect Programs in Douglas County, Nebraska" (University of Nebraska at Omaha, 1976); Garbarino and Crouter, "Assessing the Construct Validity."

27. J. Gray, C. Cutler, J. Dean, and C.H. Kempe, "Prediction and Prevention of Child Abuse and Neglect," *Child Abuse and Neglect* 1 (1977): 45–58.

28. D.G. Gil, *Violence against Children: Physical Child Abuse in the United States* (Cambridge, Mass.: Harvard University Press, 1970).

29. Ibid.

30. J. Garbarino, "A Preliminary Study of Some Ecological Correlates of Child Abuse: The Impact of Socioeconomic Stress on Mothers," *Child Development* 47 (1976): 178–185; idem, "The Human Ecology of Child Maltreatment: A Conceptual Model for Research," *Journal of Marriage and the Family* 39 (1977): 721–727; Garbarino and Crouter, "Assessing the Construct Validity."

31. National Academy of Sciences, *Toward a National Policy for Children and Families* (Washington: U.S. Government Printing Office, 1976).

32. Garbarino, "Preliminary Study."

33. A. Collins and D. Pancoast, *Natural Helping Networks* (Washington, D.C.: National Association of Social Workers, 1976).

34. N. Gourash, "Help-seeking: A Review of the Literature," *American Journal of Community Psychology* 6 (1978): 413–423.

35. In statistical terms, the multiple correlation of the economic and social variables with the rate of child maltreatment was .90. Thus these economic and social factors accounted for some 81 percent of the variation in child-maltreatment rates overall. When we used ninety-three census tracts, the strength of the relationships was somewhat diminished but the pattern of results remained the same. For census tracts, the multiple correlation was .72, accounting for 52 percent of the variance. Garbarino and Crouter, "Defining the Community Context."

36. Center for Applied Urban Research, *Housing and Community Development in the Nebraska-Iowa Riverfront Development Project Area* (Omaha, Neb.: Center for Applied Urban Research, 1973).

37. Garbarino and Sherman, "High-risk Neighborhoods."

38. M. Straus, R. Gelles, and S. Steinmetz, *Behind Closed Doors* (New York: Doubleday, 1980).

39. M. Lewis, "Nearest Neighbor Analysis of Epidemiological and Community Variables," *Psychological Bulletin* 85 (1978): 1302–1308.

40. C.J. Smith, "Residential Neighborhoods as Humane Environments," *Environment and Planning* 8 (1976): 311–326.

41. Sattin and Miller, "Ecology of Child Abuse."

42. Lewis, "Nearest Neighbor Analysis."

43. C. Stack, *All Our Kin* (New York: Harper and Row, 1974).

44. J. Garbarino and D. Sherman, "Child Maltreatment as a Research Issue in Applied Community Psychology" (Paper presented at the annual convention of the American Psychological Association, Toronto, Canada, August 28, 1978).

45. Howard, *Families,* p. 60.

46. L. Harris, "Experiences Important to Americans Indicate U.S. in Post-industrial, Nonmaterialistic Era" (ABC News-Harris Survey, May 17, 1979).

47. Garbarino Stocking, and Associates, *Protecting Children.*

48. S. Fawcett, R.M. Mathews, R.K. Fletcher, R. Morrow, and T. Stokes, "Personalized Instruction in the Community: Teaching Helping Skills to Low-income Neighborhood Residents," *Journal of Personalized Instruction* 1 (1976): 86–90; Garbarino, Stocking, and Associates, *Protecting Children;* D. Warren and R. Warren, *The Neighborhood Organizer's Handbook* (Notre Dame, Inc.: University of Notre Dame Press, 1977).

49. Bronfenbrenner, *The Ecology of Human Development.*

7 The Role of Schools in Child Maltreatment

One of the central events in American human development is the child's entrance into formal schooling. The basic change in the child's world has important ramifications for the child's development from that point onward through adolescence into adulthood. Just as the hospital offers an institutional context for childbirth and thus provides an opening to the family, the school gives the community an opportunity to establish and nurture a variety of prosocial influences in the child's life. The school can do much to establish what is normal and routine in the lives of families with older children just as hospitals can in the lives of families with infants. As we look at the role of schools in child maltreatment, we are most concerned with how well schools perceive and fulfill this responsibility.

Where do schools fit into the complex and difficult problem of child maltreatment? We begin with a brief look at how the existing literature deals with the role of the schools. Even a limited review reveals several dominant themes. These themes can be seen in a series of illustrative statements drawn from a variety of sources.

Because schools are concerned with the *whole child*, seeking help for the child in trouble is quite compatible with educational objectives.[1]

Educators and others who work directly with children have an excellent opportunity and a grave responsibility to identify and properly report suspected cases of child abuse or neglect.[2]

American education is potentially a major resource for helping abused children and their families. But this potential has rarely been tapped and, as yet, has never been fully utilized.[3]

Although school personnel are generally mandated to report suspected abuse or neglect, the requirement is widely disregarded. . . . There are seldom clear-cut channels for reporting and the extent of the school's involvement is uncertain. Yet few professionals are more genuinely concerned about children.[4]

The school system must be convinced, pressured, or even coerced to initiate parenting and early child development courses and skill learning experiences for every elementary, junior, and senior high school student.[5]

Where else may we find the legally and socially sanctioned abuse of children? I point to that social institution which, after the family, is the most important socializing agent in America, namely the school.[6]

These diverse conclusions about the role of schools in the maltreatment of children are echoed throughout the growing body of literature dealing with this topic.[7] When put together, these sources suggest a tension between two views of schools, one seeing them as part of the problem and the other, as a key to the solution. This tension is itself a complex phenomenon rooted in the ongoing love-hate relationship between reformers and schools. If there is one common theme to the extensive reformist critique of American education, it is that of unfulfilled potential. The issue of child maltreatment and the schools is no different in this respect from the issues of moral development, creativity, cooperation, reading, or redressing social inequalities.

But there is at least one way in which the problem of child maltreatment presents a somewhat different picture regarding the schools than do many other issues: It is deadly serious. Without denying the genuine importance of other concerns, we can assert confidently that the issue of child maltreatment is the bottom line in any discussion of child care and the quality of life. This factor forces us to do our best to understand both the potential and actual roles of schools in child maltreatment. Moreover, it creates a real urgency in our attempts to close the gap between them.

Issues for Schools as Part of the Human Ecology of Child Maltreatment

Given what has gone before, we must address at least four serious issues regarding the role of schools in child maltreatment. These issues can be expressed in the form of questions.

1. What is the responsibility of schools to identify and report suspected maltreatment?
2. Are schools culpable as perpetrators of or accessories to the fact of maltreatment?
3. Are schools in a position to affect significantly either the necessary or sufficient conditions for maltreatment in the home (or in other extramural settings)?
4. Can schools realistically be expected to contribute directly to the prevention or treatment of child maltreatment?

Most useful of our options at this point is to deal with each issue in a manner that links the present to the future; what we have now to what we can do. We can begin by presenting brief answers to these questions. Then we can proceed to a more general discussion of the role of schools in maltreatment.

Issue 1: Identification and Reporting

There is a legal mandate for school personnel to report suspected child mal-treatment.[8] This responsibility is often, perhaps generally, not met in practice.[9] There are efforts, both local demonstration projects[10] and national policy initiatives,[11] designed to remedy this situation. A variety of factors, including lack of clarity in defining maltreatment and reluctance to intervene in family privacy, stand in the way of these efforts. Their ultimate success is questionable.

Issue 2: Culpability as Perpetrators or Accessories

This issue revolves around the definition of maltreatment. Using the narrowest possible definition, that is, intentional bodily harm that violates community standards, schools are rarely culpable as perpetrators. Using a broader definition that sees violence against children as intrinsically abusive and refusal to provide service as inherently neglectful, many schools are directly culpable for maltreat-ment. The use of corporal punishment as a prerogative of school officials has been maintained by the U.S. Supreme Court, to the acclaim of many educators. At the same time, there is evidence that until prodded (or even forced), many schools have refused to provide service to children and youth who deviate from the normal, either by being in some way educationally handicapped or by exhibiting antisocial behavior.[12] These two facts demonstrate that schools are culpable for abuse and neglect, if a broad rather than narrow definition is adopted. By the same token, schools engage in various forms of psychological or emotional maltreatment, once again to a degree dependent upon the defini-tion employed as a basis for evaluation (see chapter 5).

The case against schools as accessories to the fact of maltreatment is less equivocal. The very poor record of schools as reporting agents is testimony to this. Here, as in many other areas, it seems the school leadership, specifically the principal, sets a tone or defines the norms. The variable performance of schools as reporting agents suggests this. Firsthand interviews with principals and child protective-service officials reinforce it.

More broadly, despite their concern for children, schools typically are very passive to parental and community standards concerning child care, particularly with respect to neglect. This passivity is reinforced by professionals in the area of child maltreatment who focus attention on infants and preschool children. This professional neglect parallels lack of interest in the broader community. For example, while a great deal of attention is given to the development of day care for young children, little systematic effort has been directed at adequate after-school care for school-age children whose parents are not home when the children return from school.[13] Schools generally do not define their mission as including the *active* pursuit of minimal care for their children once they leave the school building, and this limited outreach is a serious problem in the ecology of American children. There are, of course, many notable individual exceptions to this overall institutional pattern. But these exceptions only serve to sharpen the contrast between how we define the mission of our schools.

Issue 3: Can the Schools Help?

One could hardly pick up an educational journal in the 1970s without reading something dealing with the limits of education. If schools were seen in the 1960s as the deus ex machina of reformist visionaries, they are seen now as marginal institutions by a substantial proportion of the professional community, and perhaps the general public as well. It is in this climate that the question of whether schools can help must be addressed. Indeed, we found that two standard criticisms leveled at contemporary proposals for utilizing schools in social engineering are lack of appropriateness (I wonder if this is a realistic use of the schools anyway) and lack of potency (We see here the visionary response without any assurance that schools can accomplish these goals). Given that there is increasing concern about the ability of schools to master their core tasks (teaching basic academic skills), there are grounds for doubting that they realistically can be asked to do more.

Forgetting for a moment the general issues of potency and appropriateness, what could schools do to help? In terms of the necessary conditions for maltreatment proposed in chapter 2, they could reduce the social isolation of families and the cultural support for violence against and neglect of children. We will discuss the forces working against this at a subsequent point. The schools could, in principle, help deal with the sufficient conditions by emphasizing educational efforts that provide both parent education and life-management skills. As we shall see later, only sporadic efforts are occurring in both these areas.

Issue 4: Can We Expect Schools to Help?

Is it realistic to expect schools to contribute directly to the prevention or treatment of child maltreatment? If we are speaking about school-initiated efforts on any broad scale, the answer probably is negative. Schools seem hard-pressed to do what they see as their fundamental goal, namely, teaching basic academic skills. Except for specific individuals who develop a special commitment or expertise, or special grant programs that permit the addition of staff, schools seem unlikely to take the initiative in helping abused children. The one general exception seems to be the work of the Education Commission of the States' Child Abuse and Neglect Project.[14] It remains to be seen what effect this national-level project will have on the operations of schools.

Perhaps the more likely source of change is the application of community influence to the task of making schools a key component of prevention and treatment.[15] Our own experience suggests that an active project at the local level can be successful if it has the cooperation of administrators within a school system.[16] There are at least three points at which this extramural influence may be particularly useful: parent education, use of the student-teacher relationship as a resource in identifying developmentally dangerous conditions in the home, and use of the school facility as a center for providing services to families.

Our conclusions about these four issues can be properly understood only after a more detailed review of the interplay between the potential and the actual in shaping the role of schools in the maltreatment of children. This reverses the customary order of presentation (to have the conclusions precede the complete analysis) to be sure. However, only by suggesting where we stand, or could stand, can we see the relevance of various cultural, social, and operational characteristics of schools. We turn next, then, to a discussion of these factors in light of both our general analysis of child maltreatment as a phenomenon, and the four-part assessment of the role played by schools in maltreatment presented above.

Schools Can Help

What is the role of schools in providing cultural support for violence against children? In practice, schools present a mixed picture. As noted by many observers, American schools tend to reflect local values more than they actively seek to shape them. Where local support for violence is strong this may be a fatal liability for children. Gastil reported that there are regional differences in homicide rates linked to cultural and historical forces.[17] Straus, Gelles, and Steinmetz report regional differences in the rate of domestic violence among two-parent families with school-age children.[18] Schools appear to echo and reinforce these variations on the theme of using force in interpersonal relations.

Zigler[19] among others[20] has taken American educators to task for supporting the use of physical force against children in the form of corporal punishment. Growing concern for the lack of discipline in schools in both public and professional circles may serve to exacerbate the problem, as the challenge of disorder is responded to by a culture that offers fundamental support for violence as punishment and as a method of social control.

Schools can play an important role in defining social reality through what they model and what they reinforce, for both children and parents. Example remains the best teacher, even in the area of parent education. When schools present a model of abuse or neglect, the overall quality of life for children must suffer. The many latchkey children, estimated to number approximately 2 million, are a prime example of such neglect.[21] Left without supervision by parents (usually because of work), these children need the attention of schools, directly or indirectly, to bring nurturant control back into their late-afternoon lives. This need generally goes unmet, however.[22] Without supervision, children are prey to a host of antisocial forces and developmental problems. Schools should lead the way in demonstrating what adequate care looks like.

Perhaps most disturbing of all developments in American education is the apparently growing sense that schools are getting out of control. It is this sense of lives out of control that permeates *families* involved in maltreatment. How do schools respond to difficult or special children? In many cases they resort to behavior paralleling the behavior of families in such situations. They respond with coercion or neglect. A recent report of the Children's Defense Fund on "Children out of School in America" makes this point quite persuasively.[23] Schools tend to neglect, if not abuse, children who are socially, psychologically, and physically deviant. In this schools are both victim and victimizer.[24] In a society that demands at least minimal academic competence, we cannot afford to permit children to experience such institutional neglect.

Where do schools fit into the problem of isolation from potent prosocial support systems? First, and above all else, there is the role of the school as a support system. As Gray, Cutler, and Kempe noted, the child in America generally has no official enduring relationship with the state from the time he or she leaves the hospital until entering school.[25] During that five-year period, the child is exclusively in the hands of parents and whatever other persons (relatives and possibly day-care providers) have access to and interest in the child, through the family. As shown in chapter 4, at birth, health-care institutions have a natural "in" with families. Later schools assume that natural role.

Do schools provide the feedback and resources that are the essence of support systems? Two recent reviews lead one to doubt that they do in general as a matter of policy and routine practice, that is to say, as part of the American culture definition of what a school is.[26] Indeed, there are grounds for believing that American schools systematically opt for the role of academic specialist as opposed to family-support system.[27] The list of possible support-system functions for schools is long and includes long-term enduring teacher-family relationships initiated prior to the start of a child's school enrollment.[28] At the very least it requires both an active policy and program to assess the quality of life for the schools' families and cooperation with other agencies, such as child protective services, in treatment (that is, preventing a reoccurrence of maltreatment once it has been identified). Our thesis is that social isolation is a great danger to children. Schools have a legal, moral, and historical mandate to ensure that each and every child has a direct and enduring relationship with adults or groups of adults who have an interest in the child's welfare. The school is the child's natural link to the community. The role of student is the closest a child comes to being a citizen of the state.

Recent developments, particularly those spearheaded by the Education Commission of the States, offer some hope, at least in the realm of policy.[29] Demonstration programs provide working examples of how to translate these policies into practice.[30] The key in the long run, of course, is the degree to which the school is internally and externally defined as a family-support system. Thus we need to define responsibility for the welfare of families as a central mission, not a peripheral concern.

What can schools do about the sufficient conditions for child maltreatment? While the role of schools in the necessary conditions for maltreatment is a manageable and reasonably specific concern, a parallel discussion for sufficient conditions can get out of hand quickly. The overarching issue is the twofold problem of environmental quality and social control. The fundamental problem underlying the maltreatment of children is the interaction of stress (both personal and social) with inadequate support and control.

To cope with the sufficient conditions for maltreatment a systematic effort must be undertaken to accomplish three goals. First, the small minority of families beyond the reach of conventional rehabilitation and treatment models must be identified. These families (estimated by Kempe and Kempe to be only between 10 and 20 percent of those involved in abuse) cannot or will not provide adequate care for children.[31] Based on their experience, the Kempes and others recommend immediate action to terminate parental rights in such cases. Schools can play a role in identifying such families, in supporting the agencies charged with responsibility for terminating rights, and, perhaps most importantly, in assisting children and foster or adoptive parents. As noted in several recent studies, foster care in America sometimes itself is abusive or neglectful.[32] Schools can take an active role in assisting the thousands of children who are removed from their families because of maltreatment. These children require all that the school can offer in the way of stable, nurturant interpersonal relationships.

Second, a universal program of training in parenting and life-management skills can be developed and implemented. The role of the schools in this must, of course, be substantial. Part and parcel of this, however, is a redefinition of priorities. The role of schools in socialization to adulthood should be recognized more explicitly and with greater attention to its implications for program, curriculum, and structure.[33] Basic academic skills are, of course, an important part of the competence needed for effective life management, but are not the whole story. Education with a life-course perspective highlights the need to facilitate the development of coping skills. These skills reduce the likelihood that pathogenic stresses will build up and ultimately precipitate maltreatment.

Caregiver incompetence is a situationally defined problem of role learning and performance. It seems all but self-evident that parent education should play a role in primary prevention of child maltreatment. Although there are dissenting voices,[34] most professionals agree that a systematic program of parent education would be an effective preventive strategy.[35]

Such a program, however, must include practical apprenticeship experiences as well as and probably much more importantly than conventional classroom instruction.[36] Such an approach has the side effect of providing a programmatic need for younger children to "practice" on and thus provide day care for, and exemplary models to portray good parenting. Both of these are beneficial in that they may be expected to enhance efforts at prevention by offering families needed support and increasing the effectiveness of adult life-management skills, really the crux of the matter.[37] If schools focus on the task of socialization to adulthood, they can aid substantially in the development of needed life-management skills. There are hopeful signs that schools, students, and parents are responding positively to parent-education courses where they are offered.[38]

Third, schools can join with other agencies in cushioning the stresses accompanying change. Justice and Duncan found that families involved in abuse were going through periods of acute change in residence, income, family composition, work schedules, health, or marital relations.[39] We reported the same thing for families in high-risk neighborhoods in chapter 6. These changes can generate pathogenic stresses. Schools can take the lead in helping families cope with change, and thus with stress. This function serves the interest of the school because it improves the lot of children and enhances the school's ability to perform its primary academic mission.[40] While providing this kind of service directly is but one aspect of the larger issue of support systems addressed earlier, stimulating the community to assume this responsibility highlights a somewhat different area, child advocacy.

Although schools are in principle the natural allies of children, child advocacy has been problematic for educators who see children's rights as a threat to their authority and obligations. Nonetheless, one of the most important roles to be played by schools is as advocates for children, for their right to a secure and nurturant environment. This implies that schools should become active, and some already are, in prodding the larger community to support the basic right of children to personal security and nurturance. Involvement in community-wide child abuse and neglect councils, in legislative action on behalf of children, and in public education on behalf of child protective services all can be part of the advocate role.

Child maltreatment is a prime social indicator of the overall quality of life for families. If we view abuse and neglect from an ecological perspective, the cultural origins of the problem are apparent. The maltreatment of children requires a social context that permits it, specifically one that offers support in law and custom for violence against children and that permits and even encourages isolation of parent-child relations from potent prosocial support systems.

Schools could, in principle, have an important role to play in the human ecology of abuse and neglect. They could help defuse the sufficient causes by reducing the necessary culturally based conditions. By modeling nonviolent interpersonal relations, particularly nonviolent social control, the behavior of present and future generations could be shaped. By acting as a support system, providing feedback and resources, the school could be active in breaking down the dangerous barrier of isolation where it exists and in building social networks where the opportunity is present.

Schools can work cooperatively with other community agencies to identify the very small minority of adults who have no business being in the role of parent. Schools can provide support to the foster-care system that assumes responsibility for children removed from their parents, and that desperately needs help and close scrutiny to meet its responsibilities. By embarking on a program of parent-education and life-management skills training, schools can aid in the cause of primary prevention, particularly if such programs involve apprenticeship experiences in which modeling and direct services can occur.

Finally, by assuming an active stance of child advocacy, schools can support individuals and agencies throughout the community. The evidence makes it clear that America's children need advocates wherever they can find them.[41] When children live in a world of abnormal rearing, they require active allies if they are to survive physically and psychically. Schools have a natural place in the lives of children and thereby in the human ecology of child maltreatment. It is the responsibility of all concerned to ensure that schools play that role to the fullest. With this in mind we can return briefly to the issues with which we began this discussion of the role of schools in child maltreatment.

Based on the foregoing analysis, it is apparent that the discrepancy between the actual and potential contribution of schools to prevention, identification, and treatment is substantial. The task before us is to help schools meet those obligations they already have in law, policy, and custom, and to provide incentives for the more visionary potential functions of schools to be realized.

The school-home relationship is typically the pivotal mesosystem in an American child's life.[42] When this system is weak it undermines the child's development. When it is strong it boosts that development. Schools are important to the human ecology of children in general, but are vital to the human ecology of the abused and neglected. If schools have a natural role to play in dealing with child maltreatment, they also have a critical role to play in dealing with adolescent abuse and neglect. As we shall see, one of the themes dominating our efforts to understand and cope with the mistreatment of teenagers is the vital role played by the adolescent's participation in institutions, among which the school is first on the list. In terms of prevention, identification, and rehabilitation, the schools must be part of any community effort. This will become clear as we proceed to discuss adolescent abuse in the next chapters. To see this we first should bring together the several elements of our emerging developmental conception of the human ecology of maltreatment. We do this in chapter 8.

Notes

1. American Humane Association, *Annual Report of the National Clear-inghouse on Child Abuse and Neglect* (Denver, Colo.: American Humane Association, 1977).

2. M. Soeffing, "Abused Children Are Exceptional Children," *Exceptional Children* 42 (1975): 129.

3. Education Commission of the States, Child Abuse and Neglect Project, *Education Policies and Practices Regarding Child Abuse and Neglect and Recommendations for Policy Development* (Denver, Colo.: Education Commission of the States, Report no. 8, April 1976), p. 3.

4. J. Delaney, "New Concepts of the Family Court," in *Child Abuse and Neglect: The Family and the Community*, ed. R. Helfer and C.H. Kempe, (Cambridge, Mass.: Ballinger, 1976), p. 342.

5. R. Helfer, "Basic Issues Concerning Prediction," in *Child Abuse and Neglect*, ed. R. Helfer and C.H. Kempe, p. 370.

6. E. Zigler, "Controlling Child Abuse in America: An Effort Doomed to Failure?" In *Critical Perspectives on Child Abuse,* ed. R. Bourne and E. Newberger (Lexington, Mass.: Lexington Books, D.C. Heath and Company, 1979), p. 198.

7. D. Broadhurst, "Policy Making: First Step for Schools in the Fight against Child Abuse and Neglect," *Elementary School Guidance and Counseling* 10 (1976): 222-226; D.G. Gil, "What Schools Can Do about Child Abuse," *American Education* 5 (1969): 2-4; R. Kibby, "The Abused Child: The Need for Collaboration," *Thrust for Educational Leadership* 4 (1975): 11-13; D. Martin, "The Growing Horror of Child Abuse and the Undeniable Role of the Schools in Putting an End to It," *American School Board Journal* 160 (1973): 51-55; J. Nordstrom, "Child Abuse: A School District's Response to Its Responsibility," *Child Welfare* 53 (1974): 257-260; M. Paulson, "Multiple Intervention Program for the Abused and Neglected Child," *Journal of Pediatric Psychology* 1 (1976): 83-87; L. Richards, "Can the Schools Help Prevent Child Abuse?" *Illinois Teacher* 17 (1973): 43-52; L. Riscalia, "The Professional's Role and Perspectives on Child Abuse" (Paper presented at the American Psychological Association meeting, Chicago, August 30-September 3, 1975); L. Sanders, "Child Abuse: Detection and Prevention," *Young Children* 30 (1975): 332-338; B. Schmitt, "What Teachers Need to Know about Child Abuse and Neglect," *Childhood Education* 52 (1975): 58-62; B. Shanas, "Child Abuse: A Killer Teachers Can Help Control," *Phi Delta Kappan* 56 (1975): 479-482; M. Wald, "Legal Policies Affecting Children: A Lawyer's Request for Aid," *Child Development* 47 (1976): 1-5.

8. S. Katz, L. Ambrosino, M. McGrath, and K. Sawitslsy, "The Laws on Child Abuse and Neglect: A Review of the Research," in *Four Perspectives on the Status of Child Abuse and Neglect Research,* ed. Herner and Company

(Washington, D.C.: U.S. Department of Commerce, National Technical Information Service, 1976).

9. J. Delany, "New Concepts of the Family Court," in *Child Abuse and Neglect*, ed. R. Helfer and C.H. Kempe.

10. D. Broadhurst, "Project PROTECTION—A School Program," *Children Today* (May/June 1977): 22–25.

11. Education Commission of the States, Child Abuse and Neglect Project, *Education Policies and Practices;* idem, *Teacher Education: An Active Participant in Solving the Problem of Child Abuse and Neglect* (Denver, Colo.: Education Commission of the States, Report no. 99, April 1977).

12. Children's Defense Fund, *Children out of School in America* (Washington, D.C.: Washington Research Project, Inc., 1974).

13. O. Harris, "Day Care: Have We Forgotten the School-age Child?" *Child Welfare* 56 (1977): 440–448.

14. Education Commission of the States, Child Abuse and Neglect Project, *Education Policies and Practices.*

15. Zigler, "Controlling Child Abuse."

16. J. Garbarino and N. Jacobson, "Youth Helping Youth as a Resource in Meeting the Problem of Child Maltreatment," *Child Welfare* 57 (1978): 505–512.

17. R. Gastil, "Homicide and a Regional Culture of Violence," *American Sociological Review* 36 (1971): 412–427.

18. M. Straus, R. Gelles, and S. Steinmetz, *Behind Closed Doors* (New York: Doubleday, 1980).

19. Zigler, "Controlling Child Abuse."

20. D.G. Gil, *Violence against Children: Physical Child Abuse in the United States* (Cambridge, Mass.: Harvard University Press, 1970).

21. National Academy of Sciences, *Toward a National Policy for Children and Families* (Washington, D.C.: U.S. Government Printing Office, 1976).

22. Harris, "Day Care."

23. Children's Defense Fund, *Children out of School in America.*

24. J. Garbarino, "The Family: A School for Living," *National Elementary Principal* 55 (1976): 66–70.

25. J. Gray, C. Cutler, J. Dean, and C.H. Kempe, "Prediction and Prevention of Child Abuse and Neglect," *Child Abuse and Neglect* 1 (1977): 45–58.

26. Broadhurst, "Project PROTECTION."

27. J. Garbarino, "The Role of Schools in Socialization to Adulthood," *The Educational Forum* 42 (1978): 169–182.

28. Garbarino, "The Family."

29. Education Commission of the States, Child Abuse and Neglect Project, *Education Policies and Practices.*

30. Broadhurst, "Project PROTECTION."

31. R.S. Kempe and C.H. Kempe, *Child Abuse* (Cambridge, Mass.: Harvard University Press, 1978).

32. R.H. Mnookin, "Foster Care: In Whose Best Interest?" *Harvard Educational Review* 43 (1973): 599–638.

33. Garbarino, "Role of Schools."

34. R. Light, "Abused and Neglected Children in America: A Study of Alternative Policies," *Harvard Educational Review* 43 (1973): 556–598; S. Jayaratne, "Child Abusers as Parents and Children: A Review," *Social Work* 22 (1977): 5–9.

35. Zigler, "Controlling Child Abuse."

36. U. Bronfenbrenner, *Two Worlds of Childhood* (New York: Russell Sage Foundation, 1970); idem, "Reality and Research in the Ecology of Human Development," *Proceedings of the American Philosophical Society* 119 (1975): 439–469; idem, "Who Needs Parent Education?" *Teachers College Record* 79 (1978): 767–787.

37. Gil, *Violence against Children.* Zigler, "Controlling Child Abuse."

38. J. Meier, "Current Status and Future Prospects for the Nation's Children and Their Families" (Address to the annual convention of the National Association for the Education of Young Children, Anaheim, Calif., November 13, 1976).

39. B. Justice and D.F. Duncan, "Life Crisis as a Precursor to Child Abuse," *Public Health Reports* 91 (1976): 110–115.

40. Garbarino, "The Family."

41. Meier, "Current Status."

42. U. Bronfenbrenner, *The Ecology of Human Development* (Cambridge, Mass.: Harvard University Press, 1979).

Part II
The Maltreatment of Youth

James Garbarino and *Gwen Gilliam*
In consultation with:
Michael Cohen
Bruce Fisher
Robert Friedman
Peter Giannini
Ira Lourie
Norman Polansky

The Mistreatment
of Youth

Child Maltreatment as a Developmental Issue

Until recently, developmentally oriented thinking about child maltreatment was scarce and primitive. The topic of child abuse was nearly absent from the major professional journals serving professional researchers in the field of child development, *Child Development* and *Developmental Psychology*. These two journals contained no studies of the topic prior to 1976, and have published only a handful since then. To be sure, the problem-oriented journals such as *Child Psychiatry* and *American Journal of Orthopsychiatry* have repeatedly addressed the issue, but their interests are not so purely developmental. What is more, most of the studies deal mainly with abusive parents rather than with abused children. Indeed, the child has been largely ignored in studies (and services) dealing with child abuse and neglect.[1] This state of affairs is changing, and a more mature developmental approach to the problem is emerging.

The premier developmental hypothesis in the field of abuse and neglect is, of course, the notion of intergenerational transmission, the idea that abusing parents were themselves abused as children and that neglect breeds neglect. This idea is, by and large, firmly established in the minds of professionals and the general public alike. It makes sense intuitively; we learn how to be a parent from our parents. However, as accepted as it is among practitioners, the concept of intergenerational transmission of abuse and neglect has not really passed scientific muster. Instead, it has come under increasing attack as being (at best) unproven and (at worst) overstated so as to be misleading or even invalid.[2] As suggested in chapter 5, if anything is common to the background of most abusive parents, it is emotional deprivation or rejection. The classic clinical studies pinpoint psychological rather than physical abuse as the common culprit.[3] One such study concludes:

> Without exception in our study group of abusing parents there is a history of having been raised in the same style which they have re-created in the pattern of rearing their own children. Several had experienced severe abuse in the form of physical beatings from either mother or father; a few reported "never having had a hand laid on them." *All had experienced, however, a sense of intensive, pervasive, continuous demand from their parents.* (emphasis added)[4]

But for all its importance, the issue of abuse's passage from generation to generation is not the only pertinent developmental consideration. A more sophisticated developmental approach proceeds to investigate the changes in the causes, correlates, and effects of mistreatment as functions of development and maturation. We began to see this in chapter 7 when we looked at the role of the schools in child maltreatment. The issues for school-age children are somewhat different than those for infants or even for 3-year-olds, for that matter. The infant can do virtually nothing to protect itself from abuse and is totally defenseless against neglect. The battered baby is victimized in direct proportion to the parent's impulses and the presence of outside constraints (which are typically few). The infant experiences neglect in exact proportion to the parent's failure to provide care, thus being liable to nonorganic failure to thrive. What is more, the infant's capacity to signal its plight to others is limited and unconscious. School-age children, on the other hand, have better resources. They can adapt to the parent to minimize abuse by assuming whatever role will mollify the parent by being extremely compliant, innocuous, or responsible. They can counteract neglect by fending for themselves to some degree. Their ability to communicate their plight is greater as is their opportunity to do so, for example, in school. Finally, they are likely to have larger independent social networks from which to draw nurturance and support.

This kind of developmental perspective is still more important when we turn to a comparison of child maltreatment and adolescent abuse. In the latter case, there are myriad developmental grounds for anticipating differences in causation, correlates, effects, and effective intervention strategies. At its heart, the matter of being parent to an adolescent (and adolescent to a parent) is substantially different from the parent-child relationship in several ways.

1. The adolescent's cognitive abilities are likely to be much more advanced than are the child's. Adolescents reason much more like adults, and this injects a new element of complexity into the parent's task.

2. The adolescent's power is much greater than the child's. This includes physical power (implying the capability of effective physical retaliation if assaulted by a parent). It goes beyond this, however, to include the power to stimulate and influence family conflict, to leave the family situation, to harm self and others, to embarrass the parent, to compare the parent with other adults, as well as to help self and others.

3. The adolescent has a broader field of other significant individuals with whom the parents must come to terms. Autonomous relationships with other adults and with peers increase, including sexual relationships that many parents perceive as volatile.

These factors (and many more) come together to shift the boundaries around appropriate behavior in family relationships. Some forms of behavior by parents toward their offspring which were appropriate (if not particularly wise) in childhood may become abusive in adolescence. For example, the psychological connotations of spanking a 3- or 4-year-old are quite different from those of spanking a 15-year-old. Likewise, some types of affectionate touching and other intimate physical contact may be quite appropriate between a father and his infant daughter but inappropriate between the same father and his teenage daughter. Also efforts to exert a high level of control over every detail of a 4-year-old's daily existence may be acceptable, while the same intrusiveness with a teenager would be entirely inappropriate. These comparisons ring true intuitively, and we will explore them in subsequent chapters.

In some ways, parents have more latitude in their dealings with young children than in their treatment of adolescents. The latter have a broader base of experience with which to compare the parent's actions. If abused, teenagers are more likely than young children to perceive the deviance of their treatment. Adolescents have the cognitive equipment to better understand flaws in parental reasoning and moral character. They typically demand a more nearly equal role in family decision making. These factors, combined with differences in our culture's view of adolescents (with suspicion) and in our institutional treatment of them (with little compassion), predict that the phenomenon of adolescent abuse will differ markedly from child maltreatment. In fact, in its interpersonal dynamics and cultural interpretation, adolescent abuse more closely resembles wife abuse than mistreatment of children.

Wives and Teenagers as Victims

The adolescent-abuse problem is rooted in the child-abuse problem, if for no other reason than that roughly half the victims are "graduates" of child abuse. This much is clear. Less clear yet nonetheless revealing is the link between the abuse of teenagers by parents and the abuse of wives by husbands. This goes beyond the simple statistical association between abusing wives and children.

We recognize that there may be a political liability for likening adolescent abuse to wife abuse. In so doing we may be opening the door for others to misinterpret our model and absorb abused adolescents into an established lobby, namely, women's advocates against spouse abuse. We believe that the comparison serves a useful illustrative purpose, however, because wife abuse is much more familiar to Americans than is adolescent abuse, and the two do share some striking similarities. Since we are only describing a newly identified phenomenon that shares common traits with a familiar one, we feel confident in pursuing the comparison.

Our idea is to place abused adolescents on a continuum, midway between abused wives and mistreated children.[5] The central issue here is power, the ability to determine one's own behavior and influence the actions of others. Children are nearly powerless (though their behavior can have a significant effect on what happens to them). Teenagers gain power because of the increased ability to think, argue, and act that adolescence brings. Just as wives are powerful enough to threaten the authority of husbands, teenagers challenge parental authority. Because children are powerless, they are perfect victims: first, because they are easily victimized; second, because they elicit sympathy once they are abused. Teenagers are closer to wives in being imperfect victims, in both of these respects. One evidence of the greater power of abused teens and wives is the fact they are sometimes involved in reciprocal assault.[6] Obviously, children cannot match the strength of their parents, but abuse has been identified as a contributing factor in many assaults by adolescents, from benign self-defense to parricide.[7] Likewise, wives who murder their husbands do so often in retaliation for abuse. Domestic quarrels involving mutual assault are considered the most dangerous calls that police have to answer. A recent report from Connecticut indicates that some 20 percent of the adolescent-abuse cases reported to child protective services were initially reported to the police as assault by the adolescent on the parent. Straus, Gelles, and Steinmetz report assault by children and youth against their parents in 10 percent of America's families.[8] (In some families it seems that this mutual rough treatment is the only physical contact allowed. Faced with the prospect of no human touching, some prefer to hit and be hit instead.) The likeness between adolescent and wife abuse extends beyond power dynamics. The two groups are likely to experience similar things and face similar issues.

With both wives and teenagers, independence is often an issue. For example, when wives and adolescents assert their autonomy and the authority figure reacts with anger, violence is always an implicit possibility, particularly in a culture such as our own that condones violence as an expression of concern and as a disciplinary tactic. The independence of the previously submissive, intimate loved one particularly threatens a personality that needs absolute compliance from its dependents in order to confirm its own validity. Many authority figures simply lose control of their impulses when a challenge becomes unbearable. Teenagers are notorious for their expertise at provoking anger in their parents. Like wives, they are thus more capable of precipitating their own abuse. This does not mean that wives and teenagers are really to blame, or that they are responsible for their own abuse. However, it means that they are integrally involved in a system of relating that does not work. They will need to learn new ways to respond, as will the aggressors. Without justifying abuse, we must note that the perpetrator is often a victim of circumstances.

Both teenagers and wives are likely to suffer separation anxiety when removed from their tormentors. They may believe that powerful person's distorted view of life. They may believe the justifications that may be offered for abuse. They probably depend upon that person and may not be able to conceive of an independent life. In some cases, the anxiety associated with being separated from the authority figure may paralyze the victim and even lead to denial in order to rationalize inaction. If the thought of breaking away is too frightening, the victim may prefer to minimize or even deny mistreatment, rather than report it.

Another factor is the complexity of adolescent and wife abuse. Teenagers and wives are capable of feeling and expressing much more ambivalence toward their aggressors than can children. Often these conflicted feelings—from attachment to rejection to dependence to anger—cloud real issues and events in the minds of older victims. These feelings and their accompanying behaviors make it difficult to help the victims, be they wives or teenagers.

While sexual misuse is not limited to any one age group, it does seem to be more common among adolescents than children.[9] Most accounts of sexual abuse point to puberty as a time when both the quantity and quality of sexual misuse changes. Domestic rape threatens wives and adolescent females as well. In both cases the aggressor may be jealous of the victim's affection for others or may wish to use sex as a means for establishing authority.

Society's response to victimized children is one of uniform sympathy, if not practically then at least in principle. But we are often less supportive of wives and teenagers. They often receive less sympathy, both from individuals and institutions, because they do not conform to the image of helpless victims nearly as well as do abused children. As teenagers and adults, they are judged (and often are) able to defend themselves and are (sometimes accurately) thought to have precipitated the abusive behavior of the aggressor. Since in this view they got what they deserved, help is not justified. Finally, both wives and teenagers are presumed to have the resources at hand to enable them to leave home if they so choose. The fact that often they do not leave reinforces the image of the covertly powerful victim who is culpable, who is responsible for his or her own behavior, and who even gains satisfaction from the abusive treatment. No doubt a handful of individuals fit this characterization, but it hampers services to all who need help and currently are denied the benefit of the doubt.

While no one expects a child to be independent, we do expect independence of adolescents and wives. Thus while we expect child victims to be passively at the mercy of abusive parents and therefore in need of help, we expect wives and teenagers to be able to help themselves. This independence is elusive, however, because adolescents and wives are usually financially and emotionally dependent upon their abusers. Resolution of the domestic conflict is not easy for either group, however. For the wife it may mean divorce, counseling, separation, and threat of retribution. All these solutions have adverse financial implications that go beyond the obvious social and psychological adjustments they require. For the adolescent, resolution of the conflict may mean counseling, foster-home placement, institutionalization, or a nearly self-sufficient independent living arrangement. These solutions elicit more intense reactions from adolescents than children. We have no hard evidence that likens wife abuse to adolescent abuse. We do have some evidence, however, that shows adolescent abuse to be distinct from child abuse.

An Empirical Introduction to Adolescent Abuse

Let us begin our discussion by looking at the picture presented by reported cases of abuse and neglect around the country. To this end, we have compared child and adolescent cases in the American Humane Association's National Study of Child Abuse and Neglect Reporting. There are many methodological limitations to these data but they serve our purpose: namely, to provide an initial, gross comparison. We should note, however, that all the comparisons are gross and subject to many sources of confounding and distortion because of (1) the way the information is gathered in the field, and (2) the time aspect of the situations it describes. The data were recorded by caseworkers regarding abusive families on their case loads often before a thorough investigation had been conducted. Only two-thirds of all the states cooperated in the study. Within states, urban areas reported more reliably than rural regions. Across states, legal definitions of abuse differ. As to the time dimension, parents of adolescents are generally older than parents of young children. The age difference can partly account for any differences of income and education favoring the older group: Parents of teenagers tend to be significantly older than parents of young children, with all that greater age implies for income and education.

The available data (from 1977 and 1978) tell us that roughly a third of the reported cases of maltreatment involve teenagers. This confirms the existence of adolescent abuse. Indeed, the data suggest that midadolescence is the peak time for abuse of girls (with the peak for boys at around 2 or 3 years of age). This is consistent with other abuse data[10] and more general survey data on domestic violence.[11] Using this relative incidence rate (one-third of the cases reported) as a starting point, we can examine the differences between cases involving children and those involving adolescents.

Child- versus Adolescent-Abuse Cases

Socioeconomic and Demographic Characteristics

By and large, reported cases involving infants and young children are heavily concentrated among low-income groups. This is much less true with respect to adolescent cases. While only 13 percent of the families in which victims are infants have incomes in excess of $11,000 per year, nearly 50 percent of the cases involving adolescents come from families in which total income exceeds $11,000 per year. Likewise, while nearly 40 percent of the cases involving infants come from families receiving aid to families with dependent children (AFDC), less than 30 percent of the cases involving adolescents involve such welfare families (figure 8-1).

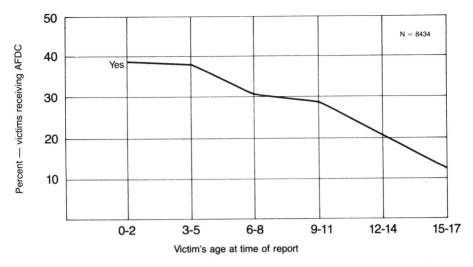

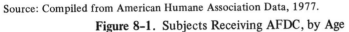

Victim's age at time of report

Source: Compiled from American Humane Association Data, 1977.

Figure 8-1. Subjects Receiving AFDC, by Age

Parental unemployment is less common for adolescent than child cases (figure 8-2). In sum, the socioeconomic measures suggest that adolescent-abuse cases are drawn more evenly from the general population, while child-abuse cases are drawn primarily from families of lower-socioeconomic status.

Demographic indicators present a picture that parallels the situation with respect to economic measures. Black children are somewhat more likely to be abuse victims than their numbers in the population would indicate when they are young (presumably because of the association between being black and being poor). During adolescence, on the other hand, blacks are, if anything, less likely to be reported victims than their numbers in the population would indicate. Whites are less likely to be reported victims than their numbers would indicate, particularly during early childhood. Hispanics are represented as victims in direct proportion to their numbers in the population across the age ranges.

The data show that young victims are substantially less likely to be living in a household with married caregivers than are adolescent victims (50 percent versus 75 percent; figure 8-3). Young victims also are much more likely than their numbers in the general population would indicate to be living in a household with only mothers, while for adolescent victims, the reverse is true. Indeed, adolescent victims are more likely than their numbers in the population indicate to be living in a household with father only.

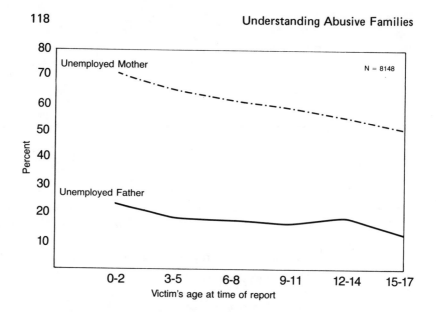

Source: Compiled from American Humane Association Data, 1977.

Figure 8–2. Parental Unemployment, by Age of Victim

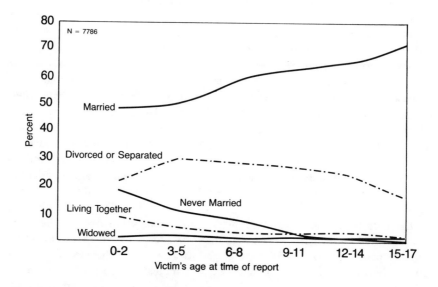

Source: Compiled from American Humane Association Data, 1977.

Figure 8–3. Parental Marital Status, by Age of Victim

In many respects, then, adolescent cases of abuse do appear to differ from cases involving young children. In general, the adolescent cases seem more representative of the general population, while the child cases are more concentrated among high-risk groups: single parents and the poor. This suggests a hypothesis for us to pursue in subsequent discussions of the sociology of adolescent abuse, namely, that families with young children are more likely to be victims of socioeconomic and demographic stresses, and that the day-to-day care of a young child is more heavily dependent on the material circumstances of life than is caring for an adolescent. Put another way, adolescent abuse may well be a more interpersonal problem than is child abuse, which is more an indicator of the quality of socioeconomic and demographic life. This is the principal developmental hypothesis generated by our review of the national data on reported cases.

Case Identification and Categorization

When we look at the source of the report as a function of victim's age, several trends emerge (figure 8-4). First, medical sources represent a declining proportion of the total across the age span. They account for more than 40 percent of the

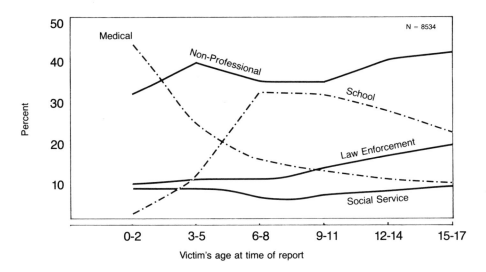

Source: Compiled from American Humane Association Data, 1977.

Figure 8-4. Source of Report, by Age of Victim

reports for infants but less than 10 percent for adolescents. Schools are major information sources for school-age children, accounting for 30 percent of the reports for 6-to-8-year-olds. For adolescents, schools report in approximately 22 percent of cases. Law-enforcement agencies represent a greater proportion of the total reports over the age span, from less than 10 to nearly 20 percent. Social-service agencies maintain a relatively constant proportion of the total reports, just under 10 percent across the age span. Finally, the relative number of reports by nonprofessional sources (friends, neighbors, relatives, and self-reports) varies somewhat across the age span but generally increases by the age of the child, from about 30 percent of cases involving infants to roughly 40 percent involving adolescents. This suggests another hypothesis: Adolescent abuse is a problem that can be attacked from many more vantage points than the mistreatment of young children, which finds its natural focal points in the health-care system and in the neighborhood.

Looking at the type of abuse and its effects, we see that young children are substantially more likely to be victims of severe abuse than are adolescents. Nearly 30 percent of reported cases of infants involve severe abuse, but only about 5 percent of adolescents. However, if we confine our attention to children above the age of 5, the proportion of severe injuries remains unchanged from this period of childhood into adolescence (figure 8–5). Sexual abuse plays an ever-larger role as children mature, particularly for females (figure 8–6). Whereas 5 percent of cases of infants involve sexual misuse, 40 percent of female adolescent

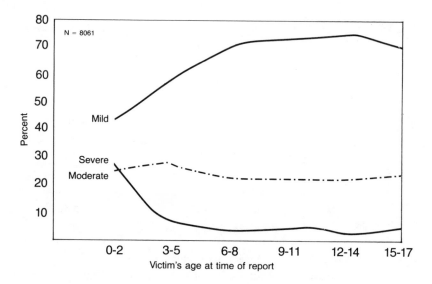

Source: Compiled from American Humane Association Data, 1977.

Figure 8–5. Severity of Maltreatment, by Age of Victim

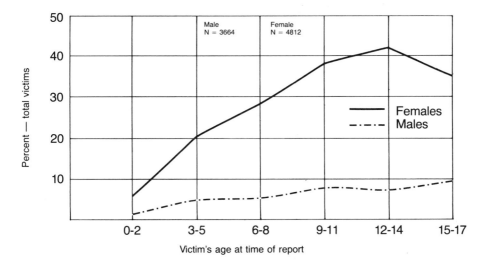

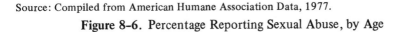

Source: Compiled from American Humane Association Data, 1977.

Figure 8-6. Percentage Reporting Sexual Abuse, by Age

cases are sexually molested. Using this knowledge, we can pursue the issues of how and why the types of maltreatment experienced by children and teenagers differ. These results tell us to look for less physically damaging victimization and for more psychological patterns of mistreatment, as is implied by sexual misuse.

Six-to-8-year-olds are most likely to remain at home as a result of a report while infants and teenagers are most likely to be placed out of the home (figure 8-7). Thus foster care is a particularly salient issue in cases involving the youngest and oldest victims. As we shall see, the issue of out-of-home placement is central in adolescent-abuse cases, be it initiated from the outside (official, as in court-ordered foster care) or from the inside (unofficial, when the teenager runs away or is thrown out of the house).

With these data as a starting point, we are in a position to move forward with our analysis, confident of our developmental hunch concerning maltreatment: namely, that the issues in the behavioral equations relating parent to child and family to environment shift as a function of age. What is more, we now have some leads to pursue: the hypotheses that adolescent abuse is less tied to material impoverishment than child maltreatment; that it touches a wider range of social contexts; that it is more psychological and less physical; that it is more likely to involve complex negotiations among parent, victim, and society over placement. With these ideas in mind, we can proceed to examine adolescent-abuse itself more closely. That is the purpose of chapter 9.

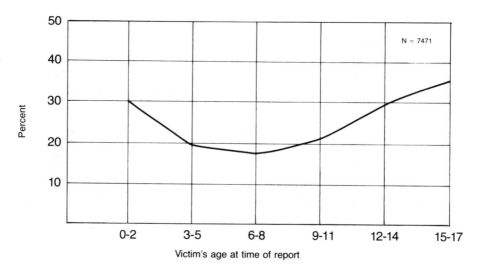

Source: Compiled from American Humane Association Data, 1977.

Figure 8–7. Out-of-Home Placement, by Age of Victim

Notes

1. H. Martin, *The Abused Child* (Cambridge, Mass.: Ballinger, 1976).

2. R. Friedman, "Child Abuse: A Review of the Psychosocial Research," in *Four Perspectives on the Status of Child Abuse and Neglect Research,* ed. Herner and Company (Washington, D.C.: National Center on Child Abuse and Neglect, 1976); N. Garmezy, "Observations on Research with Children at Risk for Child and Adult Psychopathology," in *Child Psychiatry Treatment and Research,* ed. M.F. McMillan and S. Henao (New York: Brunner/Mazel, Inc., 1977); S. Jayaratne, "Child Abusers as Parents and Children: A Review," *Social Work* 22 (1977): 5–9; M. Straus, "Family Patterns and Child Abuse in a Representative American Sample" (Paper presented at the Second International Congress on Child Abuse and Neglect, London, England, September 12, 1978).

3. B.F. Steele and C.B. Pollock, "A Psychiatric Study of Parents Who Abuse Infants and Small Children," in *The Battered Child,* ed. R.E. Helfer and C.H. Kempe (Chicago: University of Chicago Press, 1974).

4. Ibid.

5. J. Garbarino, "Meeting the Needs of Mistreated Youth," *Social Work* 25 (1980): 122–126.

6. M. Straus, R. Gelles, and S. Steinmetz, *Behind Closed Doors* (New York: Doubleday, 1980).

7. E. Tanay, "Adolescents Who Kill Parents—Reactive Parricide," *Australian and New Zealand Journal of Psychiatry* 7 (1973): 263-277.

8. Straus, Gelles, and Steinmetz, *Behind Closed Doors.*

9. American Humane Association, *Annual Report of the National Clearinghouse on Child Abuse and Neglect* (Denver, Colo.: American Humane Association, 1977).

10. J. Alley, B. Cundiff, and J. Terry, "Child Abuse in Georgia, 1975-1977," *Morbidity and Mortality Report* (Atlanta, Ga.: Center for Disease Control, January 26, 1976), pp. 33-35.

11. Straus, Gelles, and Steinmetz, *Behind Closed Doors.*

Patterns of Abuse

I skipped out of school a day and my dad found out and he really gave it to me with his razor strap. I had bruises all over my legs. So that Friday I just ran away.

They hit me with a meat cleaver. I was broiling hamburgers one night and I burned them and my mom grabbed the knife and she cut me. They don't do it all the time, only when they're mad. I've gotten a lot of bruises and strap marks since I was a little kid. I never left because I deserved every one of them.

One of these teenagers left home when she was first abused. The other tolerated years of severe mistreatment. Their stories illustrate one of the major points of this chapter, that the *experience* of abuse differs from individual to individual and may have quite different effects when it begins in adolescence as opposed to childhood. An adolescent who suffered abuse starting in early childhood lives in different circumstances than someone who is abused for the first time as a teenager. In chapter 8, we contrasted adolescent with child abuse. In this chapter, we further examine different types of adolescent abuse. These types are defined upon the basis of the child's age when abuse began.

Four Abusive Patterns

Based on the limited knowledge available, we identify four patterns of adolescent abuse.[1] In the first pattern, abuse begins only in adolescence. Presumably, this type of abuse occurs because the level of conflict rises until it reaches dangerous proportions, primarily over issues peculiar to adolescence itself, or perhaps adolescence injects some new element into the situation. Some investigators believe this pattern is most common in families in which children have been indulged by their parents.[2] This indulgent pattern causes parents to expect excessive dependency and compliance from their offspring, and that expectation in turn elicits frustration, resistance, and anger in adolescents as they begin to mature and resent their infantilized state. The behavior that characterizes a dependent teenager striving for autonomy is precisely the behavior that will enrage an indulgent parent.[3] There are many other reasons that adolescence can spark conflict in a family, including the synergistic effect of parents' and teenagers' developmental states, a characteristic economic squeeze during the children's adolescence, and the ambiguities of adolescent privileges in society (see chapter 10 for a thorough discussion). Whatever the source, we found in our small-scale study that about half of the reported cases of abused teenagers have no prior childhood history of abuse.[4]

The second pattern has only a coincidental link to adolescence. Here abuse simply continues mistreatment begun in childhood. The mistreatment is nothing new to the family and has nothing in particular to do with the victim's age or developmental stage. One may wonder how it is possible for abuse to continue throughout childhood into adolescence without outside intervention, but it happens quite a bit in the real world. Often abuse is not discovered during childhood, and even if discovered, it may continue. Success rates among abusive families that receive treatment typically are between 40 and 60 percent.[5] Particularly when the problem does not reach life-threatening proportions, chronic abuse may continue unabated as long as the child remains in the home. We hope this pattern will be a declining residual category that will continue to shrink as early identification and treatment become more widespread and effective. But it accounted for a full 40 percent of the cases in our study.[6]

The third pattern of adolescent abuse includes cases where formerly mild or moderate corporal punishment crosses the line to become abuse. It is hard to distinguish this pattern from pattern one; indeed it is perhaps better conceived of as a subvariety of it, since only at adolescence does corporal punishment, a practice widespread throughout the childhood population, become deviant. The youth who was slapped or spanked as a child is beaten or otherwise abused as an adolescent. This pattern may characterize restrictive parents who find themselves losing control as the child's strength, size, confidence, and independence increase. As a result, the parents feel more force is necessary to punish and control. This escalation of force may reflect a last-ditch effort to save the family from the real or imagined disgrace that a disobedient son or daughter could bring.

Authoritarian methods of child rearing keep youngsters from internalizing values and self-control. This lack of internal control shows up as a propensity for irresponsible behavior and may lead parents to feel they must use more force. (The thought that "he's now too big to spank" can mean a shift to more psychological discipline *or* an escalation of force.) These confrontations can be brutal and involve reciprocal assault. This pattern accounted for about 5 percent of the reported adolescent abuse in our study, but since it is difficult to document retrospectively, it may well be more common than these data indicate.[7] Indeed, given the prevalence of low-level violence against children, it may actually represent a finding contrived by our measures. No doubt most of the abused youth in pattern one were disciplined with corporal punishment as children also.

In the fourth pattern, abuse represents a return to behaviors that characterized parent-child relations when the teenager was a toddler. Many investigators comment on the parallel between adolescence and the "terrible twos," and several studies of abuse noted that these two periods are times of heightened risk.[8] In both these stages of the life cycle, parents and children are often at odds over expectations, dependency, autonomy, and social control. Parents who have difficulty with these issues when their offspring are toddlers may experience the same difficulties, perhaps in a more intense fashion, when the child reaches adolescence. The issues are the same: autonomy and independence. About 5 percent of the reported cases fit this pattern in our study.[9] Conceptually, this pattern falls somewhere between the two major types of adolescent abuse.

Two Contrasting Sets of Circumstances

We will look closely only at the first two types: abuse which begins in adolescence, and that which simply continues a pattern begun in childhood. (We have labeled short-term abuse type I; long-term abuse, type II.) These two categories account for most of the cases, and, as we have shown, they may easily subsume the other two categories. Our study suggests that families from the two major groups differ on nearly every gross measure of home life.[10] In other words, it looks like very different things are happening in these families, and for very different reasons.

In general, we found that families that became abusive for the first time during their offspring's adolescence appear to be more settled and stable than are those who have been at it for years. In fact, parents who started abusing their children when they were young appeared similar to the classic multiproblem child-abusing family described in chapter 8, characterized by unmanageable life stress and inadequate coping resources. This is no surprise, since they were probably the very same families who continued to be abusive into the child's adolescence.[11]

We found that parents of teenagers who abused their children for the first time at adolescence were much more likely to be married than were long-term abusers (figure 9-1). They were also much less transient than long-term abusers (figure 9-2). We also found that when social agencies helped families involved with short-term abuse, predominantly both victim-oriented counseling and mental-health-related services were provided, in contrast to the predominance of life-management services provided to long-term abuse families (figure 9-3). This complements the finding that emotional abuse is cited three times more often among first-time abuse cases than in long-term cases.

Parents in long-term cases had lower incomes (less than half that of the parents who did not mistreat their youngster until adolescence; figure 9-4). Parents who abused their teenagers as children were also somewhat more likely to themselves have been victims of abuse as children or to have a history of

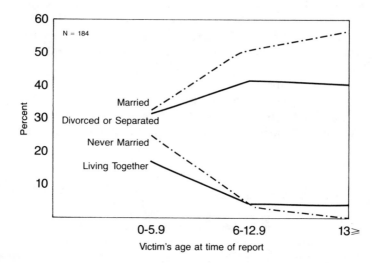

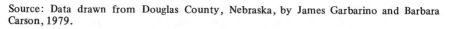
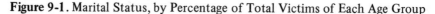

Source: Data drawn from Douglas County, Nebraska, by James Garbarino and Barbara Carson, 1979.

Figure 9-1. Marital Status, by Percentage of Total Victims of Each Age Group

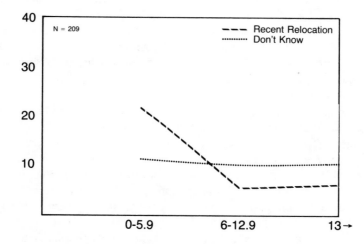

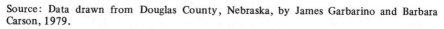

Source: Data drawn from Douglas County, Nebraska, by James Garbarino and Barbara Carson, 1979.

Figure 9-2. Percentage of Recent Relocation, by Age

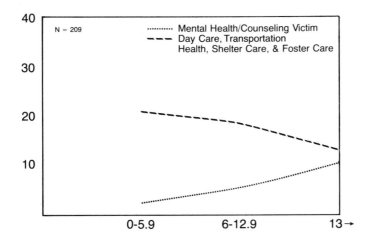

Source: Data drawn from Douglas County, Nebraska, by James Garbarino and Barbara Carson, 1979.

Figure 9-3. Percentage of Services Provided to Different Types of Victims, by Age

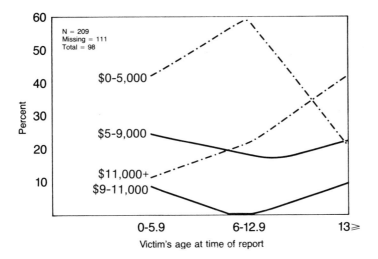

Source: Data drawn from Douglas County, Nebraska, by James Garbarino and Barbara Carson, 1979.

Figure 9-4. Family Income, by Age of Victim

spouse abuse (figure 9-5). There were more self-reports by victims with no childhood history of abuse. As we shall see, this may be evidence of stronger egos among short-term victims relative to long-term victims.

While mothers were more likely than fathers to abuse young children, that trend reversed itself for adolescents, for fathers were more often reported as perpetrators, in part, it would seem, because of the level of sexual abuse (figure 9-6). Mothers who abused their young children were more likely to be single, poor, transient, and unemployed. Among those who were married, it is possible that sex roles may have dictated that they alone would be charged with caring for the child.[12] Mothers were the ones who lashed out when caught in the squeeze between their deficient social skills and their children's imperfect behavior.[13]

Fathers (including stepfathers) play a larger role in rearing adolescents and thus a larger role in abusing them. The fact that fathers are more likely to abuse their teenagers points to the different issues that adolescence itself brings to the picture. Normal teenage developmental changes such as striving for independence, sexual maturation, and the ability to think abstractly require adjustments by parents and can create substantial conflict.[14] In normal families, both mothers and fathers may alter their behavior in response to the teenager's challenges; some, however, do not.[15] Traditional paternal dominance dictates that the father's role include asserting authority over the children. This puts him at the apex of potential abuse.[16] In most families, fathers are also more

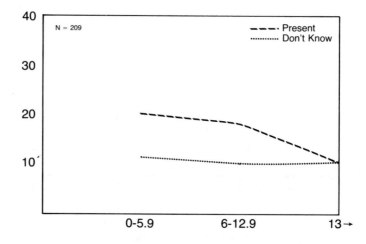

Source: Data drawn from Douglas County, Nebraska, by James Garbarino and Barbara Carson, 1979.

Figure 9-5. Percentage of Parental History of Abuse, by Age

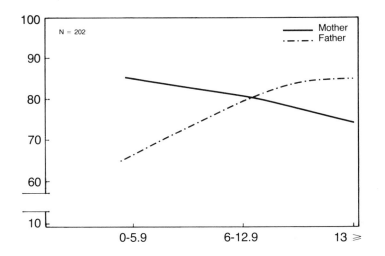

Source: Data drawn from Douglas County, Nebraska, by James Garbarino and Barbara Carson, 1979.

Figure 9-6. Parent Alleged Perpetrator, by Age of Victim

likely than mothers to let their own needs dominate their responses. Thus a father is more likely to try to physically or verbally control a teenager's behavior in this period of normal change than is the mother. Some fathers use methods that are inappropriate and damaging.

Much of the profile we have drawn is an elaborate way of describing the differential patterns and types of abuse as class phenomena. (The profiles in chapter 8 do the same thing for child as opposed to adolescent abuse.) The marital instability, transience, and unemployment we have described in long-term abuse families are all problems associated with poverty. Poor people are greatly overrepresented among the abusers of young children. We do not know how much of this is due to differential patterns of reporting as opposed to the stresses that poverty brings. Previous research suggests that any class bias in reporting is neither so large nor so simple as conventional wisdom suggests.[17] Leroy Pelton has gone so far as to refer to the "myth of classlessness" in child abuse, as a way of countering the suggestion that class differences in reported cases are invalid.[18] He argues that the reported differences reflect actual differences. The class difference makes sense when one considers the act of hitting an infant compared with hitting an adolescent. Assuming that infants are less capable of deliberately angering their parents, child abuse is mainly a result of the other environmental factors, especially stresses, surrounding the parent. Poverty limits the healthy venting of frustration in almost every conceivable way, from the amount of square footage each person is allowed to the ability to pay for diversion and babysitting to the lack of residential stability. Outside its tangible limitations, poverty has another pernicious effect: Many poor people begin to believe the values and opinions that the dominant society holds about them. If they feel that they are to blame for their under-privileged condition, the loss of self-esteem they experience can be crippling. Low self-esteem can trigger aggression if a person terrorizes others as a self-validation of potency. Once abuse has occurred, the parent loses further esteem by confirming his or her failure in the parental role. Chapters 1 through 7 dealt witn the social origins of child and adolescent maltreatment. Those origins are painfully clear. However, there are many factors that influence the quality of life that have nothing to do with social class. Abuse beginning in adolescence does not appear to have any particular link to poverty. Rather, it is spread across the community.

Implications

The differences in the class backgrounds of the two categories of adolescent abuse have some important implications for service professionals. Those who work with youth are likely to notice striking differences between adolescents from the two groups, particularly once they are made aware of these differences. In general, the later abuse began, the more whole the victim will be. One reason is the amount of development that was permitted without disruption. Another is the likelihood that the short-term abuse victim will come from a less impover-ished environment, an environment that does not itself retard development. We will discuss service implications in chapter 14.

Based upon this class difference, it appears that the remedies for child abuse are in many respects simpler to identify but harder to implement than those for adolescent abuse. The most obvious primary remedy to child abuse is to provide adequate income to all families, a step that would require nothing less than a major redistribution of wealth. In contrast, victimization of adole-scents is a more complex phenomenon than child abuse, harder to understand but, paradoxically perhaps, simpler to solve. The capabilities of adolescents themselves form the basis for approaching the problem through relatively inexpensive services, some of which address the family, others that exclude it in favor of the youth. The resources necessary for such services are miniscule when compared with those required to totally remedy child abuse. This is not to pit the needs of one age group against another. Indeed, it is unchecked child abuse that accounts for half the problem in adolescence. Child abuse has been recognized much longer than has adolescent abuse. Both are significant problems. It is true for adolescent abuse, much more than for child abuse, that awareness goes a long way toward resolution of the problem. That, of course, is the purpose of this book.

In chapter 10 we describe some of the factors that can create problems for any family with teenagers. While these stresses may even be enough to push some adequate families into abuse, these problems are most likely to compound the already serious difficulties of long-term abuse families, families whose members are ill-prepared to deal successfully with adolescence precisely because of the damage they have already sustained.

Notes

1. To the best of our knowledge, though this typology of four distinct patterns is not new, only two studies other than our own have systematically looked at this issue—I. Lourie, "Family Dynamics and the Abuse of Adolescents: A Case for a Developmental Phase Specific Model of Child Abuse, *Child Abuse and Neglect* 3 (1979): 967-974; and P. Libbey, and R. Bybee, "The Physical Abuse of Adolescents, *Journal of Social Issues* 35 (1979): 101-126. The survey data reported by M. Straus, R. Gelles, and S. Steinmetz, *Behind Closed Doors* (New York: Doubleday, 1980), deal with age differences in domestic violence, but with interests different than ours. To conduct our study, we surveyed a sample of 100 adolescent-abuse cases and 100 child-abuse cases reported to authorities in one Midwest county.

2. N. Polansky, personal communication.

3. H. Steirlin, *Separating Parents and Adolescents* (New York: Quadrangle, 1974).

4. J. Garbarino and B. Carson, "Mistreated Youth in One Community" (Boys Town, Neb.: Center for the Study of Youth Development, 1979). Other investigators reported higher figures. I. Lourie, "The Phenomenon of the Abused Adolescent: A Clinical Study," *Victimology* 2 (1977): 268-276; and idem, "Family Dynamics," found that most adolescent cases do not have a childhood history of abuse, while Libbey and Bybee, "Physical Abuse of Adolescents," report that twenty of their twenty-five cases fit this pattern. We suspect the difference in results is due to our use of a broader definition of abuse (as maltreatment) and our more broadly based sample of protective-service cases.

5. Berkeley Planning Associates, "Evaluation of Child Abuse and Neglect Demonstration Projects, 1974-1977," NTIS Report No. NCHSR 78-64 (National Technical Information Services, Springfield, Virginia); Garbarino and Carson, "Mistreated Youth"; R. Herrenkohl, R. Herrenkohl, B. Egolf, and M. Seech, "The Repetition of Child Abuse: How Frequently Does It Occur?" (Paper presented at the Second International Congress on Child Abuse and Neglect, London, England, September 12, 1978); A. Cohn, "Essential Elements of Successful Child Abuse and Neglect Treatment," *Child Abuse and Neglect* 3 (1979): 491-496.

6. Garbarino and Carson, "Mistreated Youth."

7. Ibid.

8. J. Alley, B. Cundiff, and J. Terry, "Child Abuse in Georgia, 1975-1977," *Morbidity and Mortality Report* (Center for Disease Control, Atlanta, Ga., January 26, 1979), pp. 33-35.

9. Garbarino and Carson, "Mistreated Youth."

10. Ibid.

11. On the basis of our research, we cannot say this with certainty, however. We know that the families whose children are now adolescents with long histories of abuse have similar demographic profiles to families that have just begun abusing their young children. Social-service agencies react to them in the same ways. These similarities are strong enough for us to conclude that they are people with similar problems at different stages of life. Our study is not longitudinal, so we cannot conclude unequivocally that we are seeing the same group of people in different phases of life. It makes sense, however, that this would be the case since the families are probably not experiencing any dramatic downward shifts in economic, migrational, and marital status at the onset of the children's adolescence. The fact that adolescents are more expensive to rear than young children would not affect the total financial resources of a family. Our information is also drawn from a single county. Our investigation of adolescent abuse among the data recorded by the American Humane Association's compilation of reported cases explored in chapter 8 does not permit comparisons between the key patterns I and II.

12. D.G. Gil, *Violence against Children: Physical Child Abuse in the United States* (Cambridge, Mass.: Harvard University Press, 1970).

13. C. Gray, "Empathy and Stress as Mediators in Child Abuse: Theory, Research and Practical Implications" (Ph.D. diss., University of Maryland, 1978).

14. J. Hill, "The Early Adolescent and the Family," in *Seventy-ninth Yearbook of the National Society for the Study of Education,* ed. M. Johnson (Chicago, Ill.: University of Chicago Press, 1980).

15. L. Steinberg, "Research in the Ecology of Adolescent Development: A Longitudinal Study of the Impact of Physical Maturation on Changes in the Family System in Early Adolescence" (Paper presented at the Conference on Research Perspectives in the Ecology of Human Development, Cornell University, Ithaca, N.Y., August 17-20, 1977).

16. M. Straus, "Stress and Child Abuse," In *The Battered Child,* ed. R. Helfer and H. Kempe (Chicago: University of Chicago Press, 1980).

17. J. Garbarino and A. Crouter, "Defining the Community Context of Parent-Child Relations: The Correlates of Child Maltreatment, *Child Development* 49 (1978): 604-616; idem, "A Note on Assessing the Construct Validity of Child Maltreatment Report Data, *American Journal of Public Health* 68 (1978): 598-599.

18. L. Pelton, "The Myth of Classlessness in Child Abuse Cases, *American Journal of Orthopsychiatry* 48 (1978): 569-579.

10 Family Stress and Adolescent Abuse

Abuse has many roots. Families with adolescents experience pressure from inside and from without. Internally, the changes that midlife development and puberty bring to the parent-child relationship pressure the family to adapt. Externally, stresses such as financial pressures, geographic mobility, and youthful frustration at the lack of an acceptable outlet no doubt leave their mark. These pressures are challenges that require adaptation; any sort of family dysfunction is a cumulative result of some combination of external (environmental) stress and internal (interpersonal) vulnerability. We are not sure exactly what the mixture between the two is, nor do we know the relative weighting of factors that precipitate abuse. For long-term abusing families, the situation is obviously different than for families that abuse for the first time in adolescence. Inability to accommodate to the changes of puberty is probably primarily responsible for the abuse that begins in adolescence; it must certainly exacerbate long-term child abuse.

In our view, adolescent abuse is rooted in our culture's inadequate provision for adolescence as much as in the inadequacies of individual families. The two feed upon each other, and no complete understanding of adolescent abuse can neglect either part of the problem. While the inadequacies of parents are easily recognized, society's deficiencies are often harder to see.

The developmental agendas that individual family members pursue independently can complicate their own lives as well as those of people around them. We now examine the issues surrounding the development of adolescents and their parents, as well as the culture that affects them both. This will help us understand how it is that some parents come to mistreat their teenagers; how circumstances victimize parents who in turn victimize their offspring. To understand the mistreatment of youth we must understand the human ecology of adolescence.

Adolescence

Most of us have mixed feelings about our own adolescence. We probably remember it as better and worse than it really was. More than any other period in life, the adolescent years have been alternately romanticized and feared. We hear that children today are disrespectful, idealistic, irresponsible, generous, or dangerous, depending upon the motives of the speaker. This ambivalence and confusion is not new.

Historically, adolescents have always been held in low regard. In the 1800s, young men were described as giddy, romantic, and harebrained. Youth was thought of as not merely the opposite of age but as a period of prolonged immaturity and lamentable irresponsibility.[1] The ancient Greeks could have written the pop classic, "What's the matter with kids today?"

G. Stanley Hall, one of the first people to consider adolescence as a scientific issue, described it as a period when the individual reenacts humanity's passage from savagery to civilization. In his view, any attempt to end adolescence prematurely by imposing adult values and rules was doomed to failure because it would only lead to expression of savage propensities in adulthood. As we shall see, society's view of adolescence today has not moved very far from Hall's depiction.

Erik Erikson defined adolescence as "a period of rapid change: physical, psychological, physiological, and social; a time when all sameness and continuities relied upon earlier are more or less questioned again."[2] Many definitions of adolescence emphasize the issues of change and autonomy, and it is these two issues that have the greatest effect upon the way teenagers interact with their parents and siblings. Adolescence is also a time when one learns adult roles, and that process requires some testing that may also affect life at home.[3] All these learning processes take place in adolescents who are undergoing the fundamental biological, intellectual, and social changes that define this stage of life.

Physical and Sexual Development

While a complete review of our knowledge about adolescent development is beyond the scope of this book, we will outline the physical, social, and psychological changes of puberty to put the phenomenon of maltreatment in context. The biological start of adolescence is the growth spurt that signals the beginning of puberty, and is followed by the maturation of the sexual organs (ovaries in girls, testicles and penis in boys) and later by secondary sex characteristics (facial hair and lowering of the voice in boys, breast development and broadening of the pelvis in girls, and the appearance of pigmented pubic and axillary hair in both sexes). All this growth is stimulated and accompanied by hormonal changes that may precipitate mood swings. These biological changes are really less important for our purposes than are their social implications because these social factors have a greater influence upon family dynamics.

There is a great deal of variability in the timing of the growth spurt and sexual maturation. The sexes differ as do the individuals within them. Boys may begin their growth spurt as early as 10-and-a-half or as late as 16 years old. Girls may begin their growth spurt as early as 8 and as late as 11-and-a-half. (Historically, the age when puberty begins has become ever younger, though the trend seems to have leveled off. For service professionals, this has meant an ever-younger clientele.)

The typical adolescent tends to be self-conscious about these changes, especially when he or she is early or late. It seems that early-maturing girls and late-maturing boys have more psychosocial problems later in life than their friends who developed along with the majority.[4] But there really is no perfect time to mature sexually, and most teens suffer anxiety over real or imagined physical flaws. One classic study found that 61 percent of the boys and 72 percent of the girls in the tenth grade desired some change in their physical selves: in their complexions, proportions, weight, hair, height, and so on.[5] No doubt people of all ages feel some dissatisfaction with their appearance, but adults do not have to accommodate to rapid change, and children are less self-conscious.

Menarche (the onset of menstruation) for girls and nocturnal emissions for boys are tangible proof that one is growing up. And depending on the context in which they occur, these sure signs of maturation can themselves generate either apprehension or pride both in teenagers and their parents. Parental reaction is thought to be one of the primary determinants of the psychological impact of menarche.[6] Parents are often surprised by and uncomfortable with the emerging sexuality of their offspring, perhaps because they fear that sexuality can become a vehicle by which the adolescent challenges adult authority and power.

In our society, authority and sexuality are both withheld from youth until they pay their dues, until they accept the cultural ground rules for sexuality. Some teenagers no doubt see sex as a way to separate from the adult world as represented by their parents, or to define themselves as distinct, powerful individuals. Sexual experience is now often equated with general life experience by adolescents themselves.[7] Needless to say, the issues surrounding sexuality—curfews, dating activities, and choice of friends—are a powerful force in the lives of teenagers and adults. Unseen and therefore difficult to dictate, adolescent sexual behavior can inflame families that seek, with variable success, to exert a high level of control over the teenager's social life. Parents are left to trust their teenager to uphold their wishes, to abdicate the choice to the youth, or to quarantine him or her from social contact. Whenever values as sacred as chastity, trust, and independence are involved, emotions run high and the time is ripe for abuse.

Intellectual Development

If sexual maturation and the growth spurt are the primary factors in physical development, the emerging ability to think abstractly is the salient aspect of intellectual development. With adolescence comes a significantly increased ability to deal with hypothetical problems, mathematics, philosophy, and ethics. Adolescents are also able to think abstractly about their own behavior, their families, their schools, and about society in general. Unlike children, teenagers can ponder alternative points of view, and can independently evaluate the motives of others. This means they are better able to discuss family problems and that they can have a much more objective view of their parents' motivation than ever before. While educators welcome this development because it permits more sophisticated academic work in the classroom, parents quickly realize that these new intellectual tools are soon turned toward social and interpersonal matters as well.

Most teenagers change their focus, becoming more introspective and analytical than their former childhood selves. They are typically preoccupied with defining their own individual identities, and with reconciling the enormous physical changes they are undergoing with their social experiences. Their thoughts may shift from the real to the possible, absorbing them in the pleasure of thinking for thinking's sake. As psychologist Paul Osterrieth puts it:[8]

> To reason is for the young person a need and a pleasure; the "constructs of the mind" are a delight. He reasons every which way, about subjects that are most unreal and farthest from his experience. . . . The arrival at abstraction permits the individual to delve into the systems of collective representation that are afforded him by the culture in which he is growing up, and he will gradually be carried away by ideas, ideals, and values.

But he notes that while these developments open new vistas for the youngster, they, like all opportunities, contain the seeds of trouble and conflict as well as those of harmony and improved relationships: "Everything will be food for thought, for spoken thought, for passionate discussion, for endless discussions, for preemptory affirmation, and the adult, losing his footing a little in this tidal wave, will often fail to perceive that what he takes to be vain rehashing or sterile questioning of old worn-out problems corresponds in reality for the youngster to youthful explorations and discoveries."

Finally, since they can take alternative points of view, adolescents for the first time have the ability and the inclination to take the side of the underdog. This new ability causes teenagers to side with victims of oppression, and they may even include themselves in this group. Although teenagers may use myriad techniques for gaining power within their families, they remain largely powerless politically, economically, and socially. In our society, adolescents are generally outsiders, and if their views reflect that position they may encounter grave differences with their parents, especially with parents who are well established in the society's economic and social life. Heated discussion of social and political issues has never been known for its soothing effect. Realistically, however, most intrafamily disputes do not evolve from such ethereal realms; as we shall see, the routines of daily life generate much more conflict than does ideology.

Expanded cognitive abilities and the exploration these abilities encourage have some important implications for the way teenagers act. As self-assured adults, we tend to approach new situations with some degree of confidence as well as caution, usually knowing that our behavior will probably be acceptable based upon our past experiences. Adolescents need reassurance, and may therefore try to imitate the behavior of competent people they know. It may try parental patience at times to deal with living replicas of pop singers, screen idols, sports figures, and other heroes and heroines. Although this identity sampling no doubt accounts for much of the perceived erratic behavior of adolescents, it seems to be a necessary step toward developing a stable sense of self, and generally does not threaten an underlying affiliation with parents and their basic values in most families.

Social Development

Partly as a result of their need to separate from their parents, adolescents appear to be preoccupied with their peers. Peers become the primary influence on many daily activities, and may compete with parents. Because peer influences are likely to be strong over highly visible aspects of life-style, it is easy to over-emphasize their long-term significance. The dichotomy between parental values and peer demands may be exaggerated.[9] However, teenagers who enter the world of their peers, perhaps unconsciously swearing allegiance to a new set of values (particularly if they seek to dramatize peer affiliations), see adults realistically as outsiders whose authority is to be mistrusted.

Teenagers lead much of their day-to-day lives segregated from other age groups in high schools that are a sort of youth ghetto.[10] They have created their own distinct subculture in many ways. The values and norms of this youth subculture, divergent from the adult world and uniform unto itself, constitute the context in which teenagers practice interpersonal relationships with friends, dates, and acquaintances. The personal egocentrism we noted in individual adolescent mental development extends to absorption with other teenagers. Few adults penetrate this world and feel comfortably accepted in it. Those who do can be a bridge between youth and adults. These individuals may serve as a vital link between adolescent victims and services because abuse victims are likely to have few people to whom they may turn. These youth also tend to be wary of reaching out to anyone for help.

Tasks

Many of the internal changes that teenagers undergo have a direct effect upon their attitudes about the world in general and their families in particular. The tasks that adolescents must accomplish in order to mature are not always pleasant to experience, or even to observe. One important task is that of separating from one's parents. It is a normal process. Indeed, we worry when it does not occur.

To accomplish the task of separating from one's parents, teenagers must believe that their parents are not the perfect people they had imagined them to be, after all.[11] For children, idealization of the parent is reassuring because it makes them feel safer and more secure. At adolescence, it is time to leave this security behind in favor of establishing an independent identity. Some teenagers, especially those most dependent upon their parents, need to work harder to make the separation.[12] They need to launch out farther and with more force than other adolescents. A dependent youth may be angered by his or her own feelings of dependency as he or she seeks to make the separation, and this anger may be directed back at the very parents to whom the teenager feels so strongly attached. To separate, the teenager may feel the need not only to take his or her parents off their pedestals but to go further, to the point of denigrating the powerful authority figures who have always controlled his or her life. This pattern may be a common one for American youth, who often seem to have extreme ambivalence about dependency once they reach adolescence.[13] This normal adolescent task (individualization) is probably made more difficult by our culture's obsession with independence and our unresolved feelings about dependency.[14]

Compounding the task is adolescent dogmatism. Perhaps this is partly the result of the role model experimentation we spoke of earlier. Osterreith describes "the opinions that [the adolescent] defends sometimes with as much flare as thoughtlessness" as a necessary attempt at self-definition.[15] It could also be that since the adolescent is examining so many new concepts for the first time, he or she is likely to have little capacity for entertaining alternative points of view. In any event, teenagers do seem to have a surprising capacity for fervent adherence to simplistic ideologies and beliefs. In the home setting this can mean, for example, that parents who are average individuals and who were once exalted are suddenly denounced as weak hypocrites. And, naturally, dogmatism can make the job of providing services to adolescents more difficult.

Beyond that, the whole setting of adolescence is one of ever-widening unfamiliar circles to be tested. These new situations are threatening, albeit alluring. Adolescents tend to retreat sporadically to the security of the home, even though they might be quite independent at other times.[16] This swinging from independence to dependence and back again can frustrate parents who misinterpret it as simply wanting to have one's cake and to eat it too (which may be true in some cases because the existence of a legitimate need does not preclude the use of that need for manipulative purposes). Furthermore, American families may be particularly prone to trouble with independence. In this country, most parents ascribe to a strong belief in *early* autonomy and they socialize their children accordingly. This practice makes for a prolonged period of late dependency.[17] Parents who view the situation from their own perspective without considering their teenager's needs may begin to feel that they are being used. Empathy, putting one's self in the place of another, is a primary skill for being an effective parent, particularly when one's offspring reaches adolescence.[18] Without it, many daily crises that adolescents experience must seem trivial and annoying. And in a society where there is little support for parents, empathy may become still more important.

If parents take too much responsibility for a youngster's dress and appearance, their feelings of success or failure may depend upon the ability to control the preferences of their youngsters.[19] This need to control may stem from the parent's own lack of confidence about authority and can also lead to inconsistency and use of developmentally inappropriate forms of control. Moreover, a parent's unthinking threat to control private behavior can bring out the righteous, dogmatic indignation of a teenager intent upon protecting his or her privacy. This vicious cycle can occur when responsibility has not been given out gradually as the child learns to use it. The danger of this approach is that it can cause problems in adolescence.

Because adolescence usually brings independent mobility, it is simply impractical for parents to monitor their teenager's actions away from home. Thus overcontrolling parents may end up relying upon emotion-charged interrogations in the absence of firsthand data because parents have no mechanism at this point for observing many of their children's behaviors. Such scenes can easily lead to abuse. Indeed, one study found that most adolescent-abuse cases involved mild to severe "acting out" behavior of the adolescent as an antecedent to physically abusive incidents.[20]

Parental Adaptation

Parents of adolescents must adapt to their offspring's new mental and physical competency. Healthy adaptation produces more mature family dynamics, while unhealthy adaptation can spark developmentally damaging conflict. Adolescence is a time for parents to listen to their young, to discuss family issues, to make democratic decisions, and to explain their own reasons for setting rules. Parents who ignore the teenager's capabilities soon find the new faculties can be effectively turned against them. Democratic government in the home is important for all families; it is fundamental if those with adolescents are to avoid serious conflicts. Authoritarian families, those where parents make arbitrary decisions based only upon their position of authority and upon undisclosed reasons, are particularly at risk for trouble when they encounter the intellectual developments of adolescence.

As children leave childhood, they rightly expect to wield more influence at home based upon their new abilities. Parents who have not done so already must begin to reason and consult with their teenagers when making decisions. This change disrupts (if only temporarily) even healthy families.[21] It requires listening and communication skills that parents have not needed before in order to control young children.[22] Most families experience a shift in power at this time, with the child gaining power at the expense of the parents.[23] As we shall see, those who cling to old patterns and continue to treat their adolescents as children are setting themselves up for trouble. Since they do not hand over any power to their teenagers, they must use power themselves more often and more forcefully in order to maintain control. This is a typical origin of physical abuse, and it represents a situation in which parents fall victim to their own rigidity.

Perhaps some of the problems begin in the way we socialize our young children. According to Kandel and Lesser who studied adolescence comparatively in the United States and Denmark, because Danish parents socialize their children more intensively in childhood than do American parents, Danish adolescents are more self-assured and confident than their American counterparts.[24] They found American parents more authoritarian with their teenagers and Danish parents more democratic. They found that Danish adolescents feel more independent than American youth who in turn desire that independence more. They hypothesized that American parents seem to switch techniques—treating their children as teenagers and their teenagers as children— when compared with parents in Denmark. In both countries, the feeling of being granted adequate independence was associated with positive interaction with parents. Danish parents tend to communicate more with their teenagers, to take adolescents' wishes into consideration more often when making decisions, and to provide more explanations for their decisions than do American parents.

It appears that in the absence of new guidelines, American parents are by and large sticking to the methods they used when their youngsters were children. They have solved the problem of hanging in limbo by regressing into familiarity. Kandel and Lesser go as far as to say:[25]

> The great preponderance of authoritarian patterns in the American family may be indicative of an institution that is breaking apart as a communal unit; in the absence of shared norms, parents find it necessary to institute formal rules. External controls have to be substituted for internal ones . . . the failure of such internal controls to have developed may result from ineffective socialization practiced early in life of the American child.

The faults in our patterns for rearing children may be compounded by the lack of support and guidance our culture gives to parents.

For most families (80 percent according to one study) the offspring's adolescence creates no serious difficulties. It is important to note that the adjustments we have been describing are made and made smoothly by most people, most of the time.[26] Only a minority of families have serious problems, and we do not present them as typical. We are merely trying to point out the potential points of conflict that most families overcome and that cause some families to stumble.

Midlife Development

Teenagers are not the only ones who are changing. Because of their relative positions in the life course, many parents of adolescents are sensing physical, sexual, and social change in themselves just as much as their teenagers. This point in the life course has been dubbed "midolescence," a concept growing out of Erik Erikson's model of progressive developmental challenges. Midolescence may not be a crisis, but it certainly seems to be a distinct phase that requires some adjustment. Fred McMorrow, author of *Midolescence: The Dangerous Years*, describes it this way for men:[27]

> Midolescence is that time when a man recognizes and/or rejects the truth about himself, that for better or for worse, he has reached the point at which he has achieved, if not all that he thought he *would* achieve just about all he ever *will*. For decades he has been conditioned to living in a steady ascent; everyday leads to a tomorrow, every year to a happy New Year: let's *make* it this time, let's do *better*. Now he has reached a leveling-off, the end of youth, that some mistake for the beginning of old age and the approach to death.

For women, this stage is eventually documented physically by menopause. So besides facing the psychological significance of middle age, women are faced with an added biological event that in this culture has traditionally been fraught with dread and degradation.[28]

While most parents face midolescence as their children simultaneously face adolescence, some do not. For adults who were teenage parents, the child's adolescence comes at a time when they are in their early- or mid-30s. Clinicians report a problem with young parents in this situation who are either competitive with their same-sex child, or involved in confusing, semiseductive interactions with their opposite-sex child.[29] The relationship between parents' developmental stage and child's developmental stage is not simple, but demographically the most common combination is that of an adolescent and a midolescent facing each other exactly when each most needs support, encouragement, and personal validation, but is probably least able to give it.

Just as most families manage pretty well with adolescence, neither men nor women need have problems adjusting to middle age, and most probably do not. For those who can see beyond Madison Avenue's obsession with youth, the middle part of life can be long and enjoyable, offering an economic zenith and eventual freedom from child-rearing responsibilities. But there are people who do have trouble, and that can render them less effective as parents, at just the time when they are responsible for shepherding an adolescent through puberty.

Adolescence and midolescence are inversely parallel. As Ira Lourie, the first person to apply this theory to the abuse literature, puts it: "It seems that nature has designed the changes of adolescence to rub salt into the wounds of the changes of middle age."[30]

Middle-aged adults tend to be concerned with the integrity of their bodies.[31] They may be noticing a general decline in their level of energy. Gray hairs, wrinkles, and paunches may enter the scene. In turn, they may begin to feel less attractive and desirable. During this time of self-consciousness, these parents must watch their children grow larger and stronger than ever before. Teenagers and toddlers are famous for their inexhaustible energy and both can be a trial for the exhausted parent.

Along with this physical decline, adults may be experiencing a sexual crisis. While research shows that sex in midlife may be less frequent than in younger years, sex has not been shown to be less enjoyable at this time. Still any failure to perform sexually is often interpreted as a sign of age by middle-aged men. Ten years earlier, the same inability to respond would probably have been attributed to mental pressures or dismissed as a fluke.

Of course the most prominent aspect of pubertal development is that of emerging sexuality, and parents are witness to it all. Doubts about their own libido may spur some parents to overcontrol the activities of their never-so-able youngsters. As stated earlier, a parent's perception of the teenager's sexual activity, with all the subtle nuances of things such as curfew and selection of dates, can be volatile sources of conflict.

We do not know how many adults pursue extramarital affairs at the onset of midolescence. One study shows that the probability of extramarital sex increases with the length of marriage, up to 40 percent after six years of marriage of the individuals sampled.[32] Hunt suggests this may represent an attempt to recapture the romanticism of one's own marriage through sex outside it.[33] Whether sexual adventure is an attempt to regain past romance or to confirm one's sexual attractiveness, it often puts unbearable strain on a marriage, though it need not always do so.[34] Even without sexual infidelity and the complications it can bring to a marriage, the restlessness and introspection of midolescence can lead to dissatisfaction with one's mate. Parents who are struggling with their own romantic involvements may view their teenagers' breathless first love with skepticism or even envy.

When parents examine their careers, they may or may not be satisfied with what they find. Their dreams may or may not have been fulfilled. They may feel that, for what it is worth, they have reached the pinnacle of their careers. A father may want to break out of his field and switch careers—many do—but many others feel constrained by financial commitments to the family. For the woman who has been a career homemaker, this process may be a vicarious one if she derives her status from her husband's achievements. If not, she may do it independently.

But for teenagers, life is beginning. The world spreads out before them and no aspiration seems too high. Youth, especially those in the middle and upper classes, look forward to professional careers and may be disposed to discussing their plans with parents who may not share the ebullience of youth.

We must remember that both adolescents and midolescents can be quite self-centered, so greater age does not always mean that parents will be able to accommodate for their teenagers' needs. There is another source of stress that clouds the lives of some families with adolescents.

Financial Pressure

A family with three teenagers needs 2.5 times the income that a childless couple does in order to maintain a similar standard of living.[35] If the inflationary spiral of America in the 1970s continues, parents may begin to more openly resent the financial burdens their children place upon them. Survey research shows that parents will not stop having children entirely for economic reasons, but the cost of rearing children is less than that for teenagers.[36] If a family stops having children when it begins to press the upper limits of an income, it will need more money when the children grow older. In all except upper-level white-collar and professional occupations, earnings peak early, when the worker is in his early-30s and the children are young. There is no rise in income later when more money is necessary to maintain the family's standard of living. This fact may place a burden on the family, a burden that easily turns to resentment. The strains are not only financial, however.

The Adolescent Role in American Society

American teenagers are in the awkward position of being simultaneously indulged and oppressed, by and large constrained from contributing anything meaningful, and shielded legally from the consequences of their own acts. The contrived position of youth in this society may act either as a direct irritant or as an unconscious source of frustration. In other words, adolescents may not see it as such, but their arbitrary roles limit the contributions they can make, and the effects of that limitation are the real sources of irritation they feel. We do not know how much of this frustration teenagers carry from the outside world into their homes.

In past eras, people often died young and positions of responsibility were often open to people at a very early age. Many of the founding fathers were virtually teenage parents to the nation. In 1930, a full 2 million children under 18 were gainfully employed. As the depression deepened, stringent regulation of child labor seemed a way to open jobs for adults. The crusade against child labor finally succeeded in banning the practice when it was in the economic interest of adults. At the same time, many professions started requiring more schooling in order to raise their status in the eyes of the public. (It was not until the 1920s, for example, that one needed a college degree in order to pursue legal education.)[37] The logical place to put young people who could no longer work was in schools to "prepare for life." The number of adolescents enrolled in secondary schools rose from less than 7 percent in 1890 to more than 92 percent in 1970.[38]

Incidentally, research shows that when teenagers drop out of high school they do not increase delinquent behavior.[39] Such behavior may even decrease, presumably because they have removed a major source of frustration from their lives.[40] One reason that so many youth feel frustrated is that at school there is room for only a tiny percentage of adolescents—talented athletes, gifted artists, popularity kings and queens, and the like—to contribute and feel important. This is especially true in large schools.[41] A change in the regimented structure of today's schools that would allow more achievement for more students who could thereby appreciate their own uniqueness would be a major step toward dissipating youthful dissatisfaction.

Families in Flotation

Finally, our culture provides no clear guidelines to parents and their teenagers. The dependency of adolescence has been determined by our economic and political systems, but little else has been mapped out about the stages by which one becomes or helps someone else become a mature adult. Most major privileges given to teach responsibility are granted on the convenient but inefficient basis of age rather than competence. Beyond the major milestones of a driver's license, high school graduation, and the right to vote, parents have very few guidelines for meting out responsibility, especially in the small doses that are considered most constructive. There is no authoritative, universally accepted guide for living with teenagers, no Dr. Spock for adolescence. There are programs that offer some hope in this regard. We are encouraged by the success of Parent Effectiveness Training, which teaches family members to listen competently, checking the accuracy of their perceptions of messages; and the Teaching Family Model, which teaches such social skills as giving directions and taking criticism effectively. Of course neither touches the broad social forces affecting adolescence in America, and both are more process than content, more guide than recipe. The situation is therefore so poorly defined as to allow for anything from indifferent permissiveness to concerned democracy to stern authoritarianism. This is significant because we believe that teenagers and children who are abused or neglected tend to come from families on the extreme ends of the authority scale.

In a society with clear-cut puberty rights and respect for aging process, conflicts between adolescents and their midolescent parents are probably minimized or, at the very least, ritualized. In our society, where adolescence is an ambiguous time in life and aging is looked upon with disrespect and suspicion, it is no wonder that the conflict reaches serious proportions in families without adequate coping resources.

The stresses we have mentioned cannot of themselves produce maltreatment. The issues facing family members—gaining autonomy, finding constructive outlets for adolescent energy, learning to handle one's developing sexuality, adapting to middle age, coping with economic decline—can represent challenges that a family can meet and in so doing the be drawn closer. The Great Depression of the 1930s actually benefited young girls because they became strong and capable at earlier ages than they would have otherwise; and, it knitted strong families even closer together.[42]

But sometimes adversity does not breed achievement. In some vulnerable families the pressure explodes into maltreatment. In other extremely vulnerable families it exacerbates the abuse that began in childhood. We do not know exactly what makes the difference between those who come through adolescence strengthened and those whom it tears apart, but we can hazard some guesses. Social isolation must play an important role. So must the norm of physical punishment. Marital dysfunction, low parental self-esteem, role reversal, poor communication, sending double messages with double binds (so that if Johnny obeys mommy he will make daddy mad and vice versa), parental dependence upon the child to unify the family, extreme dependency of the child upon the parents, parental rigidity and overcontrol, and a lack of trust are a few of the problems for which families seek therapeutic counseling. Although not abusive in the technical sense, these destructive patterns do take their toll and probably have a lot to do with whether a family becomes abusive or not. Frankly, we know too little about adolescent abuse to be able to identify with any confidence the factors that are associated with it. At this point, the research has yet to be done. We can only extrapolate from what we know generally about the human ecology of child rearing.

Before proceeding, we will address a particularly painful and intensely disturbing aspect of this process, namely, sexual abuse. As a society, we do not quite know what to do or say about sexual abuse; as authors we find it difficult to sort through the conflicting evidence, theory, and speculation. This confusion is, we think, an accurate reflection of reality. In chapter 11, we interrupt our narrative to bring together what we think we know about sexual abuse as a transition to our discussion of the more general consequences and service needs of adolescent abuse. Sexual abuse epitomizes several of the central themes in adolescent abuse: The demarcation between the normal and the inappropriate is often hard to pin down; the potential for developmental damage is great; the credibility of the victim is often in doubt; and the interpersonal dynamics within the family are complex.

Notes

1. J. Hawes, Lecture addressed to the young men of Hartford and New Haven, Hartford: O.D. Cooke, 1828. Cited in President's Science Advisory Committee, *Youth: Transition to Adulthood* (Chicago: University of Chicago Press, 1974).

2. E. Erikson, *Childhood and Society*, 2d ed. (New York: Norton, 1963), p. 261.

3. J. Garbarino, "The Role of Schools in Socialization to Adulthood," *The Educational Forum* 42 (1978): 169-182.

4. D. Weatherly, "Self-perceived Rate of Physical Maturation and Personality in Late Adolescence," *Child Development* 35 (1963): 1197-1210.

5. A. Franzier, and L.K. Lisonbee, "Adolescent Concerns with Physique," *School Review* 58 (1950): 397-405.

6. G. Konopka, *The Adolescent Girl in Conflict* (Englewood Cliffs, N.J.: Prentice-Hall, 1966).

7. P. Blos, *Adolescent Passage* (New York: International University Press, 1979).

8. P.A. Osterrieth, "Adolescence: Some Psychological Aspects," in *Adolescence: Psychosocial Perspectives,* ed. G. Caplan and S. Leborici (New York: Basic Books, 1969).

9. J. Hill, "The Family," in *Seventy-ninth Yearbook of the National Society for the Study of Education,* ed. M. Johnson (Chicago, Ill.: University of Chicago Press, 1980).

10. U. Bronfenbrenner, *Two Worlds of Childhood* (New York: Russell Sage Foundation, 1970).

11. D. Offer and J. Offer, "Normal Adolescent Males: The High School and College Years, *Journal of the American College Health Association* 22 (1974): 209-215.

12. H. Steirlin, *Separating Parents and Adolescents* (New York: Quadrangle, 1974).

13. D. Kandel and G. Lesser, *Youth in Two Worlds* (San Francisco: Jossey-Bass, 1972).

14. M. Rotenberg, "Alienating Individualism and Reciprocal Individualism: A Cross-cultural Conceptualization," *Journal of Humanistic Psychology* 17 (1977): 3-17.

15. Osterrieth, "Adolescence."

16. G.J. Manaster, *Adolescent Development and the Life Tasks* (Boston: Allyn & Bacon, Inc., 1977).

17. Kandel and Lesser, *Youth in Two Worlds.*

18. A. Jurich, "Parenting Adolescents," *Family Perspective* 3 (1979): 137-149.

19. Group for the Advancement of Psychiatry, *Power and Authority in Adolescence* (New York: Mental Health Materials Center, 1978).

20. P. Libbey and R. Bybee, "The Physical Abuse of Adolescents," *Journal of Social Issues* 35 (1979): 101-126.

21. L. Steinberg, "Research in the Ecology of Adolescent Development: A Longitudinal Study of the Impact of Physical Maturation on Changes in the Family System in Early Adolescence" (Paper presented at the Conference on Research Perspectives in the Ecology of Human Development, Cornell University, Ithaca, N.Y., August 17-20, 1977).

22. R. Friedman, personal communication.

23. Hill, "The Early Adolescent."

24. Kandel and Lesser, *Youth in Two Worlds.*

25. Ibid.

26. Hill, "The Early Adolescent."

27. F. McMorrow, *Midolescence: The Dangerous Years* (New York: Strawberry Hill Publishing Co., 1974).

28. C. Bruck, "Menopause," *Human Behavior* (April 1979): 38-46.

29. R. Friedman, personal communication, 1979.

30. I. Lourie, personal communication, 1978.

31. R. Gould, "The Phases of Adult Life," *American Journal of Psychiatry* 129 (1972): 521-531.

32. R. Bell, S. Turner, and L. Rosen, "A Multivariate Analysis of Female Coitus," *Journal of Marriage and the Family* 37 (1975): 375-383.

33. M. Hunt, *The Affair* (New York: World Publishing Company, 1969).

34. McMorrow, *Midolescence.*

35. Hill, "The Early Adolescent."

36. J. Blake, "Is Zero Preferred: American Attitudes toward Childlessness in the 1970s," *Journal of Marriage and the Family* 41 (1979): 245-265.

37. R. Stevens, "Two Cheers for 1870: The American Law School," *Perspectives in American History* 5 (1971): 405-548.

38. U.S. Bureau of the Census, "Projections of the Population of the United States by Age and Sex: 1970 to 2020," *Current Population Reports,* Series p-25, no. 470 (Washington: U.S. Government Printing Office), table 2, series D.

39. J. Bachman, S. Green, and I.D. Wirtanen, *Youth in Transition,* vol. 3 (Ann Arbor, Mich.: Institute for Social Research, 1971).

40. D.S. Elliott and H.Z. Voss, *Delinquency and Dropout* (Lexington, Mass.: Lexington Books, D.C. Heath and Co., 1974).

41. J. Garbarino, "Some Thoughts on the Effects of School Size on Adolescent Development," *Journal of Youth and Adolescence* 9 (1980): 19-31.

42. G. Elder, *Children of the Great Depression* (Chicago: University of Chicago Press, 1974).

11

Sexual Abuse: A Special Case?

> If I was alone with my dad, he would touch me and kiss me. I would try to please him in little ways because it was confusing to me. Then he came into my room one night. I was real scared, but he told me to relax and he wouldn't hurt me. It did hurt, but there were moments I remember enjoying. I mean, I was the ugly one and this was the closest thing I had ever experienced to love. The only affection I can remember were those times with my father. He told me he would kill me if I told, so I never told my mom. I still don't know if she knew.

Family life is intimate. Within the homes of many cultures (including our own), people live in crowded quarters, share common beds, and are regularly exposed to each other's nudity. Mankind always maintained some sort of incest taboo to protect us from the natural attraction and sexual arousal that can easily occur in such close quarters between people already bound by powerful relationships. Many who have studied the phenomenon most closely believe the urge to commit incest is deeply rooted within us all. Society's strongest sanctions are needed to forbid it. Every culture upholds this taboo in some form, though specifics vary greatly from place to place, particularly among traditional folk societies.

Both violence and sex are inevitably issues for families because when people with strong attachments are locked-in together the most powerful human forces always surface. Our isolating culture cuts families off from the outside world, and thus accentuates the degree to which members of American nuclear families have only each other. For this reason we must come to terms with domestic sex just as we must deal with domestic violence.

The National Center on Child Abuse and Neglect defines sexual abuse of children as "contacts or interactions between a child and an adult when the child is being used for the sexual stimulation of the perpetrator or another person when the perpetrator is in a position of power or control over the victim."[1] Placing misuse of power at the heart of the matter is a sound decision, in our opinion. Here, as elsewhere, exploitation is the hallmark of the perpetrator-victim relationship. Finkelhor highlights this issue when he states that adult sexual contact with children is intrinsically wrong because children are not in a position to give informed consent, be it because of their limited understanding of sexuality or because of the coercive context in which they must inevitably operate, given the dimensions of parental power and authority.[2]

151

Whether or not it involves actual incest (sexual intercourse between two people too closely related to marry), family sexual abuse is both inappropriate and damaging. Of course, much of what we consider sexual abuse, such as fondling, fellatio, and cunnilingus, falls outside incest in its strictest sense. We will refer to all incestuous and nearly incestuous activity as family abuse to differentiate between that which goes on within the family life and that which goes on outside it. (Only when we are reporting the work of other researchers who have investigated actual incest will we use the term *incest*, otherwise we use the broader phrase, *family sexual abuse*.) Some studies attribute harmful psychological effects not to the sexual acts themselves, but to society's reaction. We maintain that it does not matter. One cannot function apart from society; society will not be ignored. Whether or not incest would damage people in the best of all possible worlds is not the issue here. In this culture it presents serious problems, and it is this culture that affects the teenagers with whom we are dealing.

Incidence

Given the shamefulness and secretiveness of the acts involved, it is little wonder that estimates of the incidence of sexual abuse vary. Outdated official criminal statistics show an incidence of one to two per million population.[3] Since that number represents only the people who stood trial and were convicted of incest, and since 80 percent of all sex crimes against children occur within close-knit situations (immediate family, relatives, close friends, neighbors) where the participants have good reason not to report, the hidden rate is surely much higher.[4] The most recent effort to compile estimates of incidence and prevalence concludes that there are some 300,000 cases per year involving some form of sexual offense against children.[5] One barometer that appears to give us an accurate estimate of incidence is effective reporting among a population served by an active service program, such as that in Santa Clara County, California. That experience suggests as many as 1,000 families per million are involved in sexual abuse of children and youth.[6]

Almost all the information we cite in this section is based upon case studies by professionals. There is little else to use. Although it helps us understand the problem, this type of information is drawn from groups of people who typically are already having psychological problems, and the number of people in these groups is typically so small as to make statistical inference difficult if not impossible. (We know very little, for example, about people who are not harmed as a result of incest.) Still these studies are the best evidence that we have and we will use them to sketch a rough profile of the dynamics of incest. We note with hope that better research in this area does seem to be on its way.[7]

One issue that is unresolved is the socioeconomic character of sexually abusive adults. There are reasons for arguing that incest is more common among those most affected by socioeconomic stress—crowded living and sleeping quarters are among them—as well as reasons for thinking it more common among the affluent where fathers may be less inclined to seek sexual gratification outside the family for fear of legal and social retribution. Clinical research reflects both points of view. Recent evidence based on active community programs suggests that the victims represent a crosssection of the community.[8] Because of the psychological and cultural nature of the problem, this seems plausible. Our findings concerning the socioeconomic character of adolescent-abuse cases support this view. However, the power of situational forces linked to socioeconomic status, which play such a significant role in other forms of child abuse, should not be ruled out prematurely. Indeed, we must always keep in mind that intervention into the circumstances of life is often much more efficient and powerful than therapy with individuals.[9]

Domestic Sexual Abuse

Incest as a Form of Abuse

We have set sexual abuse apart from other types of abuse because its dynamics within the family are different. While it is often accompanied by the use or threat of physical abuse, and may grow out of a neglectful situation as well as lead to future refusal to provide care, it is not any of these things alone. The issues are not entirely the same, but do bear a resemblance. When it begins with the onset of adolescence, physical abuse usually centers around issues of adolescent autonomy and independence. It is linked to the overall family dynamic, while sexual abuse seems to spring more directly from marital dysfunction and other interpersonal problems. Emotional abuse carries messages of rejection while sexual abuse does not necessarily do so, at least initially. As in the case cited at the beginning of this chapter, it may be the only sign of acceptance a youth receives. One could not classify incest per se as a neglectful behavior, though an incestuous pattern often requires a neglectful stance by the other parent. While physical or emotional abuse may explode from conflict, incest can be an act to fill a void.

One approach identifies five necessary ingredients for incest: (1) the daughter's assumption (whether voluntary or forced) of a mother role, (2) relative sexual incompatibility between the parents, (3) the father's unwillingness to seek a partner outside the family unit, (4) family fear of disintegration, and (5) unconscious sanction by the mother.[10] While it is rare that such recipes really describe reality, in this case these dynamics may describe a special case of general parent-adolescent dysfunction. Sexual abuse is a misuse of power and failure to live up to the protective responsibilities implicit in the parental role.

Family Sexual Abuse and Adolescence

Sexual abuse of children happens between people who are not related. One study found the distribution of partners falls into a pattern in keeping with the strength of the incest taboo; uncles are more frequent partners than fathers and cousins more than brothers.[11] Three-fourths of all known offenders are among the victim's household, either as relatives or acquaintances.[12]

But sexual abuse within the immediate family is worth major consideration because there is good reason to believe that sexual abuse within a family is much more damaging than is exploitive contact with a stranger. One researcher believes that even though violence by a stranger is surely terrifying, it is less destructive than incest because at least it can be dealt with directly. Everyone can vent their rage at the offense and support the child. However, he continues, "a seduction or forcible rape by a respected authority figure is more disillusioning and the child's problems are compounded if those surrounding the victim find it so hard to accept the deviant behavior of a friend or relative that in their confusion they withhold the support that the child so desperately needs."[13]

Some students of this phenomenon believe incest is less harmful to the psyche of a young child than to an older one, with the risks increasing as he or she approaches adolescence. They argue that younger children do not recognize that taboos are being violated and have only a vague sense something is wrong. In this view it is only at adolescence that they are capable of becoming sharply aware of the norms and expectations of the culture beyond their immediate family. This, along with other developmental traits of adolescence, has motivated some researchers to call adolescence the "danger period" for incest.[14]

Unfortunately, much serious sexual abuse begins shortly before or during early adolescence. Both the incidence and the type of abuse seem to change as the child matures. As a child, contact is often limited to genital manipulation. As a girl grows older, the chances of intercourse increase, and the incidence of intercourse tends to increase along with the development of her secondary sex characteristics.[15] So her own sexual maturation seems to set up the potential victim for sexual abuse just when she is best able to understand the power of the incest taboo. The timing of these events conspires to threaten healthy development.

We will use the father-daughter dyad as a model for discussing sexual abuse within the family since it constitutes more than 70 percent of all reported cases of incest.[16] However, the problems that incest brings to sons are equally if not more severe.

Not all sexual abuse in families happens between biological relatives. Considering the current rates of divorce and remarriage in this country, reconstituted families surely form a sizable demographic group, on the order of 25 percent for adolescents.[17] The U.S. Census Bureau estimates that half of today's children will spend some of their first eighteen years in single-parent homes, and that most of these youth will eventually become part of such reconstituted families. Stepparents within these families may not be biologically related to their stepchildren but the roles they fill are similar to those of biological parents. As such, they influence the development of the child. For the new American family, then, we will define sexual abuse in terms of the role the perpetrator plays in the family rather than in bloodlines. Thus the stepfather-stepdaughter relationship seems particularly risky because it combines the authority and opportunities for exploitation that parenthood brings without the natural inhibitiions of consanguinity.

Sexually Abusive Families

Sexual abuse is typically a symptom of family dysfunction. Often the individuals involved suffer psychological traumas that warp their relationships with each other. According to those who counsel them, members of many sexually abusive families tend to be bound up in one another to an unhealthy degree. The family may not allow individuals to develop normally, consuming everyone's energy just trying to stay together. This may help to explain a victim's extreme fear of leaving the home, for to be without a family in this situation is to be without identity. The families tend to be socially isolated, and though they often show no outward signs of conflict, many are comprised of destructive relationships characterized by hate, jealously, and immaturity. Members often function within rigid sex roles.

There seems to be a high incidence of early economic deprivation among sexually abusive fathers, as well as a marked history of emotional impoverishment.[18] Many of them were deserted by their own fathers in their formative years.[19] Often they are angry with their wives or at women in general, but the typical incestuous father is not retarded, psychotic, or pedophilic (desiring, as an adult, sexual contact with children). He lacks the internal and external controls to cause him to respect the incest taboo when tempted to commit incest. Of the three patterns of incest that Meiselman identified, the one that includes the great majority (80 percent) of fathers has no hint of mental illness about it.[20] These men are often upstanding citizens, with higher than average levels of education and income. The category is called "endogamic incest," and is characterized by a turning inward of the family and by relative social isolation. The fact that incestuous fathers are so "normal" may be confusing, but it does offer hope for those who seek to help. The endogamically incestuous father depends upon his relationship with the daughter, and tries to sustain it over long periods of time. The other two categories, psychotic and psychopathic incest, each contain about 10 percent of the total reported cases. Psychotic incest is usually a spontaneous occurrence. Basically, this incest is committed only when the aggressor is in a psychotic state or otherwise out of control, for example, drunk. Finally, the psychopathically incestuous father has no particular sexual interest in his daughter. His approaches result from her availability alone. Even with its existing numerical preponderance, the secretive nature of endogamic incest suggests that, if anything, it is underrepresented in reporting rates.

Occupying the maternal position in a sexually abusive family is a difficult task. Coping with incest would exceed the personal resources of most women. However, some investigators believe the mothers in sexually-abusive homes are often complicitous in the incest, indirectly stimulating it by their sexual unavailability. Such women may have a history of emotional deprivation and be ill-equipped to protect their daughters. Often they groom their daughters to become the "little mother" of the family, reversing roles and encouraging the daughter to assume maternal responsibilities. If incest occurs, the mothers in these cases are thought to be relieved.[21] Others characterize the incest mother as passive, dependent, infantile, and masochistic.[22] It is impossible to know how many women are actually aware of sexual abuse and what their real feelings are when it occurs in their own homes. But it seems that relatively few women actually take assertive action to protect their daughters once they find out. Some experts believe these mothers are more concerned about the potential disruption in their own lives than their daughters' welfare.[23] We must be cautious about blaming the mother in these cases, however, particularly since the research on which the maternal-complicity thesis is based is suspect. Its reliance on psychiatrists' case loads weights the evidence in favor of psychologically disturbed families. What is more, the realistic nature of the fears that inhibit action, such as retribution by the husband and public humiliation, should make it somewhat understandable, and us more compassionate.

We know less about the individual personality traits of the daughters involved than we do about fathers and mothers, since research cannot separate innate traits from the psychological effects of incest. Incest is thought to have a greater potential for changing the personalities of daughters than parents, and we do not know what they were like before they were sexually abused. Some researchers (particularly those working before the current national upsurge of interest in abuse generally) have characterized the daughters as exceptionally beautiful,[24] while others contend that the typical incest victim's appearance is unimportant and that she is indiscernible from the average adolescent.[25] We assume that the latter view is correct. There is some evidence that incest daughters are lower in IQ than their nonvictimized peers, but it is unclear whether this is due to inadequate mental capability or the psychologically disruptive effects of the incestuous relationship.[26] This inability to separate cause from effect characterizes research on physical abuse as well.[27] In this, the scientific issues surrounding sexual abuse invoke our discussion of psychological abuse in chapter 5.

The Dynamics of Family Sexual Abuse. As stated earlier, the basic cause of sexual abuse is often a poor marital relationship, which itself certainly has social dimensions.[28] The individual psychological factors mentioned earlier influence whether the family becomes sexually abusive or not, but it is the relationships between the parents or the parent substitutes that are by far the most important factors. Other contributors such as emotional crises, unemployment, death or separation of a spouse, and illness are thought to precipitate the event. However, if everyone's needs were being met, there would be no incentive to break such a strong taboo. We believe this parallels research conducted by Elder and Rockwell showing that the effects of the Great Depression of the 1930s were most negative for families with a prior history of marital conflict.[29] As is so common in human behavior, we see an interaction effect, where it is the *combination* of personal vulnerability and social conditions that gets people in trouble.

Children naturally seek affection from their parents. A behavior that is innocent in a child would be seen as seductive in a teenager or an adult. Children are not without sexual drives; those drives are simply immature and generalized. As a young girl matures, it is easy to see why she might try her new charms on her father, probably the most trusted male in her life. A father who misinterprets his daughter's overtures by responding as if they were part of a mature seduction is projecting his own feelings. If he betrays her innocence by responding sexually, he puts his daughter in an impossible situation, forcing her to choose between the values of her culture and those of the most powerful male figure she knows. This problem extends to the normal heterosexual activities of the girl. One particularly difficult problem for the family is the daughter's dating. Because of their own involvement, incestuous fathers often guard their daughters from boys, accuse their daughters of sexual promiscuity, and use escalating physical force or rejection to control them. All this argues persuasively for specialized education programs aimed at helping fathers understand the nature of their role in the process of their daughter's sexual development. It also argues for programs aimed at children to teach the difference between normal nurturant touching and inappropriate exploitative touching. (The Illusion Theater in Minneapolis, Minnesota, performs dramatized vignettes in local elementary schools to this end.)

One study found that when approached sexually by their fathers, a few incest daughters willingly complied (12 percent), while others (32 percent) passively conceded.[30] Whereas 35 percent complied out of fear of punishment, 21 percent overtly resisted. The same investigator found that older daughters could and did resist more successfully than younger ones, presumably because they are more mature and may be less dependent.[31] In another study researchers found the threat or use of force a factor in 30 percent of the cases with which they dealt.[32] These figures make clear that physical abuse is often an adjunct to sexual misuse (at least as a threatened possibility).

The power balance in a father-daughter relationship is so unequal that physical force is rarely necessary to initiate incest. For the daughter, there are many reasons for compliance. Leaving home may be risky, frightening, and even illegal. As an adolescent capable of ambivalent feelings, she may love her father as a parent and even need the love and affection he gives her, especially if her mother is rejecting. Thus neglect by one parent may set the stage for abuse by the other. She may wish to remain loyal to a father who has been a source of support during childhood. Simply childhood respect for authority loads the deck. She may want to express her anger about a chaotic home life or defy her mother.[33] She may even comply in exchange for special privileges.

Apart from any conflict, bewilderment, or guilt a girl may feel about the act itself, she faces a host of other family problems. If she derives any sensual pleasure out of the incest (despite its moral repugnance), she may feel responsible for it.[34] She may justifiably worry about becoming pregnant. Family members who know about an incestuous relationship often deny it. This denial may cause the daughter to doubt her own senses, wondering why no one mentions the topic or seems to even be aware of the incest. This kind of denial appears frequently in the recollections of victims. If she wants to tell, she may be threatened with physical harm for disclosure. Even if she does tell her mother, she is usually not believed, at least initially. If she reports sexual abuse to others, the daughter faces the real possibility of breaking up the family to which she is bound. As stated earlier and as might be expected, many mothers choose to ignore, deny, or rationalize the sexually abusive situation. It is not uncommon for a woman to accuse her daughter of promiscuity outside the home or of having seduced the father. Some former victims who were sexually abused as teenagers report that the inaction by their mothers hurt them as much as their father's abuse. Many remain just as angry at their mothers as at their fathers, if not more so.

The average incestuous affair lasts about three-and-a-half years,[35] ending when the daughter struggles to establish autonomy from the family.[36] It tends to last so long probably because the endogamic incestuous father typically works hard at prolonging the affair. Traditionally, daughters have rarely ended incestuous relationships through official means. Instead of reporting sexual abuse, most daughters choose to leave home as soon as possible through early marriage or running away.[37] This course of action compounds the normal problems that the sexually abused girl may have in establishing heterosexual activity outside the home, particularly given the pool of sexually exploitive males waiting to capitalize upon her vulnerability and use her in one way or another.

Effects of Family Sexual Abuse. As noted earlier, it is difficult to differentiate the adverse effects of sexual abuse per se from those of the disturbed family environment in which it occurs. This parallels the problem of determining the effects of physical abuse as well.[38] Different adolescents react differently, of course, but there are several indicators that seem to determine the severity of damage that sexual abuse will cause. In general, the closer the relationship between the aggressor and the victim, the more damaging the abuse will be. Other considerations include the age and developmental status of the victim, the use or lack of force, the degree of shame or guilt the child feels, and the reactions of parents and professionals.[39] Where the victim does not have access to a network of family-support systems, the risk is substantially increased.[40] Social isolation here as elsewhere is a threat to development, particularly in abnormal or unhealthy families.

Many counselors mention pseudomaturity as a characteristic of sexual-abuse victims. After all, sexual experience has the effect of creating an air of worldliness even when it is age-appropriate. Many clinicians report that female incest victims have learned to relate to men only in a seductive way. This Lolita syndrome is of underdetermined prevalence, and may be much less frequent than clinical reports would suggest. One must always remember that females have not been treated fairly by clinicians in sexual matters. Freud assumed that accounts of sexual misuse were pure female fantasy. Where it does exist, however, any such pseudomaturity and seductiveness present special problems for male therapists. In addition, victims often display a wide range of symptomatic behavior, including regression, bedwetting, sleepwalking, insomnia, and nightmares.[41] These problems complicate the task of diagnosing sexual abuse in the first place.

Over time, the effects of family sexual abuse change. Drug and alcohol abuse, and self-multilation;[42] depression and suicide;[43] compulsive masochistic behavior;[44] and phobias, anxieties, and psychosomatic symptoms[45] are much more common among incest victims than among the various populations with which researchers have compared them. In general, the people in these comparison samples have emotional problems they consider serious enough to warrant professional help, since they are usually drawn from analysts' case loads. The incest victim does not compare well, even with these troubled people. It makes sense that tampering with sexuality has far-reaching implications.

Often the fears that sexual abuse elicit persist even after the situation changes. One girl, after years of incest with her natural father, accused her stepfather of incest on flimsy grounds. Another, after being removed from the home because of incest, locked herself in the closet of her foster home to sleep every night.[46] This phenomenon could account for the high incidence of fallacious charges of incest that some ex-incest victims level against their foster parents. Sadly, they are frightened and threatened by their misinterpretation of the healthy affection they need so much.[47]

Relationships with men in general are difficult to sustain for many victims. They may seek out father figures, taking a masochistic stance about relationships and life in general, unable to see their way out of abusive situations. Because of their poor self-concepts, many sexually abused women seek out partners to confirm their worst suspicions about themselves. Many will suffer anything to remain attached to a man.[48] These "worst suspicions" are often reinforced by the fact that once sexual abuse is made public a girl may be approached by other men (even other relatives) who view her experience as something that makes her sexually available. Also sexual-abuse victims are frequently victimized again as a result of their efforts to escape from the initial victimization (as when they run away from home).

The most predictable type of harm is to the victim's overall sexual adjustment. The two most common symptoms are promiscuity and frigidity. Promiscuity may simply be an expression of poor relationships with men and a lack of satisfaction in sexual activity. Frigidity seems to be more common. To escape her guilt, the incest victim may learn to deny her feelings during the incestuous relationship and to separate her mind from her body.[49] This learned response may become a habit that impairs later appropriate sexual relationships. Like many pathological symptoms, it results from natural attempts to cope.[50]

Finally, because of the damage they have sustained, incest victims are more likely to set up their own daughters for sexual abuse, often by denying sex to their husbands. As one professional puts it: "The women who accept mysogynous, imperious, or rapacious partners deserve enlightened attention, not only for their own needs but for the protection of the children in their care. Many of these women were victims of sexual, physical, or emotional abuses as children; they have an incredibly undeveloped capacity for self-perception, self-esteem, and human initiative."[51]

Treatment

Two major bodies of thought dominate the issue of treatment of incestuous families, unlike other sorts of abuse, where there is greater consensus about initial tactics. One approach advocates intervention by the criminal-justice system to protect the adolescent, while the other decries court interference as useless and damaging. The dilemma is real, and may reflect genuine differences in the service needs of incestuous families. While some point out the trauma of a trial to a daughter who must testify against her father before outsiders, others see the result of the process (prison for the father) as the only sanction severe enough to protect the daughter and to force the parents into therapy. After a girl reports incest she will have to repeat her story to strangers, often of the opposite sex, and will be asked to describe incidents in graphic detail. In court, she may be accused of initiating the incest. Confronted with the pressure to maintain her family's integrity, she may retract her complaint, labeling her initial story a lie (and thus contributing to the myth that most complaints of incest are merely lurid accusations from angry children). Involvement in the criminal-justice system puts the family into an adversary relationship in court and into financial jeopardy whatever the outcome, but particularly if the breadwinner is imprisoned.

Except for isolated incidents, our national response to help incest families has been meager. One anonymous physician asks: "If the public sector deals with the problem in a destructive way, is the therapist ever justified to bypass the 'system' and provide needed care to all members of the family, while at the same time putting an end to the sexual exploitation?" This spokesman attributes the lack of cooperation by private physicians and therapists with reporting laws to this suspicion.

Families involved in incest need counseling to resolve their hostility and resentment. Several exemplary treatment centers exist. One that has received national attention is the Child Sexual Abuse Treatment Program in Santa Clara, California.[52] It reports no recidivism among its clients who have completed the sessions. It also reports that 90 percent of the marriages remain intact. Although the validity and generalizability of these findings are open to question, they do suggest that the problem is not intractable. Headed by Henry Giarretto, the program emphasizes the social responsibility of each member to obey society's rules, and reports that it shortens the prison term of the perpetrator, while also reuniting the family. Families become involved with choosing their own alternatives, taking responsibility for their own actions, recognizing the uniqueness of each individual, and focusing on the present rather than on past regrets.[53] The reported successfulness of this program is a challenge for researchers to verify and for clinicians to replicate.

Other counselors stress the need to allow victims to grieve and to support attempts to reestablish trust. Still others see sexual abuse as a symptom of other family problems and therefore attempt to address those problems, such as social isolation, unemployment, pathological dependencies, and role distortions directly.[54] The Harborview Sexual Assault Center provides such a comprehensive, community-based program.[55] It emphasizes the need to provide acute, crisis intervention coupled with long-term support including legal advocacy.

An approach that has recently gained favor is therapy and counseling groups composed of women who were incest victims. One program stresses the need for relieving the victim of her guilt.[56] It stresses the unequal power relationships between parent and child, as well as the fact that the victim was probably too young to have an adult conception of sexuality. The realization that they are not evil and that they are not alone seems to help incest victims the most.[57] This approach is consistent with the general strength of self-help groups such as Parents Anonymous[58] and Youth Self-Help Groups.[59] Self-help is a sound strategy for many victims and perpetrators of maltreatment.[60]

For Those on the Line

Sexual abuse, as much as other types of abuse, is an expression of family dys-function. Many therapists tell us these families present some special problems. Often it is a challenge to convince these families they need therapy when they are not compelled by law to attend counseling sessions. One of the most dis-tinctive problems the professionals who counsel incest families report may be the seductive behavior of the victim toward the therapist, regardless of gender. The professional's job is to show the victim that her actions are inappropriate and to teach her new ways of relating to people. Incestuous families are often delusional, with members who suffer anything from low self-esteem to grandiosity. All these problems can be draining to the professional who en-counters them. As one clinician puts it, "no one is immune from the outrage, righteousness, morbid curiosity, sexual arousal, resentment, hostility, despair, helplessness, omnipotent rescue fantasies and the countless other surges of con-flicted feelings that the incest family elicits in the would-be helper."[61] Like those who counsel families involved in other types of abuse, the clinician work-ing with sexual abuse needs special support. We will return to this issue (helping the helper) when we deal with programmatic issues in our concluding chapter.

Notes

1. National Center on Child Abuse and Neglect, *Child Sexual Abuse: Incest, Assault, and Sexual Exploitation* (Washington, D.C.: Department of Health, Education and Welfare, Publication no. 79-30166, 1978), p. 2.

2. D. Finkelhor, *Sexually Victimized Children* (New York: Free Press, 1979).

3. S.K. Weinberg, *Incest Behavior* (New York: Citadel Press, 1955).

4. S. Chaneles, "Child Victims of Sex Offenders," *Federal Probation* (1967): 31-52.

5. E. Sarafino, "An Estimate of Nationwide Incidence of Sexual Of-fenses against Children," *Child Welfare* 58 (1979): 127-134.

6. H. Giaretto, "The Treatment of Father-Daughter Incest: A Psycho-social Approach," *Children Today* (1976): 2-5, 34, 35.

7. Finkelhor, *Sexually Victimized Children*.

8. C. Bach, and S. Anderson, "Adolescent Sexual Abuse and Assault" (Paper presented at the Second International Congress on Adolescent Medi-cine, May 6-10, 1979, Washington, D.C.).

9. U. Bronfenbrenner, *The Ecology of Human Development* (Cambridge, Mass.: Harvard University Press, 1979).

10. National Center on Child Abuse and Neglect, *Child Sexual Abuse*.

11. J. Benward, and J. Densen-Gerber, "Incest as a Causative Factor in Antisocial Behavior: An Exploratory Study," *Contemporary Drug Problems* 4 (1975): 32-35.

12. V. DeFrancis, *Protecting the Child Victim of Sex Crimes Committed by Adults* (Denver, Colo.: American Humane Association, 1969).

13. J.J. Peters, "The Psychological Effects of Childhood Rape," *World Journal of Psychosynthesis* 5 (1974): 11-14.

14. I.I. Nakashima, and G.E. Zokus, "Incest: Review and Clinical Experience," *Pediatrics* 60 (1977): 696-701.

15. J.J. Peters, "Children Who Are Victims of Sexual Assault and the Psychology of Offenders," *American Journal of Orthopsychiatry* 30 (1976): 398-421.

16. K.C. Meiselman, *Incest: A Psychological Study of Causes and Effects with Treatment Recommendations* (San Francisco: Jossey-Bass, 1978).

17. R. Friedman, "Adolescents as People: No Kidding Around" (Paper presented at a conference on A Community Response to the Adolescent in Conflict, Jacksonville, Florida, February 1978).

18. P.H. Gebhard, et al., *Sex Offenders: An Analysis of Types* (New York: Harper and Row, 1965).

19. Weinberg, *Incest Behavior.*

20. Meiselman, *Incest.*

21. I. Kaufman, A.L. Puck, and C.K. Tagiuri, "The Family Constellation and Overt Incestuous Relations between Father and Daughter," *American Journal of Orthopsychiatry* 24 (1954): 266-277.

22. B. Courmier, M. Kennedy, and J. Saugovicz, "Psychodynamics of Father-Daughter Incest," *Canadian Psychiatric Association Journal* 7 (1962): 203-217.

23. DeFrancis, *Protecting the Child Victim.*

24. L. Bender, and A. Blau, "The Reactions of Children to Sexual Relations with Adults," *American Journal of Orthopsychiatry* 7 (1937): 500-518.

25. Meiselman, *Incest.*

26. A.M. Gligor, "Incest and Sexual Delinquency: A Comparative Analysis of Two Forms of Sexual Behavior in Minor Females" (Ph.D. diss., Case Western Reserve University, 1966).

27. H. Martin, *The Abused Child: A Multidisciplinary Approach to Developmental Issue at Treatment* (Cambridge, Mass.: Ballinger, 1976).

28. S. Forward, and C. Buck, *Betrayal of Innocence* (Los Angeles, Calif.: J.P. Tarcher, Inc., 1978).

29. G. Elder, and R. Rockwell, "The Life Course and Human Development: An Ecological Perspective" (Boys Town, Neb.: Center for the Study of Youth Development, 1977).

30. Gligor, "Incest and Sexual Delinquency."

31. Ibid.

32. Bach and Anderson, "Adolescent Sexual Abuse."

33. National Center on Child Abuse and Neglect, *Child Sexual Abuse.*

34. M. Tsai, and N. Wegner, "Therapy Groups for Women Sexually Molested as Children," *Archives of Sexual Behavior* 7 (1978): 417-427.

35. Meiselman, *Incest.*

36. Cormier, Kennedy, and Sangowicz, "Psychodynamics of Father-Daughter Incest."

37. Meiselman, *Incest.*

38. J. Garbarino, "An Ecological Perspective on Child Maltreatment," in *The Social Context of Child Abuse and Neglect*, Pelton (New York: Human Sciences Press, 1980); Martin, *The Abused Child.*

39. B.M. Jones, and L.L. Jenstrom, "Introduction," *Sexual Abuse of Children: Selected Readings* (Washington, D.C.: National Center on Child Abuse and Neglect (DHEW), 1980).

40. Bach and Anderson, "Adolescent Sexual Abuse."

41. National Center on Child Abuse and Neglect, *Child Sexual Abuse.*

42. Ibid.

43. Kaufman, Puck, and Tagiuri, "The Family Constellation."

44. J. Bigras, C. Bouchand, N. Coleman-Porter, and Y. Passe. "On Disappointment and the Consequences of Incest in the Adolescent Girl," *Canadian Psychiatric Journal* 11 (1966): 189-204.

45. H. Maisch, *Incest*, trans. C. Bearne (New York: Stein and Day, 1972).

46. R. Summit, "Sexual Child Abuse: The Psychotherapist and the Team Concept," *Dealing with Sexual Child Abuse*, vol. 2 (Chicago: National Committee for the Prevention of Child Abuse, 1978).

47. Friedman, "Adolescents as People."

48. R. Summit, and J. Kryso, "Sexual Abuse of Children: A Clinical Spectrum," *American Journal of Orthopsychiatry* 48 (1978): 237-251.

49. Meiselman, *Incest.*

50. T. Millon, *Modern Psychopathology* (Philadelphia: Saunders, 1972).

51. Summit, "Sexual Child Abuse."

52. H. Giaretto, "Humanistic Treatment of Father-Daughter Incest," in *Child Abuse and Neglect: The Family and the Community* ed. R. Helfer and C.H. Kempe (Cambridge, Mass.: Ballinger, 1976).

53. Giaretto, "Humanistic Treatment."

54. Summit, "Sexual Child Abuse."

55. Bach and Anderson, "Adolescent Sexual Abuse."

56. Tsai and Wegner, "Therapy Groups for Women."

57. Ibid.

58. L. Lieber, and J. Baker, "Parents Anonymous and Self-Help Treatment for Child Abusing Parents: A Review and an Evaluation," *Child Abuse and Neglect* 1 (1977): 133-148.

59. J. Garbarino, and N. Jacobson, "Youth Helping Youth as a Resource in Meeting the Problem of Adolescent Maltreatment," *Child Welfare* 57 (1978): 505-512.

60. A. Gartner, and F. Reissman, *Self-help in the Human Services* (San Francisco: Jossey-Bass, 1977).

61. Summit, "Sexual Child Abuse."

12 Youth in Trouble Are Youth Who Have Been Hurt

They wouldn't have beat me if I didn't deserve it. They just wouldn't have done it.

Children come into this world without any frame of reference. They have no inherent scale upon which to judge their worth; they must ascertain their value from the messages they receive. Parents largely determine the ratings that children give themselves, at least until they enter school and begin to reevaluate themselves based upon the feedback they receive there. It is no wonder that youth whose parents show signs of emotional pathology have trouble making value judgments, especially when it comes to assessing their own personal worth.[1] Considering the impact that parents have upon the lives of their children, it is also not surprising that abuse and neglect can have devastating consequences that are quick to show. In this chapter, we outline the effects of adolescent abuse. When a vulnerable youth suffers maltreatment, the result can be physical damage, low self-esteem, anxiety, lack of empathy, poor social relationships, drug- or alcohol-abuse, suicide, delinquency, or homicide.

Different Effects

We identified two groups of mistreated teenagers: those for whom abuse began in adolescence and those who are former child-abuse victims. As we discuss the effects of maltreatment, it is logical to assume that abuse may affect these two groups differently. Adolescent abuse has been professionally acknowledged only very recently, and as yet has received little systematic study. Admittedly, we know very little about the mistreatment of youth in general and even less about the differences between our two newly identified groups of victims. We have, for example, no psychological profile of the parent who abuses a teenager. Except for what we can infer from general studies of troubled youth, we do not really know anything about the educational or career success of former victims, or even their marital or social adjustment. What is more, we know almost nothing about how different individuals react to these patterns of abuse. Still from the fragmentary evidence available, it seems that both the abuse itself and the environmental context in which it occurs are quite different for people in the two groups.

Based on the preliminary study cited previously, we believe the two groups of victims differ in their social class and family stability.[2] We assume that the psychological effects of long-term abuse are not the same as those of relatively short-term abuse. We assume that years of abuse during early childhood do more damage than does maltreatment that begins in adolescence. (One possible exception may be the case of sexual abuse, which does not appear to harm children as much as it does adolescents, according to the expert testimony reviewed in chapter 11.) At least the short-term group has a chance to put some psychological "money in the bank." One small sign that adolescents who have no history of abuse are psychologically stronger than those who have such a history is the fact that the former report themselves as victims nearly twice as often as the latter (22 percent versus 13 percent in our study). We suppose that teenagers who were not abused as children are not accustomed to mistreatment and they do not expect it. All the other pertinent studies support this hypothesis.[3] Reporting oneself as a victim of parental abuse requires recognition that such treatment is intolerable and undeserved. It also requires personal initiative and the ability to communicate. Long-term abuse tends to undermine such capabilities, so we would interpret the lower rate of self-reporting among long-term victims as a sign of psychological damage.

Clinicians tell us that abused teenagers who have a childhood history of abuse tend to be more crippled emotionally than those who do not. These adolescents also tend to have extremely strong dependency needs. Many youths who were abused from infancy or early childhood and were subsequently removed from the home never get a chance to deal with the abuse they suffered and, in fact, may idealize their parents and be eager to return home.[4] This has serious implications for the foster-care system.

We are addressing the issue of differential effects partly because we will be drawing links between maltreatment and delinquency. We believe youth from the two groups will have very different motivations for becoming delinquent. A middle-class teenager who has recently been sexually abused is likely to commit different sorts of offenses than her poverty-stricken counterpart who has always been beaten, and who feels forced to acquire her spending money by stealing it. We cannot ignore the effects of the impoverished environment from which long-term abuse victims are likely to come. Elmer found it impossible to do so in her data.[5] It is as if some environments are themselves abusive.[6] In a racially defined ghetto, for example, much delinquent or disturbing behavior—things like hustling, gang membership, and audacity in sexual exploits—may serve as alternative modes of attaining competence because legitimate ones are closed off.[7] Whether or not the problems that an abused adolescent suffers show up as delinquency probably has as much to do with the demands and expectations of his or her social situation as it does with any predisposition of personality. We do not know enough about the differential effects of the two types of abuse upon delinquency apart from the settings in which they occur.

This should come as no surprise when decades of research on delinquency in general have failed to resolve many basic issues of causation and consequence.

Social class also affects the destiny of an abused adolescent. Status offenses are acts legal for adults but disallowed for minors. Poor parents are more likely to file status offense petitions against their teenagers than are those who can afford to send a child to boarding school or some other private out-of-home placement. In a family setting, parents sometimes petition the state to assume responsibility for a child they cannot control. The poor have less access to psychiatric services and are therefore less able to get professional help for their problems. There are many other ways that poverty places a family in a double bind by both causing problems and preventing their successful resolution. Social-service and criminal-justice systems may react less favorably to victims from these families than to more affluent youths. This differential treatment may be partly a function of class bias as well as a response to more severely impaired psychological health among long-term victims.

The differences between the two types of adolescent-abuse cases require a differentiated response in some ways, and we will discuss some of these in later chapters. On the other hand, the developmental damage experienced by the victims is probably more similar than not. The principal difference is one of degree: low-social class and long duration of mistreatment exacerbate the problems. That said, we will deal with abused adolescents as a single group for the rest of the chapter because for all their differences, the two groups face the same developmental tasks, societal rules, and parental abuse. What is more, we simply do not have the knowledge base necessary to differentiate between the types of damage youth in these two groups may experience.

Maltreatment Deprives Youth of Basic Human Needs

There are a few basic essentials that human beings need in order to grow into competent adults. They need to feel powerful, that they can affect the world around them. They need identity, to know who they are and with whom they belong. They need acceptance from their parents, an unconditional regard that allows them to experiment and make mistakes. They need consistency in order to believe that the world is predictable. They need to feel worthwhile. They need affection.

Parents who supply these essentials tend to have competent children. As we are using the term, competence includes effective communication, ability to adapt socially, patience, high self-esteem, social responsibility, and empathy.[8] An authoritative style of child rearing (in contrast to both a permissive and an authoritarian style) tends to produce secure, happy people.[9] Authoritative parents combine support with limits, grant reasonable autonomy, and explain the rationale behind their decisions. Parents who encourage their children, who pay attention to the child's contribution in the decision-making process, who are concerned with the child's own accomplishments tend to have competent children.[10] In fact, the amount of support as opposed to severe punishment that parents give their children is directly related to the social and intellectual competence of those children.[11]

In adolescence, the essential ingredients of effective parenthood include a gradual meting out of responsibility and privilege to the child, a handing over of more power within the family. One major determinant of teenagers' mental health is whether or not they feel respected and liked by their parents.[12] Those who believe their parents think positively of them are more likely to hold prosocial value systems and to care about their own social images. Older teenagers whose parents grant them a lot of freedom tend to feel close to their parents, enjoy activities with them, ask them for advice, want to be like their parents, and fight with their parents infrequently.[13] Adolescents who are autonomous, who make their decisions independently of parents and peers, tend to come from homes with high levels of support and moderate levels of control.[14] Youth who enjoy positive relationships with their parents and other adults are motivated to avoid antisocial and self-destructive acts because they recognize the value of their social investments. It makes sense that adult disapproval would be ineffective in discouraging such acts among people who have never experienced the approval of their parents. In abusive homes the process of socialization tends to work to the child's detriment.

Processes of Damage

Perhaps the most amazing characteristic of the human being is its flexibility and adaptability. Children can learn to live with a wide range of circumstances. The price that children pay for this adaptability is often developmental damage if they must adapt to unhealthy circumstances. Those who live in abusive and neglectful environments learn to accommodate to the hurtful things they experience. There are several normal processes through which they are damaged. These processes have been described and observed by many clinicians, theoreticians, and researchers. They include processes that may be described in the specialized language of the psychodynamic, cognitive-developmentalist, and behaviorist approaches to behavior and development.

We believe there are two key processes of damage relevant to understanding the consequences of abuse and neglect. The first involves children or youth imitating and identifying with their parents. Through imitation, victims learn to be socially deficient. The second involves children or youth rationalizing family dynamics and the hurtful consequences of those dynamics. Through this process, they learn a negative self-concept.

There are many technical terms of these processes, most of which are related to particular theories of personality and psychological development. In the interest of providing the most practically useful discussion we have chosen to focus on the *behaviors* involved, linking those behaviors to some of the classical psychodynamic concepts.

One way that damage occurs is through identification and imitation. By and large, children learn to become the people they "belong" to. Children learn to be like their parents (in greater or lesser degree) because they are emotionally tied to and spend their formative years with their parents. This process involves both the accumulation of specific behaviors, habits, and characteristics (modeling) and the development of a more general identity (identification). Modeling, or setting an example, is an efficient method of teaching since it includes much more than words. A person who models a behavior is giving information through body language and voice inflection. Through modeling, children grow to become like the people who matter to them and to whom they are important. Thus these processes (modeling, imitation, and identification) are the natural avenues for social and personal development. Without them, the process of becoming human would be almost impossible, because adults could never specifically teach children every detail of personhood. By identifying with their parents' prohibitions in order to avoid punishment, children develop consciences and become effectively socialized.[15] However, the processes of identification and imitation also mean that children will absorb whatever reality is defined for them, even if it is a warped and violent one.

One expert describes the process of identification this way. The child says, in effect: "If I make my image of you part of my image of me, I can control you. Then you cannot hurt me as much" (fear of aggression), or "walk away and leave me" (fear of loss of love).[16] Ironically, the higher the level of violence or the more intense the threat of loss of love, the stronger the child's motivation to emulate the parent may become. This seems to say that abusive homes can be powerful producers of damaged human beings because they generate strong identification with people who have many negative lessons to teach. Thus children are motivated strongly to imitate their parents' social incompetence. Behavioral evidence suggests they do.[17]

If children identify with parents who are aggressors, they will incorporate those parents' hostility. Thus by attempting to gain the favor of a potential enemy, the victim may become his or her own enemy. In cognitive-developmental terms, the child's concept of self is defined in large part by the day-to-day experience of reality in the family. In an effort to gain some measure of self-protection and mastery over his environment, the child may identify strongly with the aggressor and develop a deeply set pattern of discharging aggression against the outside world in order to manage internal insecurities.[18]

Cognitive Consistency

Human behavior is largely a product of emotion screened through intellect. In encounters with other humans, intellect is often expressed as social skill. A competent person possesses both a range of social skills and a positive emotional life to motivate and regulate the effective use of those skills. Just as abuse seems to undermine the necessary social skills for effective and gratifying interpersonal relationships, so it also seems to produce a negative emotional life.

Children learn to value themselves (to develop self-esteem) by being valued. Rejection (through mistreatment) directly tells a child he or she is not worth much. Through the process of striving for cognitive consistency, a person always seeks to reconcile reality with feelings. Because of this process, there is always the possibility that a child will justify parental abuse by downgrading himself or herself. As one young victim put it: "There must have been *some* reason they beat me. Otherwise, why would they have done it?"

In addition to this downgrading of self, there is likely to be anger, rage, frustration, hatred, fear, and pain. It is impossible to fully reconcile oneself to a horrible existence. Some victims avoid their situations by compartmentalizing their emotions or by letting go of reality through drugs, alcohol, or insanity. Others simply end up with strong negative emotions that work against them. It is little wonder that the emotional life of an abuse victim is in jeopardy; "walking on thin ice" is the way one of the victims we interviewed put it.

The process begins early. Abusive parents help their young children less and show less approval than other parents. The children reciprocate by showing much less affection to their parents and expressing less pleasure in life generally than nonabused children.[19] When a child repeatedly encounters extreme punishment or the withholding of affection by a parent, the natural reaction is likely to be one of open hostility or withdrawal.[20] As we shall see in the following chapter, we need to deal with the complex emotional issues facing abuse victims if we are to resolve the threats to successful life-course development.

In light of the processes involved, it is difficult to imagine a child surviving abuse unscathed. Fortunately it does happen, and for all we know it could even be the rule rather than the exception, simply because the human psyche is so adaptable. The fact that children survived life in World War II concentration camps relatively intact psychologically is testimony to this phenomenon.[21] We really do not know how many victims of maltreatment survive psychologically and socially.[22] We know some do. There is a small group of extremely competent children who accommodate to their parents faults in a healthy way and who may even thrive. They are called "invulnerables," and they usually have some special personal and social resources to call upon: They are well-armed and well-armored against adverse parental influences.[23] But many mistreated people are not so fortunate. They are negatively affected by the mistreatment;

many grow up with some substantial emotional problems. We will discuss a few of the more common problems that abuse-victims carry, then examine the actions those problems precipitate, actions that often mean harm for others.

Physical Damage

> It didn't matter if I did right or wrong. Sometimes she would beat me for nothing, and then say it was for "in case you did anything." My mom used to hit me really hard—not just a swat—and for nothing. She even cut me a couple of times with a knife.

Although physical injury is not the overriding problem for abused adolescents that it is for infants, it cannot be ignored. Size can actually work against teenagers in this regard. Because they are harder to physically subdue than children, they are more often assaulted with weapons. One study found that only preschool males were more in jeopardy than teenage girls to die from abuse.[24] Nonetheless, adolescents are better able to defend themselves when compared with young children and most experience only minor injuries. While there is always danger of permanent damage, especially to the central nervous system, the most common danger of physical abuse remains its psychological consequences. This is evident in the informal reports we have received from victims.

Low Self-Esteem

> My mom, see, she has hit me with furniture and my dad has beaten me with his belt, hit me with his fist and everything else. . . . I took it for five years. I don't blame them for doing it because I deserved every bit of it.

Self-esteem is the value we place upon ourselves, the way we rate ourselves. It is one of the crucial determinants of our response to life.[25] People with high self-esteem feel the world is a better place because they are in it. Researcher Stanley Coopersmith studied self-esteem and formulated internal monologues of people with high and low self-esteem as a way to describe the concept. In his view, someone with high self-esteem might think, for example, "I consider myself a valuable and important person and am at least as good as other people of my age and training. I am regarded as someone worthy of respect and consideration by people who are important to me. I can control my actions toward the outside world and have a fairly good understanding of the kind of person I am."[26] Parents who instill a high level of esteem in their children give them lots of attention and praise while maintaining high standards for the children's behavior. Children with high self-esteem are better equipped to take on challenges, can better express their creativity, and are more competent than those with lower self-esteem.[27]

In contrast, Coopersmith writes that an internal monologue by someone with a low self-esteem would sound something like this: "I don't think I'm a very important or likeable person, and I don't see much reason for anyone else to like me. I don't expect much from myself, now or in the future. I don't have much control over what happens to me, and I expect that things will get worse rather than better."[28] A person with low self-esteem is in an impossible situation when faced with adversity, apt to think, "After all, how could such a worthless person as myself solve my problems?" People with low self-esteem are more likely to manifest deviant behavior patterns, including destructive tendencies toward inanimate objects, anxiousness, and psychosomatic symptoms. Between these two extremes fall people with moderate levels of self-esteem, who were raised in families that provided moderate levels of support.

For victims of maltreatment, the task of convincing themselves they are actually worthwhile individuals after having been told and shown for so long that they are not is probably the most common problem. It is natural to believe the opinions of parents and other significant people, so when such adults express a low opinion of one through their words or actions, it is difficult not to believe them. Some have even suggested that one's evolving conception of the world and one's place in it is the essence of development.[29] All the evidence that abuse presents a victim is negative; it practically preempts a positive conclusion.

According to Coopersmith, constant parental criticism "not only reduces the pleasures of the present, but it also serves to eliminate realistic hopes for the future. The corrosive drizzle of negative appraisal presumably removes the joy of today and the anticipation of tomorrow."[30] He feels the overall climate seems to be a more important determinant than outstanding events: "It is possible that by their repetitive occurrence, less severe or dramatic occurrences might well have a more depressing effect than might more isolated, dramatic episodes."[31] This supports our belief that it is the abusive climate that does the most damage.

Domination, rejection, and severe punishment—all different expressions of what we label abuse—result in lowered self-esteem. Under such conditions, adolescents have fewer experiences of love and success, and tend to be generally submissive and withdrawn, though occasionally they veer to the opposite extreme of aggression and domination. They simply have not been provided a basis for believing themselves to be secure. They have no practice in being competent. The world does not *feel* safe. Children and youth reared under such psychologically-crippling circumstances have little hope of seeing the world realistically or being effective in their everyday functioning, much less of realizing their full potential.

Anxiety

A problem closely related to low self-esteem is anxiety. Because abuse victims tend to think of themselves as not being worthwhile, they may be overly dependent upon the opinions of others. They are therefore very anxious about the cues they send out. This high level of anxiety also causes real problems to become even larger than they might otherwise be.

Anxiety is a significant reason for school failure and lack of achievement. People learn best when their minds are clear, when they feel good about themselves. Low-achieving students are more self-critical than high-achievers. This self-criticism is self-protective because it reduces anxiety. It prefaces every action with a negative appraisal and thus eliminates the hearer's option to devalue the act. Low school achievement, anxiety, and self-devaluation are interrelated, and each is in turn related to a predominance of negative reinforcement from parents, low-parental interest and acceptance, and high-parental punitiveness.[32] Having suffered severe punishment or abuse in the past seems a strong incentive to feel anxious about one's present actions, especially if that parental response is unpredictable.[33]

Anxiety about aggression can even drive a person to violence. People with a high degree of anxiety over aggression will respond more aggressively than those with low-aggression anxiety. All in all, maltreatment increases most youngsters' uncertainty about themselves and their place in the world. Neither they nor that world is reliable. This anxiety is often compounded by a genuine inability to read people and social situations accurately, by a lack of empathy.

Lack of Empathy

> That old man thought he was tough or something. Wouldn't give me his wallet, so I had to cut him up. He shouldn't be around when I need money if he doesn't want to give it to me.

Empathy is taking the role of the other, feeling what another person is feeling. Empathy plays a major role in making human society more humane. Children as young as 6 have chosen to give an adult pleasure rather than receive candy themselves in laboratory tests. They have shut off a painful noise that another child is experiencing after hearing it themselves.[34] Empathy acts as a strong motivator for social responsibility. Young children behave more morally when the consequences of their behavior are explained in terms of the effect upon others than when they are punished or simply told the behavior is wrong.[35] An empathetic person will work to help another person, even when the receiver cannot know or find out who is giving help.[36]

Empathy is so central to mental health and maturity that it is considered by some to be the key to socialization, which one researcher defines as: "largely the ability to put oneself in the position of others while keeping one's own position in mind," adding, "If understanding others is the essence of social interaction, to do so successfully means that one is able to differentiate between self and others. . . . Increasing differentiation is the process by which the mind develops what is loosely called maturity."[37]

Empathy has some other positive effects. A child who has a lot of it will be much less aggressive than one who has little.[38] Empathy is even a better predictor of school success than IQ. Empathy can provide the basis for altruism, sympathy, and help. It is the very foundation of morality.[39]

Not surprisingly, youth who are empathetic see their parents as being more supportive. Conversely, those with little empathy see their parents as severe.[40] One of the most disturbing effects of abuse is that those who have suffered it tend either to lose their ability to empathize or not to develop it in the first place. They reenact the lack of empathy their parents showed them while growing up. Mistreated teenagers tend to respond to children in a manner reminiscent of the way their own parents responded to them, with an inability to be empathetically aware of a child's needs.[41] Parents who lack empathy are liable to become abusive when exposed to social and economic stress.[42] This suggests the need to retrain mistreated youth to help them avoid a chronic pattern of unsuccessful social relationships.

Poor Social Relationships

> It's hard for me to give up part of myself to somebody and have them take it because I'm afraid they're going to take it and go "crunch." You know, wring it and throw it back at me.

Teenagers who have been mistreated are often sadly ill-equipped for meaningful relationships with other people. Low self-esteem is a major root of this difficulty with social interaction. People with low self-esteem are grateful that anyone speaks to them, no matter what is said or how it is said. By devaluating their own worth, they place themselves beneath the value they assign to others. They feel responsible for everything that goes wrong. They feel they owe everyone gratitude and would not think of asking anything for themselves; after all, who are they to ask?[43] Victims of mistreatment are thus naturally set up to become lifelong victims.

Feeling worthless can have another effect: aggression. Persons with low self-esteem may attempt to convince others that they count for something by making others obey their wishes or fear them. We know that if teenagers become aggressive, they fare less well with everyone, including their peers.[44]

Research found that rejected children do not perform well socially.[45] They face the future with less confidence and are more confused, discouraged, and insecure than children reared with parental acceptance.[46] And it is not just in early life that rejection hurts. Parental rejection in adolescence following the establishment of earlier attachments tends to produce increased dependency upon peers and other adults, and antisocial behavior as well.[47] It is only natural for people to seek support wherever they can find it. When it is not forthcoming from their parents, youth look elsewhere. This desperate need to fill a void, combined with the insecurity that results from being made to feel unworthy, causes abuse victims to be extremely vulnerable to the people around them. Take, for example, these words from a perceptive runaway: "It's terrible. Someone just has to reach out and I'm waiting for any person who walks by and will hold my hand and be my friend. They can hurt me just as much as anyone else."

The most slavish peer conformity happens in adolescents whose parents are either extremely permissive or authoritarian.[48] Extending the scale even further to include neglect (on the permissive side) and abuse (on the authoritarian side) can only have even stronger effects. This is one reason why victims of abuse in the home seem to be so vulnerable to abuse from strangers.

As shown in chapter 2, abusive families tend to be socially isolated in the sense of being cut off from prosocial support systems. We know that most neglectful parents were themselves isolated as teenagers.[49] As parents, they tend to isolate their children by discouraging friendships. Children reared in abusive homes tend to follow a self-perpetuating course of social behavior that leads to social isolation.[50] They probably have not learned how to deal successfully with other people. Since they fear dependence, they mistrust signs of love and esteem and thwart friendly relations by quick display of aggression.[51] One long-term victim described it like this:

> You get too used to being beat up. Where if you're not beat up, you don't know what the hell to do. And when I would find somebody that would not hurt me, I'd do something very fast in order to get something negative to come out of them. And then I could walk away and say "I told you so, you don't care about me." You can't trust everybody. That's a fact. It's not just a paranoid statement, it's a fact.

Coming full circle, social isolation can even make young teenagers more vulnerable to abuse. For one thing, they will spend more time at home alone. With a smaller world, they may be enmeshed in the pathological dynamics of their families. Finally, they will have no place to turn for advice on alternative ways to survive.[52] If, as a result of inadequate social skills, youth find themselves cut off from social contact and support, their isolation itself is a self-perpetuating problem. They are thus deprived of opportunities to learn the skills they would normally learn from regular social contact.

The problems that mistreated youth sustain tend to reflect the type of mistreatment they suffered. A neglected teenager will not necessarily have the same problems as one who is sexually abused. Neglected children tend to grow up streetwise, while girls who are sexually abused tend to experience problems relating to men, for example. Overcontrol is another example. Children need space to grow up. Parents who are very restrictive and who foster dependence upon adults are likely to retard the process of identity formation in their children.[53] We should therefore expect immaturity from those who have never been allowed to mature. Children from overcontrolling, authoritarian homes have been found to fight and quarrel more, to be more inconsiderate and insensitive, and less popular. Clinical studies report that those who were also punished severely show little affection, are hesitant to express themselves verbally,[54] and are extremely submissive.[55] Submissiveness around an overpowering adult is nothing more than a survival technique, a natural outcome of domination. One researcher states, "The authoritarian parent who uses his age status as a naked assertion of power over his children gets dependence and passive resistance; maybe, if he is lucky, revolt."[56] Another maintains, "the undercontrolled individual may be responsible for numerous acts that are antisocial, but the chronically overcontrolled person is much more dangerous in the long run."[57] Many people who are extremely assaultive, that is, who have committed homicides, assault and battery, and related offenses, were chronically overcontrolled as children. These offenders appear to be profoundly repressed individuals who, though outwardly controlled, are inwardly alienated and potentially capable of extremely violent, antisocial acts.[58] More than one infamous murderer has been described by his neighbors as, "Quiet. Kept to himself, mainly. Never heard a peep out of him. He was a good tenant."

The psychological problems that rejected children suffer are too numerous to explore in detail here.[59] Abuse and neglect are both evidence of rejection; even overcontrol is rejection because it expresses disapproval of the youth's independence. Briefly, clinicians have found rejected children to be sadistic, nervous, shy, stubborn, noncomplaint;[60] restless, apathetic, indifferent, impulsive, antagonistic, compulsively dependent, detached, emotionally immature;[61] less stable, and more aggressive than accepted children.[62] Rejection is a malignant force in human development.[63] As one physician puts it: "The character strivings to overcome [the victims'] sense of helplessness produce distortions in attitudes, values, and goals that engender pathological relationships with the world and with people.[64]

Escaping the Pain

Most people try to avoid pain. Those who find the whole world most excruciatingly painful tend to try hardest to escape it, either permanently through suicide or temporarily through drugs or alcohol. Although a recent study does not report more overall alcohol use among runaway and abused youth, it does report more socially disastrous problem drinking.[65] The demonstrative presence of love from both parents helps to protect teenagers from becoming involved in the abuse of drugs. Conversely, its absence is a reliable predictor of drug and alcohol abuse. Researchers have reported a connection between the misuse of drugs and impaired family relationships, particularly in father-daughter and mother-and-son dyads.[66]

The more desperate try to kill themselves. Of course, most of what we know about suicide victims comes from research done with the unsuccessful ones: "I took some pills and tried to kill myself. I had been through it so many times, I just didn't want to live. It felt that bad, the way my mom treated me."

Most children who commit suicide do so because of neglect, abuse, or bereavement.[67] Lack of family harmony, marital conflicts, isolation in the parent-child relationship, and sibling hostility have driven some youngsters to regard suicide as the only escape from acute emotional pain.[68] Adolescent suicide is often preceded by a sequence of events including a long-standing history of problems from childhood into adolescence, that mount into a chain reaction that dissolves any meaningful social relationships.[69] Many (but of course not all) suicidal adolescents come from families in which a destructive cycle of anger is established between parents and children.[70] Parental alcoholism is common among those who attempt suicide, as are extremes or inconsistency of parental control and expectations, hostility, depression, parental rejection, and extreme parental reactions to the child's behavior. One study found clear differences between teenagers who had attempted suicide and those who had not, even though both groups had experienced similar stress, including parental divorce, stepparents, and economic deprivation. Hostility, indifference, and overt rejection by the parent was the rule for the suicidal subjects, and the exception for the controls.[71]

Attempted suicide is often intended as a plea for help rather than as an act of self-destruction. Many abused youth no doubt use self-destructive behavior to manipulate other people, hoping that those people will gratify their wishes.[72] It may be a way to rectify a parent-child role reversal within the family. The suicide attempt reclaims the child's right to induce the parent to meet his or her dependent needs. This drastic step certainly removes the youth from the situation, possibly even permanently through placement outside the home.[73]

One major difference between those who attempt suicide and other troubled youth is that while neither group communicates expecially well with parents, the nonsuicides at least have maintained contacts with peers and other adults.[74] Because of their poor social skills, victims of maltreatment are set up for social isolation.[75] Many youth who try to kill themselves do not have even one person they feel they can turn to in times of trouble.[76]

Finally, many adolescents who choose to die or to try to die feel utterly helpless and hopeless. Very few adolescent suicide survivors say they have perceived a significant change in their parents' attitudes.[77] The decision to attempt suicide is often the result of a rational decision-making process,[78] attempted only after alternate solutions to the problem have failed.[79] This is a damning indictment of the community's willingness and ability to help these youth.

Troubling Behavior

Life with the psychological problems we have just chronicled is not easy. People who have them tend to have a hard time fitting into normal society. Adolescents who are having such problems tend to have trouble coping with the constraints of any environment. We often label such youngsters as troubled, at risk, alien-ated, antisocial, or wayward. Their role incompetence expresses itself in all sorts of disturbing behavior: truancy, poor school performance, substance abuse, and sexual promiscuity.[80] Besides endangering healthy adolescent development, these behaviors can cause problems that imperil the youth's future. Truancy and poor school performance can lead to low-occupational mobility. Drug and alcohol abuse can become addictive. Sexual promiscuity can produce unwanted pregnancy and venereal disease. All can lead to contact with the juvenile-justice system. Each of these behaviors can disrupt an adolescent's life, and collectively they may predict an antisocial personality in adulthood. Yahares found that theft, incorrigibility, running away, associating with other delinquent children, staying out past the hour allowed, discipline problems in school, school retarda-tion, fighting, recklessness, slovenliness, enuresis, lying for no apparent gain, failure to show love, and the inability or unwillingness to show guilt over dis-turbing behavior were all predictors of antisocial personalities.[81] He found that the *number* of symptoms evidenced was a better predictor than any one particu-lar symptom.

The Link between Abuse and Delinquency

Even if all abuse were prevented, we could not and would not predict an end to juvenile delinquency. There are numerous causes of delinquency, many of which are situational, that tend to override personal history. However, abuse and neglect are closely related to delinquency for three reasons: (1) abuse victims tend to display traits characteristic of predelinquency, (2) both abuse and delinquency spring from common environments, and (3) abuse and aggression go hand in hand.

It is hard to imagine an experience that would weaken a personality more than parental abuse and neglect. And since the nature of a parent-child relationship is a good predictor of future delinquency, maltreatment makes teenagers prone to become delinquent. If violently assaulted, they may carry the heavy weight of barely suppressed rage. If sexually or emotionally abused, they may be looking for some way to compensate or gain revenge for their feelings of self-contempt and resentment. Children who believe their parents are unaware of their whereabouts are more likely to have committed delinquent acts.[82] Neglected adolescents fall into this category, of course. In general, if a child is alienated from a parent, he will be less likely to have a feeling for moral rules or develop an adequate conscience.[83] One important consideration in predicting delinquency is whether the parent is psychologically present when the temptation to commit a crime appears, as well as whether or not the parent supports prosocial values. Whenever the bond between parent and child is weakened, the probability of delinquent behavior increases.[84] Parent-child relationships characterized by abuse and neglect are less likely to be strong enough to serve as effective deterrents to delinquency. If anything, these destructive relationships probably are incentives to misbehave, particularly if the parent models antisocial behavior.

Parents whose children become aggressive or delinquent tend to treat their children in similar ways. The fathers of aggressive boys are typically hostile to and rejecting of their sons, express little warmth for them, and spend little time interacting with them during the boy's childhood.[85] Parents of delinquent boys have also been shown to be neglectful and lax or punitive, and erratic in discipline. The fathers of delinquents were found to be cruel, neglectful, and often absent, and the mothers were judged cruel, neglectful, and passively helpless.[86] Life with these parents is a far cry from life with the supportive style of child rearing that encourages competence. It is little wonder nondelinquent sons are able to be more legitimately assertive at home than their delinquent counterparts.[87] They have been taught to express their concerns openly, and have good reason to believe their wishes will be met with a positive response. Even in infancy, parental responsiveness to the baby predicts early moral behavior.[88]

Mistreatment and delinquent behavior are part of common family environment. In one study, nearly half of the families reported for child abuse and neglect had at least one child who was later taken to the court as ungovernable or delinquent.[89] Moreover, the way that families of delinquents communicate tends to be different from the communication of families without delinquent children. The members of deviant families deal with each other much more defensively and less supportively than other families.[90] In this, their behavior resembles that found in studies of abusive and neglectful families.[91] These abusive families have been found to be dysfunctional, multiproblem families that do not fit into the normal lives of their communities (see chapter 9 for description of long-term abusing families). Children from these families who have been abused or neglected are five times as likely to be delinquent or un-governable as those from the general population.[92]

Clinicians report that male victims of mistreatment are more likely to become aggressive while females tend to become self-destructive. This sex-typed pattern is consistent with that found in deviant behavior in general. There are many physical and cultural reasons for this differential response to abuse. Psychodynamically oriented clinicians and theorists would explain this phe-nomenon through males' external orientation and females' internal orientation. Others would say that males are both programmed hormonally and permitted socially to be aggressive.[93] Behaviorists would note that because boys tradi-tionally have received less punishment for aggression than girls, they do not learn to inhibit their aggressive responses as well as girls. They would argue that it is no wonder, in view of our cultural intolerance for female aggression, that little girls develop more indirect means of self-expression.[94]

As a result, boys tend to express their anger over being abused in ways that hurt others while girls tend to turn the anger inward on themselves. Nearly 60 percent of all adolescent girls who encounter the juvenile-justice system in this country do so for basically self-destructive acts, things such as vagrancy, running away, curfew violations, drunkenness, drug-abuse violations, and prosti-tution. Fewer than 2 percent of those arrested are charged with violent crimes.[95] This only means that females in general tend to express their frustration in non-aggressive ways, and has no direct link to the level of frustration generated by abuse. The self-destructive effects of maltreatment were demonstrated by a study that showed that among one group of female drug abusers, nearly half were victims of sexual misuse.[96] Aggressive delinquency among females has recently been increasing somewhat. As traditional sex roles become less rigid, the incidence of female aggression may increase. This shift in the form of ex-pression is significant, but the underlying problem of mistreatment remains.

No one has investigated the incidence of mistreatment among female status offenders, so though we would suspect it is quite high, we have no con-crete evidence and must rely on the informal reports of caseworkers.[97] Most female juvenile delinquents (those who have committed criminal acts) report that they are not close to their fathers. It seems that the father has the greatest potential as the damaging parent for daughters. Female juvenile delinquents say that their fathers are generally not interested in them, are not loving, kind, or understanding. Many delinquent girls remember their childhoods as un-happy, with fathers who either did not live with them or did not discipline them.[98] One convicted felon described her childhood thus: "From the age of 6 to 11, I was beaten by my dad. I was hit with a belt, chains, electric wiring, and the thing is these experiences didn't make me afraid of punishment."

A large portion of a group of adjudicated juvenile delinquents (35 percent of the boys and 44 percent of the girls) were found to have been previously abused or neglected.[99] These figures may well underestimate the actual relationship because of underreporting of abuse. One-third of all the reported abuse victims later became delinquents or status offenders. Including the abused child's siblings increased this figure to two-thirds. Beyond that, the same study showed that delinquent abuse victims were far more likely to be violent offenders than nonabused delinquents. Abuse victims in one group of juvenile delinquents were twenty-four times as likely to have committed arson, fifty-eight times as likely to have committed rape, and about twice as likely to have committed assault as the rest of the delinquent population.[100] One researcher found a direct link between physical force in the home and aggressive male delinquency.[101] He found that 97 percent of his male delinquent subjects had experienced severe parental punishment. (The other 3 percent of his samples were inappropriate referrals who could not really be considered delinquent.) He writes, "I was astounded to find that the recidivist male delinquent who had never been exposed to a belt, board, extension cord, or fist was virtually non-existent."[102] This researcher also found that delinquency dropped off at about age 15, the same time that he found parents stopped hitting their sons, presumably out of fear of the son's size.[103] He concludes, "Since severe parental punishment is highly related to aggression, known abused children probably have one of the highest probabilities of becoming delinquent of all societal subgroups." Of course, there are many youth who experience severe physical punishment and who do not become delinquent. Furthermore, we cannot overlook the role of the child's own behavior in precipitating such assault.

Homicide and Abuse

When we consider the ultimate form of violence, namely homicide, the link with abuse becomes even clearer. In one study of nine young adolescents who had committed homicide, every one reported that he had been subjected to severe beatings as a child.[104] In another study of eight adolescents who had committed murderous assault, one or both parents had fostered and condoned such behavior.[105] In still another study, researchers found that 85 percent of a group of teenagers who had committed a murder that was not part of another crime had suffered severe corporal punishment during their childhood years.[106] In yet another investigation, scientists found that one-third of all homicides committed by adolescents in the state of New York were related to abuse or neglect.[107] We know that most children are on the receiving end of some domestic violence, even if it is limited to spanking and related punishment.[108] The evidence linking *severe* punishment and later serious aggression seems persuasive, however.

Many of our most infamous murderers have a long history of severe abuse. One study found that among six persons convicted of first-degree murder, four had suffered "remorseless physical brutality at the hands of parents" and the other two had been in a psychotic state at the time of the murder.[109] Charles Manson, leader of the cult responsible for the Tate and LaBianca murders in 1969, was severely abused as a child and spewed out of institution after institution as an adolescent. The link between abuse and homicide was legally recognized in 1979 when a jury acquitted a young man ("innocent by virtue of insanity") on the charge of murdering five young women due to multiple personalities created by the severe abuse he had sustained as a child.

About one-third of all the people who die at the hands of minors are family members. Perhaps the most tragic example of the effects of abuse is the youth who commits what one researcher has called "reactive parricide, a last resort to protect the psychic integrity of the perpetrator threatened with psychic disintegration due to catastrophic conflict." He believes the death of a parent is a "family-integrating experience" for the brutalized youth.[110] The saddest part is that there was no help available to these families. The study concludes, "Throughout the many years of this [parent's] sadistic behavior, societal responses were ineffective, slow, and highly frustrating. This impressed upon the perpetrator a sense of futility and powerlessness."[111] Very few abused adolescents kill their parents, but the fact that we would allow families to degenerate into such a state is a trenchant illustration of the institutionalized indifference that we address in chapter 13.

Adolescent Abuse as a Social Issue

There is hope. Human beings are extremely adaptable and capable of learning new systems of response. Victims of maltreatment need an alternative to self-blame and self-denigration. They need to have their social skills and self-concepts rebuilt. Finally, they need help sorting through their often intense and confusing emotions. One clinician calls this process "repair work with victims," as he describes a client (a 36-year-old woman) who was abused by her stepmother: "She still cries as the memory comes, unwelcome, to her mind, and one finds a mixture of guilt, sadness, terrible loneliness, and a sense of having been, in her words, 'degraded' by how she was treated."[112]

The tragic effects of maltreatment compel us to face it as a social issue, if not for altruistic motives, for reasons of self-preservation. Through the problems it presents us, abuse and neglect drain our society. They drain our criminal-justice system, our social-welfare system, and our schools. Human suffering costs us all. We all lose the productivity of the incapacitated victim. We all are potentially vulnerable to the aggressive one.

Notes

1. L. Tucker, "A Comparison of the Value Preferences of Emotionally Disturbed Adolescents and Their Parents with Normal Adolescents and Their Parents," *Adolescence* 11 (1976): 549-567.

2. J. Garbarino, and B. Carson, "Mistreated Youth in One Community" (Paper, Boys Town, Neb.: Center for the Study of Youth Development, 1979).

3. I. Lourie, "The Phenomenon of the Abused Adolescent: A Clinical Study," *Victimology* 2 (1977): 268-276; P. Libbey, and R. Bybee "The Physical Abuse of Adolescents," *Journal of Social Issues* 35 (1979): 101-126.

4. R. Friedman, "Adolescents as People: No Kidding Around" (Paper presented at a conference on A Community Response to the Adolescent in Conflict, Jacksonville, Fla., February 1978).

5. E. Elmer, "Child Abuse and Family Stress," *Journal of Social Issues* 35 (1979): 60-71.

6. H. Martin, *The Abused Child: A Multidisciplinary Approach to Developmental Issue at Treatment* (Cambridge, Mass.: Ballinger, 1976).

7. M.B. Smith, "School and Home: Focus on Achievement," in *Developing Programs for the Educationally Disadvantaged*, ed. A.H. Passow (New York: Teachers College Press, 1968).

8. D.C. McClelland, "Testing for Competence Rather Than for 'intelligence,'" *American Psychologist* 28 (1973): 1-14.

9. D. Baumrind, "A Dialectical Materialist's Perspective on Knowing Social Reality," *New Directions in Child Development* 2 (1979): 61-82.

10. H.L. Bee, "Parent-Child Interaction and Distractibility in 9-year-old Children," *Merrill-Palmer Quarterly* 13 (1967): 175-190.

11. J. Kelly, and R. Drabman, "Generalizing Response, Suppression of Self-injurious Behavior through an Overcorrection Punishment Procedure: Case Study," *Behavior Therapy* 3 (1977): 468-472.

12. Il Harris, and K. Howard, "Phenomenological Correlates of Perceived Quality of Parenting: A Questionnaire Study of High School Students, *Journal of Youth and Adolescence* 8 (1979): 171-180.

13. D. Kandel, and G. Lesser, *Youth in Two Worlds* (San Francisco: Jossey-Bass, 1972).

14. E.C. Devereux, "The Role of Peer Group Experience in Moral Development," In *Minnesota Symposia on Child Psychology,* vol. 4, ed. J.P. Hill (Minneapolis: University of Minnesota Press, 1970), pp. 94-140.

15. V.D. Hall, *A Primer of Freudian Psychology* (New York: World Publishing Company, 1954).

16. N. Polansky, personal communication.

17. R. Burgess, and R. Conger, "Family Interaction Patterns in Abusive,

Neglectful and Normal Families," *Child Development* 49 (1978): 163-173.

18. B. Steele, "Violence in Our Society," *The Pharos of Alpha Omega Alpha* 33 (1970): 42-48.

19. R. Herrenkohl, "Research: Too Much, Too Little?" *Child Abuse and Neglect: Issues on Innovation and Implementation* (Proceedings of the Second Annual Conference on Child Abuse and Neglect, vol. 1, April 17-20, 1977).

20. I. Katz, "The Socialization of Academic Motivation in Minority Group Children," in *Nebraska Symposium on Motivation, 1967*, ed. D. Levine (Lincoln: University of Nebraska Press, 1967), pp. 133-191.

21. A. Freud, and S. Dann, "An Experiment in Group Upbringing," *The Psychoanalytic Study of the Child* 6 (1951): 127-168.

22. N. Garmezy, "Observations on Research with Children at Risk for Child and Adult Psychopathology," in *Child Psychiatry Treatment and Research*, ed. M.F. McMillan and S. Henao (New York: Bruner/Mazel, 1977).

23. M. Pines, "Invulnerability: Pioneer Studies," *Psychology Today* 12 (1979): 58-60.

24. J. Alley, B. Cundiff, and J. Terry, "Child Abuse in Georgia, 1975-1977," *Morbidity and Mortality Report* (Center for Disease Control, Atlanta, Ga., January 26, 1979), pp. 33-35.

25. V. Satir, *Peoplemaking* (Palo Alto, Calif.: Science and Behavior Books, 1972).

26. S. Coopersmith, *The Antecedents of Self-esteem* (San Francisco: H.W. Freeman, 1967), p. 4.

27. McClelland, "Testing for Competence."

28. Coopersmith, *The Antecedents of Self-esteem*, p. 5.

29. U. Bronfenbrenner, *The Ecology of Human Development* (Cambridge, Mass.: Harvard University Press, 1979).

30. Coopersmith, *The Antecedents of Self-esteem*, p. 130.

31. Ibid., p. 158.

32. Katz, "Socialization of Academic Motivation."

33. N. Feshbach, "The Effects of Violence in Childhood," *Journal of Clinical Child Psychology* 28 (1973): 28-31.

34. J. Aronfreed, and V. Paskal, "Altruism, Empathy, and the Conditioning of Positive Affect," and E. Stotland, "Exploratory Investigation of Empathy," in *Advances in Experimental Social Psychology* ed. L. Berkowitz (New York: Academic Press, 1969).

35. M.L. Hoffman, and H.D. Saltzstein, "Parent Discipline and the Child's Moral Development," *Journal of Personality and Social Psychology* 5 (1967): 45-57.

36. L. Berkowitz, "Effects of Perceived Dependency Relationships upon Conformity to Group Expectations," *Journal of Abnormal and Social Psychology* 55 (1957): 350-354.

37. R. Coser, "The Complexity of Roles as a Seedbed of Individual

Autonomy," in *The Idea of Social Structure: Papers in Honor of Robert K. Merton*, ed. L.C. Coser (New York: Harcourt, 1975), pp. 256-263.

38. Feshbach, "Effects of Violence."

39. Berkowitz, "Effects of Perceived Dependency Relationships."

40. M. Keller, "Development of Role-taking Ability," *Human Development* 19 (1975): 120-132.

41. S. Bavolek, D. Kline, J. McLaughlin, and P. Publicover, "Primary Prevention of Child Abuse and Neglect: Identification of High-risk Adolescents," *Child Abuse and Neglect* 3 (1979): 314, 1071-1080.

42. C. Gray, "Empathy and Stress as Mediators in Child Abuse: Theory, Research and Practical Implications," (Ph.D. diss., University of Maryland, 1978).

43. Satir, *Peoplemaking*.

44. A. Bandura, and R. Walters, *Adolescent Aggression* (New York: Ronald Press Co., 1959).

45. R. Rohner, and C. Nielsen, *Parental Acceptance and Rejection: A Review of Research and Theory* (New Haven, Conn.: Human Relations Area Files Press, 1978).

46. P. Symonds, "A Study of Parental Acceptance and Rejection," *American Journal of Orthopsychiatry* 8 (1938): 679-88; L. Wolberg, "The Character Structure of the Rejected Child," *Nervous Child* 3 (1944): 74-88.

47. Bandura and Walters, *Adolescent Aggression*.

48. Devereux, "Role of Peer Group Experience."

49. N. Polansky, M. Chalmers, R. Buttenweiser, and D. Williams, "The Isolation of the Neglectful Family," *American Journal of Orthopsychiatry* 49 (1979): 149-152.

50. J. Garbarino, "Child Abuse and Juvenile Delinquency: The Developmental Impact of Social Isolation," in *Exploring the Relationship between Child Abuse and Delinquency*, ed. Y. Walker (Seattle, Wash.: Northwest Institute for Human Services, 1978).

51. R. White, and N. Watt, *The Abnormal Personality* (New York: Ronald Press Co., 1973).

52. B. Fisher, J. Berdie, J. Cook, J. Radford-Barker, and J. Day, *Adolescent Abuse and Neglect: Intervention Strategies and Treatment Approaches* (San Francisco: Urban and Rural Systems Associates, 1979).

53. J. Hill, "The Family," in *Seventy-ninth Yearbook of the National Society for the Study of Education*, ed. M. Johnson (Chicago, Ill.: University of Chicago Press, 1980).

54. M.J. Radke, *The Relation of Parental Authority to Children's Behavior and Attitudes* (Minneapolis: University of Minnesota Press, 1946).

55. H.W. Newell, "Psychodynamics of Maternal Rejection," *American Journal of Orthopsychiatry* 4 (1934): 387-403.

56. Smith, "School and Home."

57. R.N. Johnson, *Aggression in Man and Animals* (Philadelphia: W.B.

Saunders Co., 1972), p. 127.

58. E.I. Megargee, "The Role of Inhibition in the Assessment and Understanding of Violence," in *Control of Aggression in Violence*, ed. J.L. Singer (New York: Academic Press, 1971), pp. 125-147.

59. R. Rohner, *They Love Me, They Love Me Not* (New Haven: Conn.: Human Relations Area Files Press, 1975); Rohner and Nielsen, *Parental Acceptance and Rejection.*

60. Radke, *Parental Authority.*

61. Wolberg, "Character Structure."

62. Newell, "Psychodynamics of Maternal Rejection."

63. Rohner, *They Love Me.*

64. Wolberg, "Character Structure."

65. T. Houten, and M. Golembiewski, *A Study of Runaway Youth and Their Families* (Washington, D.C.: Youth Alternatives Project, 1976).

66. J. Streit, "A Test and Procedure to Identify Secondary School Children Who Have a High Probability of Drug Abuse," *Dissertation Abstracts International* 34 (1974): 10-13.

67. J. Duncan. "The Immediate Management of Suicidal Attempts in Children and Adolescents: Psychological Aspects," *Journal of Family Practice* 4 (1977): 77-80.

68. M. Paulson, and D. Stone, "Suicidal Behavior and Latency-age Children," *Journal of Clinical Child Psychology* 3 (1974): 50-53.

69. J. Teicher, "Why Adolescents Kill Themselves," in *The Mental Health of the Child*, ed. J. Segal (New York: Arno Press, 1973).

70. J.M. Toolan, "Suicide in Children and Adolescents," *American Journal of Psychotherapy* 29 (1975): 339-344.

71. S. McIntire, C. Angle, and M. Schlicht, "Suicide and Self-poisoning in Pediatrics," *Advances in Pediatrics* 24 (1977): 291-309.

72. Duncan, "Immediate Management."

73. D.G. Kreider, and J. Motto, "Parent-child Role Reversal and Suicidal States in Adolescence," *Adolescence* 9 (1974): 365-370.

74. McIntire, Angle, and Schlicht, "Suicide and Self-Poisoning."

75. C. Francis, "Adolescent Suicidal Attempts: Experienced Rejection and Personal Constructs," *Dissertation Abstracts International* 38 (March 1978): 4453-B.

76. Teicher, "Why Adolescents Kill Themselves."

77. McIntire, Angle, and Schlicht, "Suicide and Self-Poisoning."

78. Teicher, "Why Adolescents Kill Themselves."

79. Duncan, "Immediate Management."

80. Katz, "Socialization of Academic Motivation."

81. H. Yahares, *Why Young People Become Antisocial* (Washington: U.S. Government Printing Office, 1978).

82. T. Hirschi, *Causes of Delinquency* (Berkeley: University of California

Press, 1969).

83. F.I. Nye, "Family Relationships," in *Origins of Crime*, ed. W. McCord and J. McCord (New York: Columbia University Press, 1959).

84. Hirschi, *Causes of Delinquency.*

85. Bandura and Walters, *Adolescent Aggression.*

86. W. McCord, J. McCord, and A. Howard, "Familial Correlates of Aggression in Nondelinquent Male Children," *Journal of Abnormal Social Psychology* 63 (1961): 493-503.

87. E.M. Hetherington, R.J. Stouwie, and E.H. Ridberg, "Patterns of Family Interaction and Child-rearing Attitudes Related to Three Dimensions of Delinquency," *Journal of Abnormal Psychology* 78 (1971): 160-176.

88. D. Stayton, R. Hogan, and M. Ainsworth, "Infant Obedience and Maternal Behavior: Origins of Socialization Reconsidered," *Child Development* 42 (1971): 1057-1069.

89. J. Alfaro, "Report of New York State Assembly Select Committee on Child Abuse," *Child Protection Report,* vol. 2 (Washington, D.C.: January 1, 1976).

90. J.F. Alexander, "Defensive and Supportive Communications in Normal and Deviant Families," *Journal of Consulting and Clinical Psychology* 40 (1973): 223-231.

91. Burgess and Conger, "Family Interaction Patterns."

92. Alfaro, "Report."

93. Johnson, *Aggression in Man and Animals.*

94. P.H. Mussen, J. Conger, and J. Kagan, *Child Development and Personality* (New York: Harper and Row, 1974).

95. U.S. Federal Bureau of Investigation, *Crime in the United States, 1977* (Washington, D.C.: U.S. Department of Justice, 1978).

96. J. Benward, and J. Densen-Gerber, "Incest as a Causative Factor in Antisocial Behavior: An Exploratory Study," *Contemporary Drug Problems* 4 (1975): 32-35.

97. Fisher, Berdie, Cook, Radford-Barker, and Day, *Adolescent Abuse and Neglect.*

98. D. Lang, R. Pappenfurs, and J. Walters, "Delinquent Females' Perceptions of Their Fathers," *The Family Coordinator* 25 (1976): 475-481.

99. J. Alfaro, *Summary Report on the Relationship between Child Abuse and Neglect and Later Socially Deviant Behavior* (New York: Select Committee on Child Abuse, 1978).

100. Ibid.

101. R.S. Welsh, "Severe Parental Punishment and Delinquency: A Developmental Theory," *Journal of Clinical Child Psychology* 5 (1976): 17-21.

102. Ibid.

103. Ibid.

104. C.H. King, "The Ego and Integration of Violence in Homicidal

Youth," *American Journal of Orthopsychiatry* 45 (1975): 134-145.

105. W.M. Easson and R.M. Steinhilber, "Murderous Aggression by Children and Adolescents," *Archives of General Psychiatry* 4 (1961): 1-9.

106. E. Tanay, "Psychiatric Study of Homicide," *American Journal of Psychiatry* 120 (1963): 386-387.

107. Alfaro, "Report."

108. M. Straus, R. Gelles, and S. Steinmetz, *Behind Closed Doors* (New York: Doubleday, 1980).

109. G.M. Duncan, S.H. Frazier, E.M. Letin, A.M. Johnson, and A.J. Barron, "Etiological Factors in First-degree Murder," *Journal of the American Medical Association* 168 (1958): 1755-1758.

110. E. Tanay, "Adolescents Who Kill Parents—Reactive Parricide," *Australian and New Zealand Journal of Psychiatry* 7 (1973): 263-277.

111. Ibid.

112. N. Polansky, personal communication.

13 The Teenager as Victim

The word *victim* connotes helplessness, defensiveness, and innocence. In the public's mind, adolescents are none of these. Many of the problems encountered by mistreated youth are attributable to a lack of sympathy for their plight among both professionals and the general public. Children are appealing; adolescents are seen as obstinate, disrespectful, and aggressive. To put it bluntly: our society does not like teenagers.[1] Given this pervasive dislike, it is little wonder that abused adolescents have trouble getting the help they need and deserve as victims.

Images of Victims

The classic image of the abused child is dominated by weakness, smallness, innocence, injustice, and helplessness. Child victims are smaller than their tormentors. They are weaker and are not responsible for their actions. Their needs are unquestioned (even if in practice they are not always met). Teenagers do not fit this image. Often they are larger than their parents. They are expected to understand complex family situations. Adolescents are capable of willful provocation and revenge. Sometimes they retaliate when they are hit. One group of researchers has gone so far as to identify a syndrome of family violence they call "parent battering," in which nonabused teenagers mistreat their parents.[2] The adolescents they studied had committed a variety of threatening acts from destroying furniture to verbal assaults to near-lethal attacks upon their parents. Although these families were not previously abusive, they had disturbed authority hierarchies which made inappropriate demands on the teenager to run the family. The eventual result was violence directed at the chronically passive parents by the overburdened adolescent. Such cases, while certainly few in number, contribute to public and professional insensitivity to the genuine needs of victimized adolescents.

When we speak of the adolescent as victim we do so with full recognition of the need for two critical qualifiers. First, we must not forget that many of these adolescents play a role, often a very active role, in precipitating mistreatment through their own behavior. As noted in chapter 10, being parent to an adolescent is a challenge for most parents. We want to be clear on this point: like colicky infants and young children prone to tantrums, rebellious or otherwise troublesome teenagers are potent irritants to vulnerable parents operating without adequate prosocial support systems. We recognize this but still maintain that we need to legitimize the adolescent as victim. We do this despite our second qualifier, namely, that parents themselves are often victims of circumstances. They are frequently caught in a maze of their own personal psychologies, the interaction patterns in the family, and hostile forces outside the home weighing down upon them. Despite this situation, we believe it is important to identify the youth as a victim because getting a better social definition of the adolescent as victim is a key to solving this puzzle. We trust this will become clear as we proceed.

Bad Press

According to American folk wisdom, teenagers are intrinsically obnoxious. Because of the hormonal and intellectual changes they are experiencing, we expect them to give us trouble. The mass media and the clinical interests of many professionals reinforce this view: Both concentrate on kids in trouble, particularly kids who make trouble. As noted earlier, the transition into adolescence goes relatively smoothly for most youth. Deviance is more often the fruit of dysfunction at home than a normal consequence of puberty. But the public's *image* of typical adolescence remains one of tortured turmoil.[3] As long as that image stands as our standard, we will continue to treat teenagers as "outsiders" who are under stress and who therefore cannot be fully trusted or taken seriously. This image lays the foundation for the abused adolescent's difficulty in obtaining help, both for self and the family. When teenagers report mistreatment, they may encounter suspicion instead of sympathy. The person being told may not even believe it is possible to abuse an adolescent. Few people would assume that an infant is the cause of its own abuse (and fewer still believe an infant was to blame), but people do tend to ask teenagers what they did to deserve whatever ill treatment they received.

There are other reasons why people react less sympathetically to teenagers than to children. Many abused adolescents are not particularly appealing. When in groups, they often experience negative contagion, meaning that a group setting tends to compound the antisocial behavior of each individual, producing a frustrating morass of testing behavior and verbally obnoxious treatment of caregivers. Youth with low self-esteem may disregard their physical appearance, and are thus less appealing. If their social skills are poor, they will be handicapped in any attempt they make to ask for help. If they lack initiative, they may delay reporting mistreatment. Their stories are much less believable when they come weeks after an incident, in response to some other crisis, as is often the case.

Mistreated adolescents are likely to have been socially isolated and to have had only their parents from whom to learn to deal with other people. Learning from an abusive model, they are likely to deal with people abusively. There is no quicker way to alienate potential helpers than to reject or berate them for their efforts. In practice, this seems to be a significant barrier to meeting the needs of mistreated youth.

Perhaps most importantly, adolescents typically encounter helping systems because of their own aggressive, truant, or self-destructive acts; not because they are being abused. Violence and self-destruction elicit anger from outsiders, not sympathy, so mistreated adolescents start off on the wrong foot even when they are on the verge of receiving help because of some crisis that demands attention.

These and other reasons argue for the effectiveness of therapeutic foster care for abused adolescents because the intensive, one-to-one relationship it entails can operate as a vehicle for rebuilding skills, for readying mistreated youth to move into the mainstream of normal social life. Few victims are helpless and beyond help. Indeed, the abused teenagers we have interviewed are notable for their willingness and ability to work at rebuilding their lives.

Blaming the Victim

As a society, we tend to identify victims of social problems as "strange, different—in other words, as barbarians, as savages."[4] Although a capitalistic system requires a significant percentage of its workers to be unemployed to form a pool from which to hire, we blame the unemployed themselves for their state, not the system that requires them for its survival. Much of the common conservative rhetoric regarding the public welfare system rings with themes of the laziness and promiscuity of the poor. We do the same thing on an interpersonal level. During the famous Milgram experiments that tested human obedience to authority, subjects shifted the responsibility to the victim for the electric shocks they dealt him when he made an error. They saw him as bringing about his own punishment, blaming him for having volunteered for the experiment, calling him stupid and obstinate.[5] Victims of crime often are accused of provoking the criminal, of not resisting strongly enough, of resisting too strongly, or of being in the wrong place at the wrong time. This is most true of rape, but it applies to other crimes as well.

If we can convince ourselves that Harry's house was burglarized while he was gone because Harry talked too freely of his plans or because he failed to install a timing device on his lights, we feel confident that our own possessions will be safe while we vacation. Where the violation is more intensely disturbing, such as in rape, we go to even greater lengths to shift responsibility to the victim. Blaming the victim is the quickest and least expensive way of overcoming any threat to our just world hypothesis. In essence, if victims in some way get what they deserve, the world is still just.[6] When it comes to domestic violence, this need to justify may be overwhelming because we place such confidence in the ability of the nuclear family to stand on its own. When it falls on its face we tend to blame the victims, be they parent or child. The first step in this case is to recognize the primary victim, the teenager, and then go on to see and deal with the factors that draw parents into a pattern of abuse or neglect. In any case, to understand these forces we must return to the way the human ecology of family life isolates and closes off families, or at least permits them to cut themselves off. We must do this because families and the individuals they contain are strengthened by social connection and weakened by social isolation.

The Family in Law and Custom

Probably one of the biggest obstacles preventing adolescent victims of mistreatment from receiving help is the dominant, all-encompassing role our culture assigns to the nuclear family. In contrast to some societies, we concentrate the tasks of child rearing and socialization in the hands of parents (and often only one parent) who need, but often do not get, the support and feedback of other interested people.[7] This concentration of responsibility is coupled with a nearly absolute grant of parental authority by traditional social philosophy. Hobbes wrote, "Originally the father of every man was also his sovereign Lord, with power over him of life and death."[8] Locke, the champion of individual rights, specifically refused to extend his advocacy to minors. He wrote, "Although every man may enjoy equal rights, . . . to his natural freedom without being subjected to the will or authority of any other man, children are not born in the full state of equality, though they are born to it."[9] No one doubts that family autonomy is important for a free society, but we pay a price for this freedom when it degenerates into license.[10]

Because Americans tend to believe that children are the total responsibility of their parents, they view any intervention by outsiders, especially unrelated outsiders, as a violation of privacy and family integrity.[11] One root of this principle is a similar value: individual independence, with its corollary, refusal of help. Highly valuing independence serves to make those receiving aid feel guilty. This principle generalizes beyond the individual to the family unit. Teenagers face a special problem. Their families are supposed to handle their problems, but when the family itself is the problem, there is little recourse for them. The value we place on family privacy is so strong that many never even ask for help. When they do they may run up against a legal system weighted against them.

Our legal system views the family as supreme, and views outside intervention as a last resort.[12] This stance rests upon the typically greater experience, wisdom, and benevolence of parents compared with that of their children. Chief Justice Warren Burger expressed this position in a decision that maintained the right of parents to place their children in mental institutions without a trial. He wrote "The Law's concept of the family rests on a presumption that parents possess what a child lacks in the maturity, capacity and judgment required for making life's decisions. More importantly, historically it has been recognized that natural bonds of affection lead parents to act in the best interests of their children. That some parents may at some time be acting against the interests of their child creates a basis for caution, but it is hardly a reason to discard wholesale those pages of human experience that teach that parents generally do act in the child's best interests."[13] The dilemma is real. How do we protect the integrity of the family while not giving up the community's right and obligation to protect the child?

Children traditionally have been viewed as chattels of their parents, with few if any individual rights. Prior to recent child-abuse legislation, physical punishment, no matter how severe, was usually completely legal. In years past, for example, North Carolina had no law against abandonment, neglect, or nonsupport of minors. Only if the father's neglect to provide food, shelter, and medical care resulted in a child's death could he be prosecuted.[14] As late as 1973, Texas reaffirmed the right of parents(and guardians)to use anything short of lethal force to discipline their children.[15]

The court always has taken a paternalistic attitude toward minors. While this attitude has the effect of stripping them of their rights, it springs not so much from the tyranny of adults as from benevolent affection.[16] Judge Blackstone thought the court should secure minors from hurting themselves by their own improvident acts. Justice Wilde wrote that the purpose of the juvenile law was to protect the minor from his own imbecility. Benevolent as this intent may be, it puts everyone under the age of majority into a state of dependency with no rights of his or her own.

Minors are denied the vote, kept out of many interesting movies, forced into schools, and prohibited from buying cigarettes and alcoholic beverages. Only in the medical area have the courts begun to grant minors any rights independent of their families. [17] Ironically, those rights have been recognized on the basis of individual privacy. But generally, the value of privacy has meant that some laws were written to protect the privacy of the family at the expense of the child.

When the identity of the person making the report of abuse is kept secret, as it often is, the process of helping may be compromised. Unless that individual decides to speak publicly, he or she does not testify if the case reaches court. Without a witness, mistreatment is usually hard to confirm, particularly among adolescents where physical signs are likely to be unconvincing. Not only are juvenile cases decided behind closed doors without benefit of a jury, but all juvenile records are closed to the public and the names of all the youth involved are kept secret. These are protective measures to avoid stigmatization, but they allow the judge unchecked power in the courtroom. Without the benefit of several opinions, the door is open to capriciousness. The decision to institutionalize a child is a crucial one—at least as important to the child's future as is the decision to incarcerate an adult—yet the adult is more likely to receive due process. These legal impediments are compounded by a service delivery system that is generally recognized to be inadequate.[18] The mistreated youth is often twice victimized, first by the family system and then by the human-service system.

Inadequate Services

> While I was on the run I went to the welfare and this chick who worked there was saying, "Excuse me. I have to do something." Then she'd come back, saying, "Okay, now what were you saying. Oh, wait a minute. I have to call somebody. What were you saying?" You know, I'm going, "You don't really want to know. I'll catch you later." And I walked out and before I left she said, "Well, give me a call and let me know what happens." And you know, I just went, "You don't understand. I'm not going to call you. You might be busy."

The sad truth is that very few services are generally available to meet the needs of mistreated youth. We have not done nearly enough for abused and neglected children, but we have done even less for adolescents. Runaway shelters, crisis hot lines, and group homes are helping the teens who approach them, but these services are new, few, and usually overburdened. The child-maltreatment problem is not being solved, and this failure means that the pool of adolescents with a history of abuse continues to fill, like a spring-fed lake. Ray Helfer, a leader in efforts to deal with child abuse, sees the situation this way: "Every year 1.5 to 2 percent of our children are reported as suspected victims of child abuse. While social agencies are working to help this year's 2 percent, they are still trying to figure out what to do with last year's 2 percent and are pleading with legislators for more money to deal with next year's 2 percent. The problems of abuse and neglect accumulate at the rate of 1.5 to 2 percent more children each year."[19]

Many of the very services that could help in the least restrictive way, such as emergency caretakers, parents aides, group homes, and parental self-help groups, are least available.[20] Conventional child welfare services (casework and foster care) are of dubious effectiveness[21] and may often operate for their own survival and that of their staff at the expense of the children and youth in their care.[22] What is painfully true of services for children is disastrously true of services for abused adolescents. The level of unmet need is staggering.[23] Teenagers want quick action and they want to feel like they have a committed ally in their caseworker, not a cool professional. One reason that they are served so poorly is simply the fact that it is bureaucracies that serve them, and bureaucracies are characteristically slow, inefficient, and overburdened. In Pennsylvania, for example, one report showed that fewer than half of all reports of child abuse were investigated within the thirty days that the law required. Fifteen percent were wiped from the records without ever having been investigated.[24] In New York during the 1970s, 62 percent of all child-abuse reports led to no further action. About 12 percent led to supervision of parents, and only 1.2 percent to other services.[25] Very few services exist that social-service workers can offer abused teens. The services that do exist are generally horrendously overburdened. They form a patchwork that loses people in the gaps, especially people whose problems do not fit a familiar label. This is another reason why we believe the first step in meeting the needs of mistreated youth is validating and legitimizing those needs by defining the adolescent as a victim rather than a cause of mistreatment. Once that is done, we can proceed to a more mature appreciation of the family as an interactional system. Here is an extreme example of how tragedy can strike when the adolescent is closed out of the helping systems.

> Gloria DuPont ran away from home because she felt unloved and alone. She went straight to the local runaway shelter, where the staff set about finding help for her. The protective services unit said it couldn't help, as did the state's youth services department. So did the city welfare department. A private home for girls was out because of expense. She left the office despondent. A week or so later, her body was found floating in the river.[26]

Community-based group homes generally are thought to be a good way to care for teenagers. These homes usually are supervised by social-service workers who counsel youth and help them learn living and communication skills. The difference between life in such homes and life in a conventional institution can be enormous. It lies primarily in the fact that in the former, people are able to form close interpersonal relationships in a setting similar to a home, sharing domestic duties and living in regular neighborhoods, while in the latter there is an almost irresistible trend toward rigidity and depersonalization. Unfortunately, there are not enough group homes to provide secure and developmentally enhancing care for all the youth who would benefit by living in one. Some group homes that are opening to serve teenagers are private. As such, they are beyond the financial means of many families. In many cases, the only choice is between institutions and conventional foster care, a grim choice between two evils in many cases.

Especially when teenagers are involved, the foster-care system is a problem in its own right.[27] Many adolescents are removed from their homes as a result of mistreatment. The protective-service system places more of them in foster care than any place else. Placements are difficult to arrange and even harder to maintain for teenagers, for if they are not happy, adolescents are fully capable of running away or otherwise undermining the placement. Few professionals are pleased with the foster-care placements for adolescents available in their community. Across the nation, placements often do not receive periodic review, and effective grievance procedures are virtually nonexistent. So if a teenager is unhappy in a foster home, there is often no legitimate way to get out. Often no one seeks the consent of the teenager when the placement decision is made. Willing relatives usually are not allowed to house the teenager unless they can absorb the cost themselves. Friedman developed the concept of "therapeutic" foster care as one way of responding to these problems (see chapter 14).[28]

Other sources of help are only effective with parental cooperation. In Nebraska, for example, even a court order for family counseling does not ensure parental compliance. No one evaluates the progress of the abuse case that generated the order until six months after the case is closed. Even then, the only censure for parental noncompliance (nonattendance) is a contempt-of-court citation.

Another possible solution to family disturbances involving adolescents is independent living for the teenager, but this option is almost totally dependent upon parental approval. The only time a minor can legally live away from home is when he or she is emancipated with the termination of parental rights, but emancipation is not easily accomplished. It usually requires parental approval. Some human-service professionals involved in this problem see themselves as able to intervene but powerless to help. One worker put it this way: "Here we are with the power to meddle in people's lives but no control over what happens to them."[29] All these stiuations leave abused teenagers out in the cold. They are unable to improve their homes or to find a suitable alternative. Many decide to leave anyway. With no place to go, they turn to the open road.

Alternative Options

Running Away: The High-Risk Option

> We never really talked until he caught me going out the door. He yelled and screamed at me for two-and-a-half hours straight. Finally, he just said, "You go out that door and you're not my daughter. I don't know you. I never had you for a daughter." And I said, "Fine. If that's the way you want it, then let it be on your conscience, because I'm telling you I want a relationship with you and I can't have it living with you. If you can't deal with that, then I can't either." And then I left.

Nobody knows how many runaways there really are, but one source estimates that one out of ten American youths aged 12 to 15 has run away from home at least once.[30] Another, based on a youth survey, puts the figure much lower, around 2 percent for the 10- to 17-age range.[31] Even this lower figure represents nearly 800,000 runaways annually. Indeed, one of the better treatments of this topic focuses on the nonreturners, the nearly 25 percent of runaways who are serious about leaving and seriously troubled.[32] While most runaways are gone less than a week and travel less than ten miles from home, the nonreturners make a major break with home and community and tend to become part of the street scene. They are likely to have been rejected and abused at home and to be involved in delinquent behavior outside the home.

In New York City alone, the police contacted more than 14,000 runaways under age 18 in a single year.[33] Others estimate that as many as a million children are on the run in this country at any given time.[34] No one knows for sure. Sensationalized reports mix with reasoned estimates. What we do know is that teenage runaways represent a significant social problem, particularly when they run to escape abuse at home.

Teenagers who leave their home have many of the same problems that we identify with victims of mistreatment. This should not be surprising since there is a great deal of overlap between the two groups. Compared with youth who have not run away, runaways hold less favorable self-concepts, have more anxiety and self-doubt, have poorer interpersonal relationships, and are more defensive. They report getting less support and more punishment from their parents than nonrunaways. They report parental rejection, differential treatment among siblings, and feelings of powerlessness and failure.[35] Runaway girls report excessive parental control and boys inadequate control.[36] This kind of sex difference is found often among youth in trouble: the female adolescents being overcontrolled; the males, undercontrolled. This is consistent with the finding that teenage boys with single parents and teenage girls with stepparents are at greatest risk for outpatient psychiatric and mental-health referral.[37] Again the former is likely to be an undercontrol situation; the latter, overcontrol.

No doubt many runaways come from basically healthy families that are going through troubled times. Many families permit minor conflicts to escalate and become major confrontations.[38] Disputes over issues like eating dinner with the family, length of hair, and curfew hours sometimes divert everyone's attention away from the more basic issues of love and respect, provoking an incident of running away.[39] There are three types of runaways: those who seek adventure, those who run because of emotional problems, and those who are escaping mistreatment.

Although the adventurer leaves because of problems at home, this teenager is a casual runner who seeks excitement as much as respite from family conflict. The interpersonal relationships in this nonabused-runaway's family may be somewhat weak, but the problems tend to be those of communication and are likely to be temporary. One study found that among runaways from these families, only 23 percent ran away again after becoming involved in a youth program.[40]

Other runaways have more serious problems, running because they feel acute depression or rejection or because they want to escape a psychotic parent.[41] This type of runaway leaves home because of a mixture of personal problems at home and school. In many ways, theirs is the least positive of the three types of runaways.

A third group runs away to escape physical, emotional, or sexual abuse. The federal government estimates that one-half to one-third of all runaways are victims of mistreatment.[42] The bitter truth is that many teenagers run away for good cause: to escape intolerable conditions. The world outside looks safer to these youth than their own homes. Based on their study, Houten and Golembiewski concluded that more than 80 percent of all serious runaways flee because of family problems, including alcoholism and abuse.[43]

Another small group has no choice but to leave home. They are the "throwaways" whose parents will not allow them to live at home. One runaway house reported that one-third of its clients fit this pattern. Sadly, the victims of such complete rejection are often incapacitated. Their ultimate expulsion has been preceded by months, possibly years, of failure and rejection. Often friendless, they may be emotionally disorganized, grasping for some claim on life[44] and primed for repeated victimization.[45]

The World Outside

> You know, needing a place to stay when you're desperate puts you in a vulnerable position. Luckily, I lived with this man and he had a girl-friend and I was just his clean-up woman. And I would stay there and clean up and I didn't have any money. And he never had any food. All there was was some onions and some corn meal and so I would make these terrible onion rings. That was the only thing there was. And after a couple of months I met these neat people who asked me over for some gourmet spaghetti. It was spicy, and my body rejected it because all I had eaten was onion rings.

Once on their own, teenagers find the world outside is no haven. Adolescents on the run are raped, maimed, and murdered with grim frequency. Without transportation of their own, youngsters must trust their safety to those who will pick them up hitchhiking. Unable to find legitimate employment, they are left to scrape together an existence. Delinquency is a fact of life for runaways, both as cause and effect. Chicago police report that 70 percent of all delinquents it contacts have a history of running away. It appears that the higher incidence of drug abuse and police contacts that runaways experience is a result of their situation in life, rather than of any particular criminal inclination. Living on the street means survival through crime for teenagers on their own. It means becoming streetwise. Teenagers run con games and shoplift. They try to support themselves by writing bad checks. Often they become dependent upon someone who can benefit from their services. Many survive by stealing, selling, and transporting drugs. Others turn to burglary. Still others sell their bodies. All these means of survival drain society. We are actually subsidizing runaways through the cost of their crimes, even though we have officially allocated little for their care. It is a distasteful form of subsidy, however, since it falls randomly upon victims of purse snatchings, store owners who cash bad checks, or people whose homes are burglarized. When legitimate means of survival are closed, these teenagers may feel they have no place to turn but to illegitimate ones.

No one knows how many boys and girls support themselves as prostitutes and as models for pornography. The system that accepts them offers them the shelter and even emotional support that they can find nowhere else. Because of their typically low self-esteem, victims of mistreatment who run are likely to place themselves in self-destructive, degraded positions. Those who have suffered sexual abuse at home are especially vulnerable. The combination of a personality that is primed for exploitation and a lack of any means of support yields a predictable result.[46]

Some people who encounter runaways have specific plans for exploiting their vulnerability.

> I wasn't in the city long before a guy riding in the back of a big car pulled up and asked if I wanted a ride. I wanted to look around, so I said sure. Bam. The moment I got inside he pushed my head down and the car took off. They took me to a fancy room with a lot of other girls. They all told me that if I would work the street with them, that they'd take care of me, be my family. That felt pretty good, so I relaxed. Then they said they were going to make me feel like part of the family. They held me down—I was terrified—and shot me full of smack (heroin). After that, I was hooked and I was a working girl. Fourteen, and a working girl.

Twenty-seven boys were murdered in Houston one summer. All were thought to be runaways with no visible means of support.[47]

If apprehended while committing an illegal act in order to survive on the streets, the weight of responsibility falls upon the runaway's shoulders. In a broader sense, these youth have been cast off by society. They are symptoms of a larger problem: the failure of families to meet the challenge of child rearing, and communities of providing feedback and nurturance to all their families.

Forced out of inadequate families, barred through their numbers and their own suspicions from understaffed and underfunded agencies, youth on the run are routed toward delinquency and eventual confinement. With no rights, no meaningful options, and no advocates, they are losers in every way.[48]

Mistreatment and the Status Offense

For many reasons, abused and neglected adolescents, particularly females, tend to encounter the juvenile-justice system as status offenders. One reason is their own troublesome behavior. But other reasons are even more direct results of mistreatment. For one thing, running away from home itself doubles as a status offense and is a logical reaction to abuse within the home. Not surprisingly, one study found that mistreated adolescents were twice as likely to be detained for running away than nonabused delinquents.[49]

Another reason abused teens tend to be labeled as status offenders is the in-need-of-supervision petition, a process whereby a defeated parent asks the state to take responsibility for the child. Parents often use the court to frighten the child when they know of no other place to turn for help. The main problem with the system as it now operates is that it is weighted so heavily in the parents' favor. Even if a probation officer thinks that a petition is unnecessary, a parent has full legal rights to insist that it be drawn up anyway, and this permits the parent to avoid assuming responsibility for his or her role in a deteriorated situation. One study found that in over a third of all such petitions, the parents could have been charged with abuse or neglect.[50] If the petition is granted, the child becomes a ward of the state. Those who know the juvenile-justice system know that parents usually win in court. Because of this perceived judicial prejudice, many human-service professionals prefer to seek a more easily obtained status offense petition against the *teenager* even in cases that are clearly abusive or neglectful rather than one of maltreatment against the *parents*, as the latter would involve producing convincing evidence acceptable to a court, a lengthy and difficult process. Thus they prosecute the victim instead of the abuser.[51]

One father in New York filed such a petition on his son because of truancy from home. The son had been "on discipline" for more than a year. That meant that he was not allowed to go to movies or out with friends, and that he had to be home by 6 P.M. every weeknight. On the rare occasions when he managed to get out of the house, the boy would stay away for days while still attending school (the petition was dismissed on these and other grounds).[52]

This is partly a class phenomenon. The people most likely to petition the court are those who cannot afford other alternatives, such as boarding schools and private therapists. Thus the lower the family's income and the more reluctant the community to assist low-income families, the greater the rate of such court referrals tends to be.[53] The court is really responding to the troubled youth whose predicament arises from social and economic instability in their homes and from the failure of community institutions to serve them.[54]

Part of the problem is that the status-offense concept itself is not grounded in a firm foundation of social theory and practice. Designed to recognize the special mix of independence and dependence characteristic of adolescents in America, the status offense has come under attack by those who dispute the merits and wisdom of involving noncriminal youth in the juvenile-justice system (based in part upon doubts that it is either just or a system). We are persuaded that it is possible to serve these teenagers and their families through a variety of responses that do not involve the juvenile system at all, including in-home counseling and support services. These services are provided in direct proportion to the intensity of the crisis by one exemplary program, The Homebuilders.[55] Also therapeutic foster parents (mentioned earlier in this chapter) who are specially recruited, trained, paid, and supported to provide alternative living arrangements for adolescents placed out of home offer another solution.[56] We will address these options in greater detail in chapter 14. The point here is that viewing the troubled adolescent as "in need of services" improves the prospects for the adolescent.

The Institutional End

> You gotta act like you don't hate it here. They lock you up if you got a smart mouth. That's the worst, when they close the door and it's you and the walls.

According to our study, adolescents are more likely than children to be institutionalized as a result of abuse.[57] Once institutionalized, teenagers are vulnerable to all forms of mistreatment from other inmates and the staff. So the very improvements in identification and reporting of maltreatment that we so often advocate would only serve to set up more teenagers for institutional abuse and neglect if things remain as they are now. The dangers of reporting without the resources to provide genuine help are quite real.[58]

Nobody knows exactly how many minors are institutionalized, but one informed source estimates that 754,000 children and youth live in residential institutions, temporary and long-term shelters, detention centers and homes, centers for the mentally retarded and disabled, and group homes.[59] It is frighteningly easy for a youth to end up in an institution in this country. One study found that fewer than half the states in its sample made it possible for minors to have access to counseling before they are committed to an institution because of a psychiatric diagnosis.[60] It also found that preventive services are not necessarily provided to abusive or neglectful parents prior to the removal of a child from the home, even in nonemergency situations. We already have outlined the secrecy that surrounds the decision to institutionalize a minor through the courts. The lack of public scrutiny permits injustice. Four percent of all children in institutions today are there specifically because no one wanted them.[61] Once inside, teenagers come face to face with the dismal realities of life in American institutions.

These tall walls coming in on me, and that ceiling looking like it was going down on top of me real slow. Inch by inch. And it was so wet in there; like I was sweating and there was no place for the sweat to go so it just stayed there with me. Then it got hot, and then it got cold. Holy God, it was the worst thing I even knew about. . . . They wouldn't put a sick dog in one of those and still they had no problem sticking me in there.[62]

Adolescents within this country's institutions have suffered shocking abuse.[63] Precisely because victims of maltreatment are likely to be more psychologically damaged than their nonabused peers, they are more likely to be placed in institutions. We do not know the exact percentage of abuse victims among the young inhabitants of institutions, but logic leads us to believe that abused teens must surely gravitate there. One probation worker puts it this way, "Most of the really deeply troubled kids who have grown up in the worst environments are rejected by the voluntary agencies and there's nothing we or the courts can do about it."[64]

Government investigators have documented some shocking incidents in institutions that hold teenagers, although systematic efforts to study these problems are just beginning.[65] Kenneth Wooden, in researching his journalistic investigation of the conditions in institutions that detain minors (*Weeping in the Playtime of Others*) found some shocking abuses.[66] While his account is impressionistic and not necessarily representative, it does reveal some grisly details about the worst in the institutions investigated. He found that children were punished by holding their heads under water or forcing them to run past a line of boys who were required to strike their peer from the waist to the shoulder with closed fists. He recounts instances where youngsters were forced to eat their own feces, or their vomit. One child's head was used to mop urine from the floor.

It is not that those who run these institutions are innately sadistic individuals who delight in fulfilling their sick fantasies on their captive clients (though such people no doubt exist). Former workers report that strong peer pressure among staff combined with constant challenges to authority by clients cause those who survive the job to become callous and rough.[67] What is more, the negative-contagion phenomenon means that troubled adolescents in groups are likely to cause trouble for caretakers. One anonymous expert who is familiar with this problem frankly admits that, "One of my concerns is how easy it is to abuse adolescents, particularly when groups of teenagers with special problems are together."

The institutional system itself effectively takes normal healthy individuals and enables them to commit inhuman acts that they would never otherwise consider by giving them complete power over troublesome youth. One psychologist tested the effects of an institutional way of life upon people who had never before encountered it.[68] He paid students to role-play as guards and inmates in a closed stiuation. The experiment had to be abruptly terminated because half the mock prisoners were having severe emotional disturbances such as uncontrollable crying, rage, and disorganized thinking. The students merged reality to their roles so much that the guards naturally dehumanized their wards. Those who have looked have consistently found such dehumanization in nearly every sort of institution that houses youth.[69] Our country's guidelines for institutional treatment encourage insensitivity and mistreatment on the one hand, and antisocial and psychologically disordered behavior on the other.

The policies and administration of these institutions often lead to unpleasant, unhealthy conditions. Many of these official abuses flourish in the secrecy typically afforded institutions. At one detention home for girls in New York, there was barely enough meat to go around and there were rarely any fresh fruits or vegetables on the tables. Medical care was inadequate, large amounts of medication were dispensed daily in a careless way, and even the most seriously disturbed girls received no real psychiatric care. Many staff members frequently used vile and obscene language to the girls, cursing, belittling, and threatening them.[70]

Surprisingly, the most violent penal establishments are not those providing long-term maximum security for serious offenders, but short-term detention facilities, often the county jail.[71] In such transient situations people have no time to become familiar and can form only tenuous interpersonal relationships.[72] Detention is a waiting period of enforced idleness, usually employed because of overloaded court schedules. It is destructive to youth and is of little value to the criminal-justice system. Of these tanks for those awaiting trial, few (less than 20 percent) have recreational facilities, almost none (10 percent) have vocational programs, and half do not even have medical services. Although 80 percent of the children in these facilities are emotionally disturbed, less than half receive any psychiatric or psychological evaluation. Only a quarter of these holding units employ any full-time helping professionals.[73]

But administrative policies and staff abuses are not the only problems facing youth within institutions. Many fall prey to the exploitation of other inmates, adults who have committed serious crimes. "They were worse to me because I was a kid. It was easier to push me around. They called me names and threw me against the wall. They scared me. They threatened me. It kept getting worse. They kept hitting me a little harder every time."[74]

Although federal law has mandated the states to move minors out of adult jails, many states have dragged their feet. Across the country adolescents have been placed, as punishment, in dormitories with older inmates who raped and abused them.[75] Under extreme circumstances, running away, attempting suicide, and resorting to drugs seem the only available response.[76] We simply do not provide treatment for youth during their stays in these and other institutions. At best, they are subjected to repeated batteries of tests and interviews. At worst, they are isolated for misbehavior, forced to account for every minute of their time, denied their privacy, subjected to having their mail censored, and refused all contact with members of the opposite sex.[77] As Rena K. Uviller, director of the American Civil Liberty Union's Juvenile Rights Project puts it: "What kids learn from these institutions is how to adapt to institutions, and they do that just because it's the only way not to get hassled at a place that regulates their lives from seven o'clock in the morning to nightfall."

One group of researchers tested the effect of institutionalization upon adolescent victims of mistreatment. They found that the institutionalized victims expressed more abusive attitudes toward parenthood and child rearing than did noninstitutionalized, nonidentified abused adolescents.[78] Things rarely go well for teenagers who are released. They are likely to encounter the criminal-justice system again. To survive within institutions, adolescents learn behaviors that often assure their failure in the outside world. Some play the game successfully while inside. "The only way to get by in here is to be the meanest bastard around. I never liked to scare people but now I do it a lot, 'cause otherwise you got people scarin' you." As one former staff member of a detention center puts it: Those who demonstrate a modicum of willfulness wind up back in the institution. The behaviors they adopt for survival make them chronic inmates, outsiders in a society unprepared to come to terms with them.[79]

No Place to Turn

As abysmal as conditions inside institutions are, there are those who prefer life within an institution to life at home. One researcher identified a group of boys who expressed a low desire to be released from a correctional camp. Not surprisingly, they were likely to have a history of parental abuse.[80]

We have no reliable and comprehensive system for *helping* abused adolescents.[81] They need protection from their parents, from themselves, from predators, and from institutionalization. They need to learn to understand their parents. They need dignity and respect and the right to look after their own interests. They need counseling to let them know they are not intrinsically bad. Very few mistreated youth get what they need. Often they are thrown into society's dumping ground for undesirables, the criminal-justice system. They emerge indiscernible from the rest of the heap, ready to become adults primed for failure in life's major roles: worker, citizen, and, perhaps most importantly, parents.

This brings us to the end of our exploration of maltreatment. Our ecological and developmental perspective on the maltreatment of children and youth has led us through the institutional life of our communities (from hospitals to jails), through the complex dynamics of the developing family as a microsystem, through the complex networks that can link together child-rearing and support systems that provide nurturance and feedback, and through the web of values and cultural principles (the blueprints) that shape our very perception of reality. We are ready to draw some conclusions about helping abusive families and the individuals within them, but we can see clearly now that this goal challenges our science, our morality, and our politics as much as any other on our civilization's agenda.

Notes

1. E.Z. Friedenberg, *Dignity of Youth and Other Atavisms* (Boston: Beacon Press, 1965).

2. H. Harbin, and D. Madden, "Battered Parents: A New Syndrome" (Paper presented at the American Psychological Association, September 1-5, 1979, New York, N.Y.).

3. John P. Hill, "The Family," in *Seventy-ninth Yearbook of the National Society for the Study of Education,* ed. M. Johnson (Chicago, Ill.: University of Chicago Press, 1980).

4. W. Ryan, *Blaming the Victim* (New York: Vintage, 1976).

5. S. Milgram, *Obedience to Authority* (New York: Harper and Row, 1974).

6. J.L. Barkas, *Victims* (New York: Charles Scribner and Sons, 1978).

7. J. Korbin, "Very Few Cases: Child Abuse in the People's Republic of China" (Paper presented at the annual meeting of the American Anthropological Association, Los Angeles, California, November 1978).

8. T. Hobbes, "Leviathan," *Great Books of the Western World,* vol. 23 (New York: Encyclopedia Britannica, 1952), p. 59.

9. J. Locke, "A Letter Concerning Toleration," *Great Books of the Western World,* vol. 35 (New York: Encyclopedia Britannica, 1952).

10. J. Garbarino, and U. Bronfenbrenner, "Research on Parent-Child Relations and Social Policy: Who Needs Whom?" (Paper presented at the Symposium on Parent-Child Relations: Theoretical, Methodological and Practical Implications, University of Trier, West Germany, May 1976).

11. J. Garbarino, "The Price of Privacy: An Analysis of the Social Dynamics of Child Abuse," *Child Welfare* 56 (1977): 565-575.

12. B.G. Fraser, "A Glance at the Past, a Gaze at the Present, a Glimpse at the Future: A Critical Analysis of the Development of Child Abuse Reporting Statutes," *Chicago-Kent Law Review,* vol. 54, 1978.

13. *Commissioner Parham, Department of Human Resources of Georgia, et al.* vs. *J.L. et al., Supreme Court Bulletin,* 39 CCH B 3484.

14. M.P. Thomas, *Child Abuse and Neglect, Part II: Historical Overview, Legal Matrix and Social Perspectives in North Carolina,* vol. 54 (Chapel Hill, N.C.: North Carolina Law Review Association School of Law, 1975 and 1976), pp. 744-753, 766-773.

15. B. Justice, and R. Justice, *The Abusing Family* (New York: Human Sciences Press, 1976).

16. Fraser, "A Glance at the Past."

17. Institute of Medicine, *Issues in Adolescent Health: Preliminary Conference Report* (Washington, D.C.: National Academy of Sciences, 1978).

18. B. Fisher, J. Berdie, J. Cook, J. Radford-Barker, and J. Day, *Adolescent Abuse and Neglect: Intervention Strategies and Treatment Approaches* (San Francisco: Urban and Rural Systems Associates, 1979).

19. R. Helfer, *Prevention of Serious Breakdowns in Parent-Child Interaction* (Chicago: National Committee for Prevention of Child Abuse, 1978).

20. Joint State Government Commission, Administration of Pennsylvania's child-abuse law (General Assembly of the Commonwealth of Pennsylvania, Harrisburg, January 1979).

21. Berkeley Planning Associates, *Evaluation of Child Abuse and Neglect Demonstration Projects, 1974-1977*, NTIS Report no. NCHSR 78-64 (Springfield, Va.: National Technical Information Services, 1978).

22. Children's Defense Fund, *Children without Homes: An Examination of Public Responsibility to Children in out-of-home Care* (Washington, D.C.: Children's Defense Fund, 1978).

23. R. Friedman, personal communication.

24. Joint State Government Commission, Administration of Pennsylvania's child-abuse law.

25. J. Alfaro, "Report of New York State Assembly Select Committee on Child Abuse," *Child Protection Report* vol. 11 (Washington, D.C., January 1, 1976).

26. K. Wooden, *Weeping in the Playtime of Others: The Plight of Incarcerated Children* (New York: McGraw-Hill, 1976).

27. Children's Defense Fund, *Children without Homes.*

28. R. Friedman and C. Zeigler, "Therapeutic Foster Homes" (Unpublished paper, Florida Mental Health Institute, Tampa, Fla., November 1979).

29. L. Harris, "Persons in Need of Supervision," *New Yorker* 54 (August 14, 1978): 55 ff.

30. R. Allison, ed. *Status Offenders and the Juvenile Justice System: An anthology* (Washington, D.C.: National Council on Crime and Delinquency, 1978).

31. Opinion Research Corporation, *National Statistical Survey on Runaway Youth*, part 1 (Princeton, N.J.: Opinion Research Corporation, 1976).

32. T. Houten, and M. Golembiewski, *A Study of Runaway Youth and Their Families* (Washington, D.C.: Youth Alternatives Project, 1976).

33. M. Raphael, and J. Wolf, *Runaways: America's Lost Youth* (New York: Drake, 1974).

34. U.S. Senate, Subcommittee on the Judiciary, *Protection of Children Against Sexual Exploitation Act of 1977*, report on S. 1585 (Washington: D.C.: U.S. Government Printing Office, 1977).

35. T. Brennan, F. Blanchard, D. Huizinga, and D.Elliott, "Final Report: The Incidence and Nature of Runaway Behavior," Prepared for the Office of Assistant Secretary for Planning and Evaluation, Department of Health, Education and Welfare (Boulder, Colo.: Behavioral Research and Evaluation Corp., 1975).

36. S. Wolk, and J. Brandon, "Runaway Adolescents' Perceptions of Parents and Self," *Adolescence*, vol. 46, 1977.

37. N. Kalter, "Children of Divorce in an Outpatient Psychiatric Population," *American Journal of Orthopsychiatry* 47 (1977): 40-51.

38. L. Troll, "Is Parent-Child Conflict What We Mean by Generation Gap?" *Family Coordinator* 3 (1972): 347-349.

39. P.M. Kimball, "Revitalization of Values Will Help Bridge the Generation Gap," *Phi Delta Kappa Bulletin* 36 (1970): 49-52.

40. T.P. Gullotta, "Runaway: Reality or Myth," *Adolescence* 13 (1978): 843-849.

41. P. Reilly, "What Makes Adolescent Girls Flee from Their Homes?" *Clinical Pediatrics* 17 (1978): 886-893.

42. Department of Health, Education and Welfare, *Runaway Youth: A Status Report and Summary of Projects*, report of the Intradepartmental Committee on Runaway Youth, March 31, 1976.

43. Houten and Golembiewski, *A Study of Runaway Youth.*

44. Gullotta, "Runaway."

45. Houten and Golembiewski, *A Study of Runaway Youth.*

46. J. Meyerding, "Early Sexual Experience and Prostitution," *American Journal of Psychiatry* 134 (1977): 1381-1385.

47. Meyerding, "Early Sexual Experience."

48. Department of Health, Education and Welfare, *Runaway Youth.*

49. F. Bolton, J. Reich, and S. Gutierres, "Delinquency Patterns in Maltreated Children and Siblings" (Paper, Arizona Community Development for Abuse and Neglect, Phoenix, Ariz., 1977).

50. R. Andrews, and A. Cohn, *PINS Processing in New York: An Evaluation.* In *Beyond Control: Status Offenders in the Juvenile Court*, ed. L. Leitelbaum and A. Gough (Cambridge, Mass.: Ballinger, 1977).

51. Harris, "Persons in Need of Supervision."

52. Ibid.

53. Ibid.

54. R. Sarri, and Y. Hansenfeld, eds., *Brought to Justice? Juveniles, the Courts and the Law* (National Assessment of Juvenile Corrections, Ann Arbor, Mich.: University of Michigan, 1976).

55. J. McLeave-Kinney, B. Madsen, T. Fleming, and D. Haapala, "Homebuilders: Keeping Families Together," *Journal of Consulting and Clinical Psychology* 45 (1977): 667-673.

56. R. Friedman, J. Quick, S. Garlock, M. Hernandez, and S. Lardieri,

"Characteristics of Adolescents Entering the Child Welfare System" (Paper, Florida Mental Health Institute, Tampa, 1978).

57. J. Garbarino, and B. Carson, "Mistreated Youth in One Community," (Paper, Boys Town, Neb.: Center for the Study of Youth Development, 1979).

58. D. Divoky, "Child Abuse: Mandate for Teacher Intervention?" *Learning* (April 1976): 14-20.

59. A. Martinez, Testimony taken at the Senate Human Resources Subcommittee on Child and Human Development hearings, San Francisco, January 4, 1979.

60. Children's Defense Fund, *Children without Homes.*

61. Ibid.

62. Ibid.

63. "Human Ecology Forum," *Child Abuse and Neglect in Residential Institutions: Selected Reading on Prevention, Investigation and Correction* (Washington, D.C.: National Center on Child Abuse and Neglect, DHEW Publication no. 78-30160).

64. Harris, "Persons in Need of Supervision."

65. Martinez, Testimony.

66. Wooden, *Weeping in the Playtime of Others.*

67. Ibid.

68. C. Henry, C. Banks, P. Zimbardo, "Interpersonal Dynamics in a Simulated Prison," Stanford, Calif., n.d., mimeographed.

69. Harris, "Persons in Need of Supervision."

70. Ibid.

71. Wisconsin Health and Social Services Department, *Juvenile Detention in Wisconsin 1976: Final Report*, 1976.

72. D. Pappenfort, and D. Kilpatrick, *A Census of Children's Residential Institutions in the United States, Puerto Rico, and the Virgin Islands: 1966, vol. 7: Detention Facilities* (Chicago: School of Social Service Administration, University of Chicago, 1970).

73. Ibid.

74. Children's Defense Fund, *Children in Adult Jails* (Washington, D.C.: Children's Defense Fund, 1976).

75. Wooden, *Weeping in the Playtime of Others.*

76. C. Bartollas, S. Miller, and S. Dinitz, *Juvenile Victimization: The Institutional Paradox* (New York: John Wiley, 1976).

77. Harris, "Persons in Need of Supervision."

78. S. Bavolek, D. Kline, J. McLaughlin, and P. Publicover, "The Development of the Adolescent Parenting Inventory (API): Identification of High-risk Adolescents Prior to Parenthood" (Paper prepared at the Utah State University, Department of Special Education, 1978).

79. Harris, "Persons in Need of Supervision."

80. J. Grisso, "Conflict about Release: Environmental and Personal

Correlates among Institutionalized Delinquents," *Journal of Community Psychology* 3 (1975): 396-399.

81. Fisher, Berdie, Cook, Radford-Barker, and Day, *Adolescent Abuse and Neglect.*

14 Conclusion

Meeting the Needs of Mistreated Children and Youth

The maltreatment of children and youth is a problem that reaches beyond victims and perpetrators in its scope. It touches the lives of all professionals and private citizens who are concerned with the quality of life in America's families.

Warren Long is a social worker in a small Midwestern city. As part of the County's Child Protective Services Unit he manages cases of child maltreatment. He feels deeply frustrated about his job. The reports keep coming in and he keeps investigating them. Despite long hours and a strong commitment to his work, Warren keeps wondering how he can influence the parents he works with. Some parents will not let him into their houses, let alone their lives. Others are so disorganized it is hard to make out the shape of their lives at all. He wants to help, but Warren sometimes feels like it is a losing battle. What strategies should he use?

Lucy Todd is the mother of three young children. Her husband works for the phone company and they are saving for a new house. All in all, her life seems to be in pretty good shape. However, there is one thing that bothers her these days, and that is her friend Betty. Betty also has three children and her husband works for the phone company, too. Maybe that is why they became friends in the first place. Lucy likes Betty, but she is disturbed by the way Betty hits her kids. Sometimes the oldest one has bruises, and there was that time last month when the youngest one had a black eye. Betty said the little girl fell. Lucy was not really convinced, but how do you go about asking your friend if she beats her kids?

Robert Lane works for the federal government in Washington, D.C. His job is to develop plans for his agency's family-assistance program to deal with child abuse and neglect. The available money seems large on paper, $3.7 million. But when it is spread across the country and filtered through the bureaucracy, it may disappear. How can he propose a plan to use the money so that it will reach the families in greatest need? What route should he take and how can he justify his decision?

Elsie Makins lives in rural New York State. She was born less than twenty miles from where she lives today. Last Sunday after church she almost stopped to talk to the minister about her problem, but then did not. That is just it.

Is it her problem, or should she mind her own business? The problem is her husband's sister, Maggie, who lives down the road about six miles. There really is not room for the four kids even if they kept the place clean, which they do not. The kids look like they never get a bath, and they are always sick or getting hurt falling over the trash. To top it off, Maggie left the kids with the 7-year-old in charge while she went out barhopping. Elsie's husband says his family always does things their own way, but she wonders how those kids will grow up healthy considering the way they live. Who can she talk to about her problem?

William Larson is a family practice physician in northern Florida. He is a bit worried about Flora Jones and her baby. He delivered the baby, so he feels some responsibility for it. Flora had a difficult pregnancy and the birth required a cesarean section. The baby was small; five pounds and two ounces. Mother and baby left the hospital together, but only after nearly two weeks. Larson has not seen either since, and it has been nearly six weeks. With nothing but his uneasiness to go on, where can he turn?

Ellen Rogers is a graduate student in child and family development at a major West Coast university. After six months of intensive reading, it is time for her to write a proposal for her doctoral dissertation research. She knows she wants to study child maltreatment but has not been able to get any more specific than that. She had hoped her reading would clarify things, but instead it has filled her head with a whirl of hypotheses, data, and theories. She needs someplace to hang what she has learned so she can see what comes next. How does she ask the right question to get her research project off on the right foot?

Steven and Betty Smithson live in Wichita, Kansas. Their three children have grown up and their furniture business is running itself these days, so they can devote themselves to the community-service projects they feel give them a sense of real accomplishment. They attended a public lecture on child abuse and now they want to do something to help. But what?

The Maze of Maltreatment

The social worker, the friend, the policymaker, the relative, the physician, the researcher, and the concerned citizen are all grappling with the problem of child abuse and neglect. Each has special needs and interests. Each perspective is different. What do they have in common? They all are stymied by the social and psychological complexities that surround maltreatment. How do you help when you cannot even gain access to the family? How do you help when to offer may break up a friendship? How do you help when you do not know where to put your resources? How do you help when you are told it is none of your business? How do you help when you do not have hard evidence? How do you help when you do not know what questions to ask?

How do we get from here to there? How do we pull together all we know to provide a map to use in our efforts to help and to understand?[1] The burgeoning of policies, programs, and research dealing with child maltreatment over the past fifteen years has provided some clues, but we still do not have a comprehensive language for describing child abuse and neglect that cuts across professional lines. Many of us are searching for such a common language. We need an understanding of abusive families that is both ecological and developmental. In this book we have tried to provide some of the vocabulary and principles for such a language. In this chapter we sketch some of our conclusions on solving the problem of maltreatment. Although most of the issues are relevant across the age span from childhood to adolescence, many are somewhat different for different stages in the life course. As stated in chapter 8, some factors are more relevant to the maltreatment of children while others apply more to adolescents. This, coupled with the very marked difference in the amount of research-based evidence to build upon, was the rationale for so clearly dividing this book into two parts.

In this concluding chapter we seek an overall ecological integration (from microsytems to macrosystems). We couch our conclusions in terms of suggestions (even exhortations) for change because we believe understanding comes from actually working with the phenomena in question, as implied in both Dearborn's Dictum (if you want to understand something, try to change it) and Lewin's Law (there is nothing so practical as a good theory). Thus to understand abusive families is to try to change them for the better (surely no one would suggest we try to change them for the worse, though the skeptic would say that many of the intervention strategies used thus far have done precisely that).

Our task, then, is to bring together an agenda for social reform that does justice to the evidence, to the moral principles involved, and to families needing assistance. We do not offer the usual shopping list of social changes needed to better approximate the millenium. We believe the evidence argues persuasively that no quick fix or band-aid intervention program will do. There are some fundamental cultural, socioeconomic, and political forces at work here. But this recognition is consistent with a very pragmatic program of social reform accomplished on the local level, in the communities and neighborhood ecological niches where families play out the dramas of their lives.[2] Perhaps our best course is to be cautious and pragmatic visionaries.

Evidence of Progress

Developing a social conscience is no small accomplishment. It is a major step in the normal development of an individual.[3] Social conscience is an important step for a whole civilization to take as well. As the often grisly history of child-hood makes abundantly clear, social conscience is a relatively recent invention with respect to the treatment of children in many cultures, including our own.

Without a concept of the child's right to nurturance and integrity (freedom from violation), there is no way to even define abuse and neglect as a problem, let alone solve it. In that sense, then, this discussion is at once both a challenge and a hopeful conclusion. It presumes that there is a social conscience to be appealed to, and that the basic right of children and youth to integrity, as we use the term, is recognized and accepted by our civilization. While both of these presumptions are not completely accurate, it would be wrong to totally deny their validity. We work from them, both because we need to believe in them and because the available evidence documents their existence, albeit in less than perfect form. This fact is a necessary resource in meeting the prob-lem of maltreatment. Our other efforts are designed to build upon and expand the integrity of children as guaranteed by individual and collective social con-science.

Having argued that there is a basis for meeting the problem of maltreat-ment, we must immediately refine the issue. The first step in this process is to be cautious in our claims and our rhetoric. One way of doing this is to refrain from indulging in the now all too familiar crisis motif in which social problems are typically cast, and then cast off.

Are we facing a child abuse and neglect crisis? Does the problem demand an immediate and massive national intervention campaign? Nearly two decades of this kind of rhetoric have led us to believe that an issue is serious only when it is proclaimed a crisis, particularly in conjunction with a congressional hearing, and is solved only when a government agency is directed to respond by politi-cians prodded into action by a spirited public demonstration of interest and support for intervention. Hunger, child pornography, declining test scores, poverty, pollution, and many other genuinely serious issues have gone this crisis-intervention route. While it may be useful and even essential for real progress, this sequence is not in itself the solution. The crux of the matter lies in the activities of what in economic terms is called the private sector.

This economic analogy is worth pursuing. Direct government efforts to deal with the problem of unemployment are marginal when compared with the impact of private enterprises: jobs numbering in the tens of thousands versus the millions. Thus government is generally recognized as the employer of last resort, at best. Moreover, its performance as an employer is not always a sterling example of efficiency or productivity. Likewise, government efforts to intervene dramatically in the problem of maltreatment are necessarily limited, both in scope and effectiveness. These limitations come from both the nature of the problem and the principles of a free society. As noted in chapter 3, we certainly do not want to pay the price of totalitarianism to deal with the problem of the maltreatment of children and youth. Those who fear we are doing this in efforts to coordinate reporting procedures and central registries are certainly right to fear such an outcome. Overall, however, we think our problem is one of too little rather than too much collective action on behalf of children. At this point, let us say that to protect the integrity of children and avoid totalitarianism we must rely upon a mix of formal and informal family-support systems, collaborative networks of good citizens, private-service agencies, relatives, neighbors, and friends to support families. In such a scheme, and only in that case, can public agencies effectively perform their function as parent of last resort, without violating the essential principles of a democratic society.

We believe that in the matter of maltreatment we have little to gain from further involvement in the crisis-intervention dynamic. This problem is so insidiously woven into the fabric of daily life, that no single dramatic intervention is likely to succeed. The necessary conditions for maltreatment—an antichild ideology and isolation from potent, prosocial support systems—inextricably link the prevention of maltreatment of children and youth with the development of a more socially integrated and humane society. Having become civilized enough to recognize abuse and neglect as a violation of a child's right to integrity, we must now build the mechanisms to guarantee that right. It is thus a chronic rather than an acute problem. It is not and never will be enough to simply and dramatically remove children from abusive homes, for example. The real test comes in the weeks, months, and years that follow. Are the family's fundamental problems addressed?

Many of our most fundamental values, institutional arrangements, and patterns of daily behavior are implicated in the problem, and in any genuine solution. Successful coping with the problem does not require some dramatic action by an agency or group of agencies to solve the crisis, once and for all. It does not depend on dramatic upheaval. Rather, it calls for a determined effort to readjust many of the day-to-day patterns of our life as a society. This is a task that can only be accomplished in small pieces. It is a matter of individuals and communities amplifying some patterns and suppressing others. It means building up community systems of support for families: values, informal relationships, and institutional structures. It means prevention.

Resources for Protecting Children and Youth

Where can we find the resources necessary to meet the problem of maltreatment? To answer this question we must compile an agenda for individuals and communities. The solution, like the problem, lies in ourselves, both individually and collectively. We can begin with five items of the highest priority.

1.   Defusing and controlling family violence.

2. Establishing and maintaining high standards for the care of children and youth, including a right to permanence for children and a measure of self-determination for adolescents.
3. Demonstrating the community's interest in its children and their families.
4. Encouraging social values and structures that strengthen families throughout their life course.
5. Studying the human ecology of the maltreatment of children and youth to improve the reservoir of research-based knowledge.

Violence in the Family

Violence is so much a part of our way of life that we hardly notice anything but the most extreme examples. Recent studies by Straus, Gelles, and Steinmetz document the pervasiveness of domestic violence.[4] They report serious domestic violence (punching, hitting with an object, and the like) occurring in 30 percent of America's families in a given year. We believe this pattern of violence is related to the problem of child maltreatment.

While the connection may seem obvious to some, it is not clear in the minds of many; one person's discipline is another's abuse.[5] Psychologist John Valusek explored this dynamic in depth and detail.[6] In his essay on the topic, Valusek argues that once we justify any act of violence against children we are clearing the way for child abuse. In fact, we are making it all but inevitable that some children will be seriously injured through the common use of force, as when a slap in the face becomes a damaging blow to the side of the head because the child turns suddenly, or through the actions of parents who lose control during the process of physically disciplining a child. Moreover, once physical force is legitimized and established as a pattern in one arena, it tends to permeate throughout a social system. Rather than defusing hostility and tension, the expression of violence tends to increase the likelihood of future violence.[7]

The old woman in the shoe is a prime example of just how dangerous it is to maintain physical force as a legitimate weapon against children. She did not know what to do so she spanked them. Some parents become involved in abuse because they do not know what else to do. But why is violence a natural response when we are frustrated in matters of child control? We believe the answer lies in one of our central hypotheses: Maltreatment is fundamentally a cultural problem. By defining the world in such a way that violence seems natural as a tool in family relations, we have set up a situation in which the possibility of abuse is always there, lurking in the background, ready to happen if touched off by a parent-child encounter that pushes the right button.

There are two things we can do. First, we can join in creating an ethic of domestic nonviolence. Spare the child. Valusek's essay is a good beginning.

We can try to live by the principle that "people are not for hitting and children are people too." Such an ethical commitment is not enough in its own right, of course. But just as progress in civil rights for racial minorities was aided by public declarations, so public expressions of an ethic of nonviolence may contribute to a climate of private nonviolence. This is the spirit of Sweden's much maligned law against spanking. Certainly we cannot fully legislate morality (as Barry Goldwater reminded civil rights activists in the mid-1960s), but we can legislate a climate that nurtures morality. Although the incest taboo does not preclude sexual encounters between prohibited family members, it does serve as a counterweight to inappropriate expressions of sexuality. The likelihood of sexual misuse does appear to be controlled in direct proportion to the closeness of the family tie and thus the cultural forcefulness of the taboo. It works better for natural fathers than for stepfathers, for example.[8] In a sense, we are looking for something in the area of family violence to serve the function of the incest taboo. Presently, one is more rather than less likely to be assaulted the closer the relationship.

Second, we can learn to control children without the use of violence. Everyone knows that children need limits to grow up successfully. But how does one provide discipline without physical punishment? How does one manage without spanking? There are alternatives. From the field of applied behavioral analysis have come many nonviolent techniques for dealing with problem behaviors in children. Some are presented in the form of effective-parenting programs offered by Family Service Associations, churches, schools, and other groups concerned with parent education. Promoting these nonviolent disciplinary techniques is one of the most important, practical ways to prevent abuse. Using them will result in living proof that nonviolent child rearing is possible and will teach by example. What is more, it will provide a stimulus for changing values and attitudes to conform to new behavioral realities. Finally, these techniques fit well with programs designed to improve the overall quantity and quality of parent-child interaction.[9] They can thus provide a strategy for creating a pattern of more adequate care in families where neglect is present.

High Standards of Care

If the old woman in the shoe is involved in child abuse, she is also involved in neglect. Child protective services document the joint occurrence of abuse and neglect in nearly 50 percent of their cases.[10] Therefore, defusing domestic violence is not enough. For one thing, it does not speak directly to the problem of neglect. Like abuse, however, neglect is fundamentally a social problem. The key is the standards we set and maintain for minimal child care. If we are to make progress in meeting this aspect of the maltreatment situation, we need to set these standards as high as is scientifically and practically possible.

Thus we must make some collective decisions about the legitimate basic needs of children and stick to those decisions. While this may sound simple in the abstract, it is difficult to accomplish in the concrete world. The politics of child care are as labyrinthine as almost any (with the exception of energy, perhaps). This, coupled with the low status of children's issues in politics, makes for an uphill fight.[11] It should make us appreciate and support the efforts of child-advocacy organizations, such as the Children's Defense Fund.

What are the minimal standards for the care of children and youth? They fall into three areas. First, we must insist that every child and adolescent has access to basic preventive health care, education, immunization, clothing appropriate to the weather, dental care, adequate nutrition, and so on. A side benefit of these efforts can be greater integration of the family in potent, prosocial support systems. As things stand now, many children and youth lack these elementary aspects of adequate care. Second, we must insist that every child is provided with adult supervision appropriate to his or her age and level of development. Young children should not be left unattended by an adult or by an adolescent. Teenagers should not be thrown out, left to their own devices, nor should they be denied the freedom to explore the broader world outside the home. As we pointed out in our introductory discussion defining maltreatment, the issue of appropriateness takes on special meaning during adolescence. Preadolescent children should receive the supervision of an adult. The several million latchkey children who return from elementary school to an empty house run the risk of being neglected. The remedy for this situation also has the effect of increasing the family's integration with prosocial support systems.

Third, we must insist that every child be involved in an enduring relationship with a responsible, caring adult. This is particularly a problem for institutions that offer substitutes for parental care, such as foster care, schools, and day care. There is growing concern that much institutional treatment[12] is systematically abusive and that much foster care is neglectful.[13] Without a guarantee of permanent placement in a stable and supportive environment, removing children from their homes is itself abusive in most circumstances. If all we can offer is institutionalized neglect, we might better leave all but those children in acute life-threatening circumstances alone. "Above all else, do not harm" is a good motto here as elsewhere.

We must insist upon an environment that is responsive to the child. In infancy this means reacting positively to the social stimuli of smiling and vocalization. Later, it means taking an interest in the child's activities, thus avoiding emotional neglect. Where there is anything to work with at all, a creative program of skills development can probably serve to enforce these standards and improve the child's life.

It is easy to say that every child must have these things. How are we to translate such moral injunctions into day-to-day policy and practice? It requires a cooperative effort among professionals, public servants, and, most importantly, concerned citizens. There must be community discussion followed by authoritative action to promulgate these standards. Parent education is as important here as it is in defusing family violence.

When we look beyond childhood to adolescence, the issue of appropriately high standards of care includes a requirement that teenagers be given information with which to evaluate their lives and their families for any deviant or socially risky patterns of behavior they may have learned at home, particularly when it comes to norms for family life.

We must recognize the existence and prevalence of adolescent abuse and help teenagers deal with the problem in a climate of support. We have yet to face the reality that by insisting on adolescents being dependent upon and answerable to their parents, we lock some teenagers into abusive environments. We must expect disruptive, self-destructive, and even bizarre behavior from youth who are caught in a web of inappropriate and destructive parental behavior. We need to validate them as victims as a starting point in establishing higher standards of care for adolescents. As things stand now, abused adolescents have few places to turn, especially if the abuse they suffer leaves no blatant physical wounds.

There are some encouraging signs. Several communities have organized programs to help abused teenagers by recognizing them as persons in need of assistance. The federal government has taken the initiative in beginning to assess the needs of mistreated youth.[14] Overall, however, the picture is a bleak one. Most mistreated youth, in most communities, have nowhere to turn. They are in a kind of social and cultural limbo without access to supportive community values or institutions.

Schools and courts can play an important role in establishing the validity of the adolescent as potential victim. Probably the most urgent need is for the people within each of these systems to become more aware of adolescent abuse, and become informed of its central role in the lives of many youth in trouble. Many victims are not even aware that the treatment they have received is unjustified and rarely volunteer details. We found in our informal discussions with teenagers that in classrooms containing mainly academically and socially troubled youth, the most common answer to the question, about how many out of each 100 kids are abused or neglected? was between eighty and ninety, while for general high school classrooms the answers clustered between two and ten. Standards of care need to be communicated to youth as well as to parents.

We need to recognize the fact that one aspect of caring for adolescents is respecting their emerging independent rights and their right to independence. This realization implies some significant changes in the way our laws define and treat adolescents. These changes would help all teenagers, but for mistreated youth they could mean a legitimate way out of an abusive situation. The cards must be stacked differently between parents and their adolescents. The balance of power in court must be more even, for not all parents can or will provide what is best for their offspring, particularly in adolescence. As things stand now, outside of severely injuring or sexually abusing their teenagers, parents may do almost as they please. Laws have been written to protect youth from neglect and emotional assault, but they generally are interpreted in a framework of nearly supreme parental authority (despite the impotence some parents feel and express). We must be sympathetic with parents who cannot handle the challenge of being responsible for the care of an adolescent in America in the future. Parents are often correct in thinking they have too little control and too much responsibility when it comes to their teenagers. Families need help as families, but we must also recognize (if only as a practical necessity) the independent needs and rights of adolescents, particularly those in abusive situations.

Demonstrating the Community's Interest

Psychologist Urie Bronfenbrenner uses the following question to highlight his analysis of America's children: Who cares for America's families?[15] This is the question we must continually ask of our communities and ourselves. Do we care? How can a community demonstrate its interest in all its children?

Several things stand out. First, a community can provide adequate financial support for the professional agencies providing child care, parent education, and child protective services. While professional services cannot be the answer by themselves, they are an essential part, particularly when they work collaboratively with informal-support systems (such as neighborhood social networks) and self-help groups (such as Parents Anonymous) to bring about higher standards of child care and children's rights.[16]

When it comes to the special needs of adolescents, the logical place to begin is with those who are already responding to other human needs, namely, the mental-health and social-service establishment. Barring some fundamental change in the delivery of human services, this is the mechanism that will provide help to abused youth if such help is to be forthcoming.[17] These agencies are mandated to serve troubled people. Their operations are established. They need only to direct their attention to abused youth, and modify programs, policies, and procedures to accommodate them. Although dealing with and preventing adolescent abuse will require changes in many other sectors and in our attitudes as well, we may as well start where we can accomplish the most in the least amount of time, with the least effort and expense possible. Workers are already trained and settled. Less lead time is necessary than would be the case in creating new agencies. While this is not always the best course of action, in the case of services for adolescents we think it more effective to tinker than to manufacture.

When we speak of services for adolescents, people often conjure up images of yet another group of clients that will burden an already overloaded system. The burden is real, but in part the task is one of shifting resources away from efforts to cope with abused adolescents as "trouble" and toward efforts to help them as "troubled." We advocate two routes for change: tailoring existing agencies to meet adolescent needs; and broadening the capacity of the services that are already offered to make room for all who need help. The first would require little or no extra funding. The second would require an expansion or shifting of resources. The struggle for adequate funding of youth services is a long-standing effort that needs to continue, for even in financial terms the cost of helping pales when compared with the cost of ignoring, particularly if a flexible strategy utilizing volunteers and self-help groups is adopted.[18]

A good first step in adapting the existing social-service structure to the special needs of adolescents is for professionals to become aware that many of the troubled youth with whom they deal are victims of abuse and as such have special needs. With that in mind, established agencies could modify their services to meet the needs of these youth. Crisis hot lines can be expanded to offer twenty-four-hour service, so that a voice is available when needed. Residential units can begin to offer part-time help, allowing teenagers to make regular visits during predictable trouble times, weekends, for example. This would allow youth to remain a part of their communities and help them avoid the dangers of institutionalization. There is a crying need for short-term respite shelter, in which youth can receive no-questions-asked protective care away from home when domestic problems (particularly chronic ones) reach occasional, acute crisis proportions. Another way for the community to demonstrate its concern is for mental-health and other agencies to ask their younger clients about abuse at home as part of regular counseling and preventive programs.

The Problem of Categorization

One reason our nation's social-service system fails to meet the needs of mistreated youth is because of the way it developed, a little at a time, along a rehabilitative medical model.[19] Each agency was established in response to a specific problem and was organized around meeting a specific need. As a result, our system is based on categorical programs that deal exclusively with alcohol or drug abuse, or that only aid in family planning, vocational guidance programs, and so on. Professionals within the system need to be able to label the problem before they can assign the person to services and services to the person. Although they may want to help the whole person, individual helpers in these agencies must swim against a strong bureaucratic tide.

This segmented structure causes many abused adolescents to plug into the system through their own deviant behavior, be it drug dependency, truancy, or running away. Caseworkers know that most of the problems that a given family may present to a variety of different agencies often stem from the same source of dysfunction. A single problem can have many symptoms as well as multiple consequences. A single-parent family headed by an unemployed alcoholic, for example, can (and often does) wind up on numerous case loads. If our agencies were designed to deal with any need a family may have, that family would be served both more comprehensively and with less stigmatization. Some alternative agencies for youth have taken this generic approach, offering medical, legal, and mental-health services to any teenager who needs them, regardless of the nature of the problem that brought him or her through the door. This is the philosophy behind multiservice centers such as The Door in New York City and Face-to-Face in St. Paul, Minnesota. The recent national review of services for abused adolescents endorsed this approach.[20] Supporting such programs is one way a community can show that it cares for its youth.

Second, a community can make it clear to all families that it abhors domestic violence and insists upon adequate child care. This means electing public officials whose views on these matters clearly support a nonviolent, caring environment for children. It means insisting that the schools be positive models of both nonviolent discipline and active care so that they do not exemplify abuse or neglect. As noted in chapter 7, this positive modeling is not to be taken for granted. It means employing judges, county attorneys, and police who implement this goal in their day-to-day handling of child-maltreatment cases. Third, it means providing active support for communitywide child- and family-advocacy efforts such as an official family week or child-abuse-awareness week which includes explicit statements by community leaders (particularly from business and government) in support of nonviolent family relations and high standards of child care. Civic groups must take the lead in shaping community consciousness using "spare the child" as a slogan for community awareness. In addition, the community can demonstrate a special concern for adolescent victims.

Reported adolescent abuse is the province of the community's protective service, typically part of the welfare or social-services department. As things now stand, these agencies are up to their ears—or worse still, over their heads—providing short-term intervention for families that abuse young children. As a result, these agencies tend to defer adolescents in favor of children. There are several reasons. Children who are physically abused generally sustain more severe injuries than do adolescents. They are more physically vulnerable. Their crises usually seem more acute and more immediate than the typical teenager's. Caseworkers may feel more sympathy for them, and the community certainly does. Instead of requiring caseworkers to make choices between children and adolescents, we advocate that communities underwrite the appointment of one or more staff members as specialists in adolescent abuse. These people would receive all reports involving teenagers and deal with them exclusively. Such specialists need to be temperamentally and programmatically prepared for the challenges of working with adolescents.[21] Protective-service agencies usually can authorize some services (such as day care for young children) but they generally provide little treatment on their own. Their role is closer to brokerage, advocacy, or referral, both on behalf of the individuals with specific agencies and on behalf of adolescent victims in general with the total community, and it is just what is needed in many adolescent-abuse cases.

Another thing that communities can do is support protective-service agencies in monitoring recidivism by checking on old child-abuse cases to see if abuse has recurred. More than half the families officially reported for abuse have done it more than once before.[22] The success in dealing with child abuse is one of the principal causes of adolescent abuse. Virtually every state has a central registry that contains information about the incidents that have generated reports of abuse. This can prevent "hospital shopping" (taking a repeatedly injured child to more than one medical facility), and can provide the basis for the kind of follow-up we envision. It may also aid in verifying whether an abuse case involving an adolescent began in childhood or in adolescence. This, like many of the needed expansions of service, requires a strong coordinating force empowered by the community to promote cooperation and sharing among agencies.

Protective services cannot handle the multiple problems of abusive families. In one metropolitan community two-thirds of the cases were referred to one or more human-service agencies.[23] The success of protective services depends upon the success of these referrals. This highlights the need for informed and trusting relationships among agencies.

Right now, most communities offer sporadic, short-term services to abusive and neglectful families. These services are sometimes independent of other community-service programs, in part because referrals often fail: Clients refuse service, agencies refuse to serve because criteria are not met, liaison is inadequate. Many families in trouble need lots of help, from psychotherapy to budget management to family planning. Being crisis-oriented, child-protection services generally are not designed to meet such divergent long-term needs. Other agencies must help. Unfortunately, the current structure of most social-service systems encourages competition instead of cooperation. Professionals often are forced to compete for funding and clientele. If all service agencies functioned as a unit (the generic approach) devoted to helping any problem, people might receive more cohesive and comprehensive service.[24] This would require organizational changes, for unless all a community's helping agencies are one in fact, they will have a hard time functioning as if they are one in spirit. The community-council approach in which the community's power structure is drawn into a regular relationship with the network of social-service agencies around the issue of maltreatment is one way to forge this alliance.[25] Such an organization can establish and support norms and structures of cooperation, and can provide the muscle needed to make cooperation happen where it otherwise might succumb to interagency rivalries.

Whenever abuse is reported, there are many tough decisions that must be made. Working with needy families entails making judgments in many areas: medical, legal, psychological. No individual or agency acting alone can do a good job making these far-ranging decisions. Without community-support systems providing feedback and nurturance to the protective-service agency and others involved, it is unlikely that either the best interests of the youth or the community will be served. All of this points to asking several people, each with expertise in a different area, to decide collectively what services a given family should receive. The multidisciplinary team concept is a strong one for child-abuse cases and has special relevance to cases involving abused teenagers. Unfortunately, the concept is too often given only lip service in actual practice. Multidisciplinary teams can assess the situation and make recommendations for both long-term rehabilitation and short-term crisis management.[26] The major participants on such teams are protective-service workers, but other professionals such as nurses, pediatricians, foster-care staff, lawyers, law-enforcement officials, and psychologists may participate part-time. The team generally is not involved with direct service; it decides which course of action is best and ideally performs the all-important function of following up on cases. Central to these deliberations is the role that out-of-home placement will play in the case. Unless the foster-care implications are realistically considered, case management will be a figment of the team's imagination. Given the special problems of foster care when it comes to teenagers, this is specially important in adolescent-abuse cases.

Even though adolescents are injured less severely than infants, they end up out of their homes just as often. We do not know exactly where they are going, but any setting without counseling will not help abused youth understand themselves or their parents. As noted earlier, institutions that provide their clientele with thorough counseling and support services are the exception. Also there is little or no provision for counseling within foster care.[27] No one advocates taking youth from their parents needlessly, but teenagers frequently are placed outside their homes.[28]

One of the primary responsibilities of the social-service community is to make sure that no one is institutionalized needlessly. Mistreated youth are at high risk for institutionalization primarily because of the psychological damage they have sustained, their frequent bouts of unmanageability, and parental inclination to reject them. They are more likely to behave in some deviant way, and they are also less likely to "play the game" well when dealing with a bureaucracy. Service professionals must make sure that institutionalization is only a last resort. Community leaders must work to increase the number and quality of alternative placements so that the last resort is not the first by default.

During the past ten years, agencies have sprung up to help adolescents with all sorts of problems. These agencies often are classed as alternatives since they offer services outside the established system.[29] They have taken the form of runaway houses, crisis centers, drug-rehabilitation programs, family-planning clinics, hot lines, and referral agencies. Their presence has no doubt improved the lot of troubled youth, but three main problems block their effectiveness: (1) there are not enough of them and they are practically nonexistent outside metropolitan areas; (2) most are on shaky fiscal grounds; and (3) many do not have smooth working relationships with the regular social-service agencies in their communities.

One of the most important functions that an alternative agency can have is that of advocacy. On a collective basis, this means lobbying for the legitimate rights of young people. Individually, it means watching after the interests of the adolescents who have sought help at the agency's door. Both processes can set the alternative agencies in conflict with the established ones. Both processes can work if the agency has good connections with sympathetic professionals and community leaders.

One needs a roster of sympathetic individuals within other community agencies to provide access to speedy and competent help. Individuals within agencies account for much of the success or failure of a particular referral. Workers also need to act as intermediaries between the different institutions that may be dealing with a given teenager. Running interference for a client is a necessary service, and is the common denominator of youth-advocacy services. The roster of sympathetic professionals is an essential part of such advocacy efforts if they are to be more than sound and fury. Such a roster should include people who work in the settings where adolescents normally spend time (schools and youth groups) as well as in the settings for troubled youth.[30]

A national survey of how communities were serving abused youth found a rift between many established child protective-service units and their local alternative counterparts.[31] Whether because of differences in life-style or philosophy or because of simple territoriality, these agencies do not seem to be working well together in many communities. The problem would arise less often if social services formed a network that could be entered at any point, that dealt with any problem from school failure to drug abuse to physical injury to running away. Youth hot lines and other referral services could then offer generic service. It is imperative that child protective-service units and alternative agencies function cooperatively. A caring community can take the lead in forging such cooperative relationships.

In part because of the inadequacy of community support, the average social-service caseworker does not last long in the field, particularly in protective services. Burnout, the much-discussed problem that stimulates such a high turnover rate, is caused by the burden of large case loads and other stresses that overwhelm workers and make them feel incapable of doing a good job. Professionals who are in the process of burning out tend to exhibit some common symptoms: They tend to minimize involvement with the client through physical distancing, fail to maintain eye contact, shorten interviews, label the client in a derogatory manner, begin to treat their clients as mere cases, going by the book in every detail; yet they often work excessive overtime.[32]

Of all areas of social casework, child-protection services must be one of the most arduous. In addition to the normal feelings of responsibility that providing human services brings, workers must literally make life and death decisions. They must decide who gets removed from the home, who gets what type of care, and who gets helped at all. These professionals are given the task of salvaging human beings from very painful circumstances. No training can ever fully protect them from the emotional drain that trying to help so many desperate people will cause. This sort of stress has some predictable effects, including denial and inhibition of anger, anxiety about physical harm, need for emotional gratification from clients, feelings of incompetence, anxiety about the effects of a decision, denial and projection of responsibility, feeling totally responsible for the assigned families, having difficulty separating personal from professional responsibility, needing to be in control, and even feeling victimized.[33] These workers will probably doubt their own professional and personal fitness at times. They need support.

We need to recognize that it is not humanly possible for people to function well under such crushing responsibility for extended periods of time without a great deal of compensatory feedback and encouragement. We must provide these workers with some sort of occasional diversion to prevent them from systematically burning themselves out. They need breaks: time to attend in-service training or catch up on their paperwork, for example. Another tool is the professional support group. In these groups, those who deal with abuse professionally share these experiences, frustrations, and solutions. A support group can be no less helpful for those who must experience abuse vicariously several times a day than it is for actual victims and perpetrators.[34] Important as such support groups are, however, a supportive community is of equal or greater importance.

As mentioned earlier, one reason why abused youth do not receive better help is that our system of helping them is so fragmented. A teenage prostitute who has run away from sexual abuse at home and who also has a drug-dependency problem could be processed through the courts, a residential institution, a chemical-dependency treatment program, and foster care without anyone ever realizing that she was abused. Until a community makes a concerted effort to coordinate the way it deals with adolescent abuse, people will continue to wind up buried in the files. The problem of family violence touches nearly every social-service agency. The people who must help people cope with these problems need to function within a coherent framework, for regardless of its dedication, no one agency can ever hope to help abused youth alone.

Someone needs to call the local service professionals together. It makes very little difference who does it. Alternative agencies, child protective services, the juvenile court, mental-health agencies, volunteer groups, and schools are all capable of calling these professionals together. Organizations, such as the National Committee for the Prevention of Child Abuse, could play a role through affiliated local organizations. Different agencies have taken the lead in different communities.[35] The important thing is that someone does it.

The first step this coalition should take is to find out what is going on in the community. We do not really have a national social-service system. It is instead a patchwork of more than 3,000 county systems. That entails a local survey of the available resources. Many groups have already surveyed the services available to youth in their cities: San Francisco, New York, Charleston, and Tacoma, to name a few. This initial survey should be fairly swift. It is, after all, only a means to an end, and an in-depth scrutiny could block the whole process because of the time involved. Once such a survey is done, the organizing force can call a communitywide conference to discuss adolescent abuse and the local response to it. This group could then map out a strategy for dealing with teenage victims of abuse. The idea is to create a system that makes sure that no matter where youth enter it, they will be guided to the help they need.

Once basic decisions are made, this group can offer training to the local service community designed to raise their consciousness of adolescent abuse as well as to help them deal with it. It can also begin to involve other local groups. For example, it might offer an intensive workshop on empathy for child protective-service workers or on outlining the symptoms and dynamics of abuse for mental-health counselors. It might sponsor a training session for foster parents on building interpersonal skills and raising the self-esteem of victims in their care. It might gather administrators, commissioners, legislators, and law-enforcement officials to discuss their adversary roles with regard to abuse, weighing protection against rehabilitation. Those individuals who process abuse cases through the courts could be asked for their opinions on specific problems, such as the precise ingredients that a doctor's statement in court should include.[36]

One essential task for this group is public education. Letting people know that they do not need to be mistreated does no good if there is no place for them to go for help. However, since the image of youth and adolescent victims among professionals is part of the problem here, changing that image among those who deal professionally with youth is part of the solution. Communities that have started public awareness campaigns report a predictable increase in reporting. The machinery to respond must be in place before the public is informed. A foundation of public sympathy and concern, not a knee-jerk response, is the goal. The needs exist, and they will overwhelm the system if it is not securely in place and ready to deal with the cases. For this reason, any public education program should emphasize the importance of self-help groups and volunteers as adjuncts to professional service programs.

Strengthening Families

One way to help prevent child maltreatment is to support families in times of crisis, such as when unemployment or illness produces acute stress. A second way is to provide special services to families at high risk for maltreatment because of the values or prior experience of the parents, or some special developmental difficulty of the child. A third is to strengthen the family as a social entity. This last area is at the heart of the matter and can be accomplished in several ways.

It is easy to see how strengthening families is an essential part of our efforts to solve the problem of maltreatment. If we increase the psychological and social resources of parents, we increase the likelihood that they can and will provide adequate care for their children. But we cannot ignore the fact that our analysis clearly points to a need to go beyond conventional notions of strengthening families by equipping them to stand on their own alone and be self-sufficient. Indeed, it is precisely this go-it-alone mentality that we have repeatedly criticized. We believe one of the most important ways to strengthen families is by building bridges between their members and the outside world. Positive dependency (interdependency, really) is our goal, in addition to individual coping skills. Our ecological perspective tells us that families *are* dependent upon other social systems, like it or not. These connections must work for rather than against families. This idea undergirds our ideas about opening up and building social bridges as a way of strengthening families.

1. Use the health-care system as a support system for families. The birth of a child is an event that offers a special opportunity to promote social connection. Even isolated and alienated families can be ready for increasing their social relationships when a child is born. We can capitalize on this receptivity. We could provide a "health visitor" to every family when a child is born. This person would begin visiting even before the baby is born and continue well afterward. Paraprofessionals, even volunteers can perform this role in most cases, and leave specially trained professionals to deal with only the most difficult or risky cases. The key is to provide an enduring relationship with the same caring person. This can be extended to other institutions as well, such as

schools. In fact, our goal should be a seamless social fabric in which the family is smoothly handed over from institution to institution as the child and family move through the life course. The physician or midwife bridges to the health visitor who bridges to the preschool teacher or day-care center worker who bridges eventually to the elementary school teacher. Such an approach builds strength into the family-community relationship, and stands on firm ground as a part of the ecology of the child's life.[37]

This health-visitor approach is part of a broader concept, however. Many observers have commented that our approach to medicine tends to focus on curing diseases rather than promoting health. The former is much less useful in dealing with child abuse and neglect than is the latter. If we think of the health-care system as a family-support system, we quickly recognize that it goes hand-in-hand with preventive medicine, for example, well-baby visits, immunization, dietary counseling, and life-style management. In both cases, the family develops a relationship with health-care providers. For our purposes, however, that relationship is best when it combines connections to specific individuals over a long period (to develop feelings of attachment) with contact with a variety of individuals (to add a note of objectivity). Let us be clear that we are not talking about some intrusive Big-Brother approach, but rather a natural extension of our traditional family practice, ministering to the family's needs. This begins with the birth of a child.

As we have learned more and more about childbirth and early infancy, it has become apparent that the more actively involved and in control of the situation the parents are, the greater is their feeling of attachment to the infant. The stronger these feelings, the less likely it is that the family will have trouble caring for the baby. Thus family-centered childbirth (such as the Lamaze method), father involvement in delivery, breast-feeding, and parent-infant contact in the first minutes of life, all can be used to promote a stronger family bond. Here, as in all our efforts, the goal is to increase the family's social and psychological resources. By viewing birth as a social event and capitalizing on its implicit power, we can take advantage of the opportunity it presents us with.

2. Recognize and encourage the role of natural-helping networks and natural neighbors. Where do most people get most of the help they need and receive on a day-to-day basis? Most of us rely mainly on friends, relatives, and neighbors. Just as our economy depends on the free enterprise system, so our social services are mainly provided by exchanges of assistance that are not professionally run. Once we recognize this, we have taken an important step. Several questions leap out at us: What are the existing networks in which the family is already or could potentially become involved? Are there individuals who are particularly adept at or interested in helping others in their neighborhood? Can they provide the missing link between the professional

responsible for child protection and the families in a given area? If we invest the time and energy to gain the trust of an area's natural-helping networks, we can use that relationship to enhance prevention, case identification, and treatment.[38] All our efforts are a coherent campaign aimed at increasing the professional's access to the community's social resources and the community's access to the professional's expertise. Everybody needs a friend, and every friend sometimes needs help to be both a good friend and a good citizen. Alice Collins and Diane Pancoast call this strategy the consultation model.[39] In it, the professional works with key citizens and neighbors on behalf of children and their families.

3. Wherever possible, use trained volunteers and self-help groups. Self-help groups, such as Parents Anonymous, are effective and cost relatively little to operate.[40] This cost effectiveness promises to be of increasing importance in coming years. But volunteers, no matter how well-trained and how highly motivated, and self-help groups, no matter how emotionally involved and caring, are not going to solve all problems. No one specific strategy will. They can, however, handle many situations, thus freeing the professional for the situations that are too volatile or too unattractive for lay intervention. Moreover, professional resources can be concentrated in a way that is rarely possible now. Programs, such as Homebuilders in Tacoma, Washington, can be used more widely. In the Homebuilders Program a team of counseling specialists can rally around a family in trouble when all conventional approaches have failed and family breakup is imminent. The therapeutic team spends all its time with the family—for up to six weeks if necessary—trying to rescue parents and children from dysfunction. The available evidence argues that this approach works.[41]

In discussing adolescent abuse in chapter 9, we identified two patterns of abuse affecting adolescents. The first was child-abuse victims grown older, and the second was composed of youth who are abused for the first time during adolescence. As stated earlier, according to the very limited evidence available, adolescent abuse is neatly divided between the two patterns. Teenagers from the two groups are likely to present professionals with very different problems, problems that require different treatment. This fact has direct implications for service delivery. For one thing, the later abuse begins, the less likely it is to result in physical and intellectual damage, and the more likely it is to involve sexuality in one way or another. The families involved with child abuse seem to be quite different from those that become abusive at adolescence, at least when viewed from the outside.

Long-term abuse, as stated earlier, generally comes from families with many more social and economic stresses than are found among families that abuse the child for the first time in adolescence. Families in which abuse began in childhood are more likely to have only one parent, to be poor, to be transient, and to have an intergenerational pattern of child abuse. By the time the children of such families reach adolescence, their parents may have exposed them to more than a decade's worth of inadequate care. Neither the teenagers nor the parents are likely to feel good about their relationships, nor will they be particularly disposed to discuss the matter, a source of failure, with outsiders.

In contrast, while parents who have never abused their child before may not have had an idyllic family life, they have refrained from abuse for at least ten years. This means that they have managed as parents (at least in comparison with those who began abuse during childhood) until they fail to meet the challenge of coping with a teenager. They may be more inclined to discuss parenthood because they have some positive feelings about parenthood and they may therefore be more willing to change their behavior in order to regain their original state of equilibrium. The task here may be much more one of rehabilitation. One very important aspect of the problem is the need to work with parents while a teenager is out of the home (for example, because of running away) to smooth the youth's reentry into the family.[42]

Clinician-researcher Jo Ann Cook has gone so far as to recommend differential treatment of families, based upon the age of the child at the initial abuse.[43] She believes that while the prognosis for families whose abuse began with adolescence is good, it is bleak for those who have developed well-established patterns of abuse. In light of the limited resources available, she recommends that clinicians reserve their family-oriented work for families that are basically sound. For chronic, long-term abuse families, she recommends that professionals concentrate on the child rather than attempt family remediation. In some cases, removal of the child in preparation for independent living may be the best move, she believes, though this measure is not always necessary. This proposition deserves serious consideration and further study. If a well-designed group home or therapeutic foster care is available, it may well be the best course of action for long-term victims. The relative wisdom of removal is in part a developmental matter; it may be more appropriate for teenagers than for children, more for chronic than for acute problems.

There are many specific services that local agencies could provide to abused youth and their families, some to one group more than another. Mental-health agencies could offer peer self-help groups for abuse victims.[44] They could also offer support groups for abusive parents.[45] They could counsel the parents of a runaway while the youth is absent in order to smooth the eventual reentry.[46] They could offer training in development for families that would include information about the adolescent and midolescent stages in the life cycle. They could also alert concerned parents to the consequences of physical punishment, promote nonviolent forms of conflict resolution, and deal with the knotty problems of adolescent sexuality, particularly where stepparents are concerned.

Agencies dealing with the foster-care system should treat the placement of an adolescent for what it is: a deal. Teenagers are completely capable of leaving any setting they do not like. With adolescents, a foster-care relationship is a mutual arrangement in that the youth's consent must be received if it is to be successful. Caseworkers also should consider the possible wrenching effect of placing a teenager in an unfamiliar community. Greater attention to an adolescent's own social network might pay off in terms of more durable and effective placements. Concerned relatives may offer an untapped resource to workers making placements, but legislative and policy revisions may be necessary to make use of them. One particularly promising concept for successful placement of teenagers is therapeutic foster care. One of its proponents, Robert Friedman, describes it like this.[47]

> Therapeutic foster homes differ from traditional foster homes in that the foster parents are specifically recruited to work with the seriously disturbed children, they are paid a stipend above and beyond the money paid to regular foster parents, they receive special training, and additional professional and social supports are built in. In most cases only one child is placed per home, and rarely would there be more than two children per home. The foster parents generally go through a minimum of twenty hours of preservice training beyond the general orientation to foster care, and then are expected to attend periodic inservice training sessions. A professional counselor or caseworker is assigned to from eight to twelve youngsters, generally, with the expectation of conducting at least one treatment session per week for each youngster. In addition, the foster parents receive the benefits of a face-to-face contact with the professional staff member weekly. This is a marked contrast with regular foster care where the foster parents may go several weeks, or even months in between visits from caseworkers. A specific attempt is often made in therapeutic foster homes to build amongst the various families a cohesive network that provides emotional and social support for its members. This is almost akin to creating an "extended family" for each household, since the foster parents are encouraged to assist each other in ways that extended family members have traditionally done.

But all the important changes that agencies and institutions combined can make are probably insufficient. Our ecological perspective points out that there are sources of risk in our macrosystem, in the blueprints we use to define and organize our lives. We need to make the difficult and slow progress on these basic cultural issues. There are two major areas that deserve attention here: Our criteria for determining personal worth and our standards of acceptable behavior during family conflict.

Our materialistic ethic undermines the sense of self-worth in people of moderate means and contributes to family conflict. People who feel they are not good enough, based upon their lack of accumulated wealth, will not feel especially good about their activities. This applies to parenthood. For the economically secure, ascription to this materialistic ethic is lamentable. It may cause needless problems since a strong sense of self-worth is the key element in sensitive, responsive parental behavior.

Obviously, a shift in values would solve the problem for the middle class. But for the poor this is not enough, and poverty remains the central problem facing child-abusing families.[48] In our materialistic society, economic inadequacy is widespread and is related to social impoverishment. It is no wonder people who are reminded every day that they are worth less than most other people because they earn less do not always feel or act like competent parents. In this way, child abuse really is a class phenomenon. Certainly adolescent victims who have a history of abuse come from this context. Every time abusing parents hit their children, they reinforce their own conviction that they are inadequate parents. Rejection of our materialistic ethic and redistributing the wealth of this country are goals that many have and will continue to work for. The role of these goals in defusing the problem of abuse is just one more reason for advocating them.

In terms of direct impact upon abuse, however, the ground rules we set for family conflict are more important than the economic issues. We do not get upset about family members hitting or slapping each other the way we would if strangers were to be similarly assaultive: the first is normal, the second, criminal. If someone will not listen to reason, we generally permit a family member to use violence.[49] We must take violence within families as seriously as we do violence between strangers. To do that we need to provide families with nonviolent mechanisms for resolving conflicts. The family-teaching model offers real hope in this area.[50] Others exist.[51] People need to learn to fight fairly and to air their grievances in a controlled, nonviolent way. To do this we need greater reliance on the rational presentation of grievances without value judgments, on bargaining toward compromise, and on effective action that carries out the dictates of the resolution. Parents need practical suggestions to do this, particularly when the natural forces at work in the family facing adolescence work in the opposite direction.[52]

Studying the Human Ecology of Child Maltreatment

No discussion of child abuse and neglect is complete without a request for more thoughtful research on the topic. The methodological problems involved are staggering.[53] Finding an adequate sample to study, devising appropriate measures to use, and designing valid comparisons between groups and treatments is enough to drive the investigator either into despair or into some less-than-adequate compromise between expediency and validity.

The very difficulty of the challenge makes it more important that communities support further research. The evidence so far is helpful despite its limitations and inability to provide comprehensive answers. We know much more than we did about the prevalence of routine domestic violence because of Straus and his colleagues.[54] We know much more than we did about the possibilities and limitations of using questionnaires to predict who is at risk for becoming involved in abuse from the work of Helfer[55] and others.[56] We now know something about the elements of effective treatment programs,[57] the characteristics of families seen by hospital-based service units,[58] and the background of neglecting parents.[59] And as we have tried to show in our own discussions, we know a little about the neighborhood ecology of child maltreatment.[60] All this is encouraging, and there are other examples of research programs that are shedding light on child maltreatment. Still we need to know more, and our discussion thus far contains many hypotheses for studies of how to prevent child maltreatment by working on the human ecology of the family from the microsystem to the macrosystem. This need for improved information is particularly pressing when it comes to adolescents.

We began our discussion of adolescent abuse in chapter 8 with a cautionary note regarding the dearth of reliable research dealing with adolescent abuse. We have precious little to use beyond the gross information contained in the American Humane Association's National Clearinghouse of reported cases. As we noted, these data do not address the vital issue of whether or not there was a childhood history of abuse, and therefore are of diminished value for our purposes. There are only a handful of studies specifically directed at adolescent abuse.[61]

We need studies that examine exactly the problem's relationship to adolescent and adult sexuality. We need to know just how much of the trouble is accounted for by stepparents and single-parent families (with and without some second adult in the household through a relationship with the parent). We need to know how often midolescence figures into the problem. Further research is needed on how youth-saving institutions and agencies fit into the picture. We need answers to questions such as: Can the school fill a preventive role by sponsoring classes on nonviolent conflict reduction? How can child protective services work more effectively with alternative agencies to meet the needs of mistreated youth? What kinds of foster care work best with adolescents?

Bringing the Developmental Perspective to Fruition

In this chapter we presented an agenda for change that can harness our practical social conscience in pursuit of an idealized world in which community and family work together on behalf of the development of children and youth. Some of the issues have greater relevance for children than for teenagers (and vice versa), though most are important across the board. We believe basic economic issues are most important in protecting young children, while "rights" issues are most important for adolescents who need the community's support in negotiating ground rules with parents. The special issues for adolescents come from the poor credibility of the adolescent as victim and the necessity of "empowering" adolescents (to use Albee's term) in their own defense. In the matter of prevention, the two central issues are (1) providing more effective community responses to child maltreatment to cut off the flow of "child-abuse cases grown up" and (2) increasing the social skills of both parents and youth to aid them in navigating the tricky currents and crosscurrents of early adolescence.

The mistreatment of youth is a social problem. Manis proposed three criteria for assessing the seriousness of social problems: (1) primacy, or how much the problem acts as a cause of other problems and is the result of multiple factors; (2) magnitude, which refers to the extent or frequency in the population; and (3) severity, which concerns the degree or level of harmfulness.[62] In these terms, maltreatment is a serious problem primarily because of its primacy and severity. It stimulates many other problems (including running away, delinquency, future child abuse, and psychological deficiencies), and it evolves from a complex set of social and psychological forces at work in the family. It is a severe problem because it appears that many of its victims experience highly impaired functioning that may well continue into adulthood. The least serious aspect of the problem is its magnitude. Most families do not mistreat their offspring. However, the primacy and severity of the problem, even in the realtively small percentages of the population involved, make maltreatment a very serious problem.

As we see it, we need to change many things on many levels to cope with this problem. We need to make some organizational changes in our social-service systems. We need more information about it. We need to mobilize the resources of our schools. We need some legislated change in the status of youth in general, and in relation to their families in particular. More fundamentally, we need to change the way we think about families, violence, power, and youth. As always, we must examine these patterns in the social contexts in which they occur.

Teachers, counselors, probation officers, and police need to be constantly alert to the possibility that the youth with whom they are dealing may be abused or neglected. This parallels the need for these gatekeepers to consider the role of learning disabilities in the behavior of troubled youth. The experience of a national program to increase this awareness among police suggests it can help teenagers to be served rather than merely processed when they exhibit delinquent behavior.[63] It is especially important that key people in the schools and law-enforcement agencies know the local social-service system and its people. No effort to change the way a community deals with adolescent abuse can afford to ignore these two institutions and the people who run them. There is no substitute for personal connections.

The Role of Schools in Prevention

Schools have made great gains in some aspects of helping abuse victims, primarily in compliance with mandatory reporting laws. Nearly all large school districts, and most small ones, now provide referrals and some counseling services for abuse victims. Most school districts now have a formal policy on abuse.[64] And more than half of our large school districts have even conducted their own campaigns to educate the public about abuse, though few small ones have done so.[65]

But the school can perform its most effective role in the area of prevention. Schools cannot be ignored in any community campaign that hopes to improve the lot of abused teenagers. Through the schools we can reach nearly all youth without any fear of labeling. Preventive efforts can take many forms. Concerned schools can attune educators in elementary and junior high schools to issues of parent-child conflict, so they can better address those issues informally with students. Teachers can also become more sensitive to the special needs of abused youth, even providing them with special in-class attention.

Parent-teacher organizations could sponsor classes for parents in nonviolent conflict resolution, sexuality, and the dynamics of reconstituted families involving stepparents, and take an official stand against physical punishment at school. The National Parent Teachers Association is preparing an educational program for parents, informing them of the hazards of corporal punishment at school, as well as viable alternative disciplinary measures.[66] The training would reach parents in the social mainstream and could begin to turn our collective attitudes toward more reasonable methods of conflict resolution. Schools can offer classes in life management and human development; some already do. These classes can begin to prepare youth for the decisions they will need to make as parents.[67] By showing teenagers exactly what babies are capable of doing, the classes also could help eliminate the unrealistic expectations held by many abusing parents.[68] A course in adolescent development could give students insight into themselves. If they gain a thorough understanding of adolescence, such a course might even help when their own children reach that age, though the long-term effectiveness of parent education is undocumented. Schools might also help teenagers in foster care or in group homes to become integrated into classroom life. Such help is crucial for youth returning to schools from institutions.

But there is another way that the schools can help teenagers: by recognizing the fact that traditional education is frustrating to those who do not succeed at it. People do not like to encounter their defeats on a daily basis. Yet those who do not perform well academically are expected to attend regularly and behave themselves properly while in school. Instead of planning some alternate form of education for these students, the school often expells them. A report by the Children's Defense Fund charges that the youth most in need of help are likely simply to be excluded from schools.[69] Schools also can become active in promoting youth self-help groups and general awareness of adolescent abuse so that the powerful processes of the adolescent peer group are working on behalf of victims.[70]

The Juvenile-Justice System

The other major secondary-service system, dealing even more directly with abuse, is the criminal-justice system. Since many abused youth come to the courts because of their own offensive acts, attorneys and judges need to be alert to abuse symptoms. The correlations we drew earlier between abuse and serious hard-core delinquency (particularly if it involves violence) are so strong that it is not unrealistic to recommend an attitude of *assuming* the youth has been mistreated until proven otherwise. The assumption of "innocent by virtue of abuse" is a good starting point because it simultaneously tells the court that intervention is required and that rehabilitation of the offender's social skills is a precondition for future good behavior. The acknowledgment and introduction of a juvenile's family history in the courtroom can change the disposition of his or her case dramatically. The juvenile-justice system itself is slow. Adolescents who encounter the court solely as a result of abuse also should be given priority on the docket because of the potential for developmental damage. Cases that involve both adult criminal charges for the parents and child-dependency hearings for the adolescent should be coordinated to avoid undue delay. This is the thrust of new initiatives in the area of legal services to mistreated youth.[71]

Because the system is so complicated, teenagers need someone to help them navigate it. Courts could provide volunteers to watch over a given case and appear in court with the youth to make sure his or her interests are protected. Such services are becoming more common. The volunteers are called guardian *ad litem*, and they usually need some legal or paralegal training.[72]

The burden of proof must be lightened in abuse cases. Since teenage bodies are less likely to show physical damage, the grounds for providing services to adolescents need to be broader. Someone must be empowered to make the decision of whether or not the family can be helped. Once that decision is made, the wheels should move quickly. The multidisciplinary team we described would best be able to make such a significant decision. The whole adversary proceeding through the court should be used cautiously.

One little-used response to dysfunctional families with adolescents is emancipation, the process that allows minors to live independently of their parents, giving them the rights they would need to do so. Many states have emancipation procedures, but almost all require parental consent. When the home is inhospitable and the youth is capable of living alone, emancipation is a nonrestrictive solution. Providing the small amount of support that an older teenager would need to maintain a household takes much less time and energy than does placing him or her in the care of an adult or an institution. It also increases the likelihood that the adolescent will not be mistreated by the person who is supposed to be providing care. For many youth, especially those who have suffered severe, prolonged abuse, independent living may present an insurmountable challenge because of their damaged social skills and psyche. But there are adolescents who could manage quite well independently. Obviously, parental permission is often an obstacle that prevents such an arrangement, and laws might be changed so that a neutral third party can play a larger role. This is the thrust of recent Swedish legislative initiatives dealing with procedures to permit children to be divorced from their parents. When circumstances permit, independent living is a legitimate solution that should be an option. We need every option to meet the wide range of needs manifest among mistreated youth.

In the same vein, we need to recognize that runaway youth are functionally emancipated. As things stand now, a lack of rights and resources leaves runaways with no means of legitimate support. We must recognize that regardless of the reason for leaving home, these youth are living independently, and we may need to allow them to do so within the law. Underage runaways should be able to attend school, enter into contracts, rent housing, consent to the provision of medical care, and work nights. We need to allow youth to get help without their parent's permission. In Nebraska, for example, a teenager cannot even receive counseling for more than ninety days without parental consent. Granting these rights would not condone or encourage running away, it would merely allow those who have left home to survive. It would recognize the fact that many runaways had no other choice but to leave their parents. It would begin to lift a little of the burden of the situation from the teenager. As one child advocate puts it: "The onus of responsibility (for children's running away) needs to be shifted, at least in part, from the minor to the other systems in society—most notably, the family."[73] Counseling parents of runaways while the youth is out of the home could help to determine the underlying causes of the behavior as well as smooth the runaway's reentry into the family, when such a reapproach is possible.

The jailing of children is a repugnant practice that has been terminated on the federal level and in many states. Youth advocates now are pressing states to comply with the federal directive to deinstitutionalize status offenders, a group that includes many victims of abuse. We need also to protect youth from abuse when they are institutionalized outside the penal system as well as within it. Studies are underway to investigate abuse and neglect within residential institutions that seek to develop procedures for handling complaints of abuse within institutions, as well as finding out the nature, causes, and effects of such abuse. They will design ways to encourage reports of abuse, to establish ways of dealing with reports, and to take corrective action.[74]

The federal government also is encouraging states to establish youth-advocacy programs. Primary prevention is largely a matter of preventing a misuse of power.[75] Through its Developmental Disabilities program, federally-supported action has helped New Jersey, Michigan, and Illinois to establish advocates for youth in residential institutions (Delaware, Indiana, and New York are currently in the process of establishing such programs). One proposal to improve institutions relies on a voucher system to increase the power of client satisfaction. While this is of limited relevance to mistreated youth, it could serve as one way to help empower these teenagers and, if properly handled, be a good vehicle for teaching social skills. Finally, investigative reporters in the mass media have reaffirmed and expanded their commitment to accurately expose institutional abuse.[76] Institutional abuse, like parental abuse, flourishes in secrecy and isolation. We need to more consistently open institutions if we are to strengthen them in fulfilling their missions.

Mobilizing as a Community

If our understanding of abusive families is to be of benefit, it must become the foundation for action. The ecological perspective developed in this book implies that the action cannot be limited to intervention strategies designed to directly change the family or the environment at only one level. As frequently stated, the maltreatment of children and youth is a social indicator describing the quality of life in a community or a society. The problems of maltreatment, then, cannot be adequately addressed by only one segment of a community, be it helping professionals, abusive parents, or researchers. Based on this knowledge, we define our ultimate goal as the primary prevention of child maltreatment, and we foresee it being accomplished by the mobilization of the total community.

One model for such total community organization relies on concepts from the fields of evaluation research and marketing. Michael Patton developed an approach toward evaluation that involves the users of the evaluation throughout the process of research.[77] Applied to community organization for the primary prevention of child maltreatment, this concept means involving the total community in such a way that people are committed to and invested in the process of making society more supportive of effective child rearing.[78] From the field of marketing we draw on Philip Kotler's principles for nonprofit organizations.[79] These principles provide a systematic conceptual framework for selling and implementing a program of primary prevention in a given community. The initial step in the process of community mobilization for primary prevention is the identification and organization of relevant decision makers and information users.[80] We would suggest attempting to identify community people from among social-service professionals, city and county government officials, business and labor representatives, leaders in education and health care, and family members from diverse neighborhoods (including adolescents). An educational group-process with these people could be implemented to focus evaluation questions. This group would study, among other things, the insights into the developmental process as it relates to maltreatment and the ecological perspective proposed in this book.

The second stage of the process would break the larger group into smaller task groups which would view the geographic area of the community as a market and segment it into neighborhoods which would be defined around such variables as age, life style, socioeconomic status, and employment characteristics. It would also define formal and informal social networks around variables such as kinds of services and demographic characteristics. The task groups would then choose the targets for action. At this point ownership of decisions by community members is crucial. These decision makers and information users must identify the systems and the neighborhoods needing change and those already functioning in a preventive mode. Financial and policy support can be planned and given to those systems in the community identified as already providing child care, homemaker, home health, parent support, and recreation services. Of course, the community needs to identify and empower a leader to be responsible for coordinating the works of the task groups, monitoring the functioning of the subsidized services, hiring other part- or full-time workers to carry out the plans of the group, and coordinating public relations efforts.

As unmet needs are identified and commitment to programs for change are developed, they are presented to the total community in a systematic way through the use of a marketing model. The philosophy of primary prevention and our ecological perspective demand that these programs be planned to be supportive of all families rather than just those identified as high risk.[81] Possible agenda items include: identifying natural-helping networks and providing consultation services to them;[82] initiating a program of family-centered childbirth; developing exosystem supports particularly between family and school; planning a campaign to change the image of teenagers as troublemakers; or developing youth self-help and support groups.[83] Informal social systems such as neighborhood or support groups can be targeted and described according to demographic and other characteristics. Decisions related to the promotion variable revolve around use of mass media, face-to-face, and small group contacts to advertise the product. While mass media are important for public education, face-to-face contacts are essential for consultation in natural-helping networks. Finally, it is crucial that psychological as well as financial costs are studied, especially in such a sensitive area as family support for the protection of children and youth.

Hope for the Future

If people can be convinced that the wrong treatment they have received is really behind them and that they are not substandard individuals because they were abused, they tend to recover from the effects of abuse. We must get that message across to abuse victims and to the helping community as well so it will attempt to give them realistic grounds for believing that help is available. We are in the hope business if we are anything at all. Our interviews with mistreated youth convince us that it does happen.

Q. Do you think other kids who have had the same kind of trouble that you've had—is there any hope for them?
A. There is if they're strong. You gotta be very strong to handle something like that. You gotta be able to let the past be the past, not the present. Which I have. I have faced up to the fact that things like this do happen. And I'm not the only one. And I know it. The other kids that won't say nothing or won't do nothing about it are the ones who are hurting the most.

Q. Who helped you?
A. If it wasn't for the school counselor and the teacher and my girlfriend's mother, I wouldn't have made it through high school and got my diploma. I would have just ended it all.

Q. What was most helpful to you during this time?
A. I'd have to say my social worker. She was the greatest help. I don't know. It wasn't really my social worker, just the attention I got from her. She treated me like a human being. Not just like a little gnat that you walk over like my parents did.

Q. Was that really a big change?
A. Oh, yea. It really was. It changed my whole outlook on life. I thought I was just not good. She changed my whole outlook. I felt like a human being. I felt like I had something to live for.

These young people are making it because they found the caring community through its formal- or informal-support systems. Everyone needs this caring community, but the victims of maltreatment are critically dependent on it.

Q. Does it feel pretty risky?
A. Yea. It's like walking on thin ice. You gotta remember that the past is the past, too. And you can't walk around with these parents that are beating you up all your life. You can grieve over it, but grieve and then walk, you know. Go away from it. Yea, just don't get stuck there.

Our hope is that by approaching maltreatment ecologically and developmentally we can all get unstuck in dealing with this problem.

Notes

1. J. Garbarino, and U. Bronfenbrenner, "Research on Parent-Child Relations and Social Policy: Who Needs Whom?" (Paper presented at the Symposium on Parent-Child Relations: Theoretical, Methodological and Practical Implications, University of Trier, West Germany, May 1976).

2. J. Garbarino, S.H. Stocking, and Associates, *Protecting Children from Abuse and Neglect* (San Francisco: Jossey-Bass, 1980).

3. J. Garbarino, and U. Bronfenbrenner, "The Socialization of Moral Judgment and Behavior in Cross-cultural Perspective," in *Moral Development and Behavior*, ed. T. Lickona (New York: Holt, Rinehart and Winston, 1976).

4. M. Straus, R. Gelles, and S. Steinmetz, *Behind Closed Doors* (New York: Doubleday, 1980).

5. D. Walters, *Physical and Sexual Abuse of Children: Causes and Treatment* (Bloomington: Indiana University Press, 1975).

6. J. Valusek, *People Are Not for Hitting* (Wichita, Kan.: McCormick Armstrong, Co., 1974).

7. Straus, Gelles, and Steinmetz, *Behind Closed Doors*.

8. J. Benward, and J. Densen-Gerber, "Incest as a Causative Factor in Antisocial Behavior: An Exploratory Study," *Contemporary Drug Problems* 4 (1975): 32-35.

9. U. Bronfenbrenner, "Reality and Research in the Ecology of Human Development," *Proceedings of the American Philosophical Society* 119 (1975): 439-469.

10. J.R. Lebsack, "The American Humane Association's National Study on Child Abuse and Neglect" (Paper presented at the National Conference on Child Abuse and Neglect, April 17-20, 1977, Houston, Tex.).

11. L. Featherstone, "Family Matters," *Harvard Educational Review* 49 (1979): 20-56; E. Zigler, "Controlling Child Abuse in America: An Effort Doomed to Failure?" in *Critical Perspectives on Child Abuse*, ed. R. Bourne and E. Newberger (Lexington, Mass.: Lexington Books, D.C. Heath and Company, 1979).

12. "Human Ecology Forum," *Child Abuse and Neglect in Residential Institutions: Selected Readings on Prevention, Investigation and Correction* (Washington, D.C.: National Center on Child Abuse and Neglect, DHEW Publication no. 78-30160).

13. Children's Defense Fund, *Children without Homes: An Examination of Public Responsibility to Children in out-of-home Care* (Washington, D.C.: Children's Defense Fund, 1978).

14. B. Fisher, J. Berdie, J. Cook, J. Radford-Barker, and J. Day, *Adolescent Abuse and Neglect: Intervention Strategies and Treatment Approaches* (San Francisco: Urban and Rural Systems Associates, 1979).

15. Bronfenbrenner, "Reality and Research."

16. Garbarino, Stocking, and Associates, *Protecting Children.*

17. Ibid.

18. J. Garbarino, and N. Jacobson, "Youth Helping Youth as a Resource in Meeting the Problem of Adolescent Maltreatment," *Child Welfare* 57 (1978): 505-512.

19. National Academy of Sciences, *Toward a National Policy for Children and Families* (Washington, D.C.: U.S. Government Printing Office, 1976).

20. Fisher, Berdie, Cook, Radford-Barker, and Day, *Adolescent Abuse and Neglect.*

21. Ibid.

22. R. Herrenkohl, R. Herrenkohl, B. Egolf, and M. Seech, "The Repetition of Child Abuse: How Frequently Does It Occur?" (Paper presented at the Second International Congress on Child Abuse and Neglect, London, England, September 12, 1979).

23. J. Garbarino, and B. Carson, "Mistreated Youth in One Community" (Paper, Boys Town, Neb.: Center for the Study of Youth Development, 1979).

24. National Academy of Sciences, *Toward a National Policy.*

25. Fisher, Berdie, Cook, Radford-Barker, and Day, *Adolescent Abuse and Neglect.*

26. R. Helfer, "Basic Issues Concerning Prediction," in *Child Abuse and Neglect: The Family and the Community,* ed. R. Helfer and C.H. Kempe (Cambridge, Mass.: Ballinger, 1976); H. Martin, *The Abused Child* (Cambridge, Mass.: Ballinger, 1976).

27. R. Friedman, "Adolescents as People: No Kidding Around" (Paper presented at a conference on A Community Response to the Adolescent in Conflict, Jacksonville, Fla., February 1978).

28. Garbarino and Carson, "Mistreated Youth."

29. Fisher, Berdie, Cook, Radford-Barker, and Day, *Adolescent Abuse and Neglect.*

30. Garbarino and Jacobson, "Youth Helping Youth."

31. Fisher, Berdie, Cook, Radford-Barker, and Day, *Adolescent Abuse and Neglect.*

32. K. Armstrong, "How Can You Avoid Burnout?" in *Child Abuse and Neglect: Issues on Innovation and Implementation,* vol. 2, ed. M. Lauderdale, R. Anderson, and S. Cramer, Proceedings of the Second Annual Conference on Child Abuse and Neglect, April 17-20, 1977 (National Center on Child Abuse and Neglect, DHEW, Washington, D.C., 1978), pp. 230-238.

33. S. Copans, H. Krell, J. Gundy, J. Rogen, and F. Field, "The Stress of Treating Child Abuse," *Children Today* (January-February 1979): 22-35.

34. Ibid.

35. Fisher, Berdie, Cook, Radford-Barker, and Day, *Adolescent Abuse and Neglect.*

36. R. Helfer, and R. Schmidt, "The Community-based Child Abuse

and Neglect Program," in *Child Abuse and Neglect*, ed. R. Helfer and C. Kempe.

37. U. Bronfenbrenner, *The Ecology of Human Development* (Cambridge, Mass.: Harvard University Press, 1979).

38. Garbarino, Stocking, and Associates, *Protecting Children.*

39. A. Collins, and D. Pancoast, *Natural Helping Networks* (Washington, D.C.: National Association of Social Workers, 1976).

40. A. Gartner, and F. Reissman, *Self-help in the Human Services* (San Francisco: Jossey-Bass, 1977).

41. J. McCleave-Kinney, B. Madsen, T. Fleming, and D. Haapala, "Homebuilders: Keeping Families Together," *Journal of Consulting and Clinical Psychology* 45 (1977): 667-673.

42. R. Friedman, personal communication.

43. J. Cook, senior analyst, Urban Rural Systems Associates, personal communication, June 7, 1979.

44. Garbarino, and Jacobson, "Youth Helping Youth."

45. L. Lieber, and J. Baker, "Parents Anonymous and Self-help Treatment for Child Abusing Parents: A Review and an Evaluation," *Child Abuse and Neglect* 1 (1977): 133-148.

46. R. Friedman, personal communication.

47. R. Friedman, and C. Zeigler, "Therapeutic Foster Homes: An Alternative Residential Model for Emotionally Disturbed Children and Youth" (November 1979). Reprinted with permission.

48. K. Kenniston, *All Our Children: The American Family under Pressure* (New York: Harcourt Brace Jovanovich, 1977); National Academy of Sciences, *Toward a National Policy.*

49. M. Straus, "A Sociological Perspective on the Causes of Family Violence" (Paper presented at the annual meeting of the American Association for the Advancement of Science, Houston, Tex., January 6, 1979).

50. E.L. Phillips, E.A. Phillips, D.L. Fixsen, and M.M. Wolf, *The Teaching Family Handbook*, rev. ed. (Lawrence, Kans.: Bureau of Child Research, 1974).

51. A. Jurich, "Parenting Adolescents," *Family Perspective* 3 (1979): 137-149.

52. J. Hill, "The Family," in *Seventy-ninth Yearbook of the National Society for the Study of Education,* ed. M. Johnson (Chicago, Ill.: University of Chicago, 1980).

53. R. Friedman, "Child Abuse: A Review of the Psychological Research," in *Four Perspectives on the Status of Child Abuse and Neglect Research*, ed. Herner and Company (Washington, D.C.: National Center on Child Abuse and Neglect, 1976).

54. Straus, Gelles, and Steinmetz, *Behind Closed Doors.*

55. R. Helfer, "Report on the Research Using the Michigan Screening Profile of Parenting (MSPP)" (Washington, D.C.: National Center on Child Abuse and Neglect, 1978).

56. S. Bavolek, D. Kline, J. McLaughlin, and P. Publicover, "The Develop-

ment of the Adolescent Parenting Inventory (API): Identification of High-risk Adolescents Prior to Parenthood" (Paper prepared at the Utah State University, Department of Special Education, 1978).

57. A. Cohn, "Essential Elements of Successful Child Abuse and Neglect Treatment," *Child Abuse and Neglect* 3 (1979): 491-496.

58. E. Newberger, and R. Bourne, "The Medicalization and Legalization of Child Abuse," *American Journal of Orthopsychiatry* 48 (1978): 593-607.

59. N. Polansky, M. Chalmers, R. Buttenueiser, and D. Williams, "The Isolation of the Neglectful Family," *American Journal of Orthopsychiatry* 49 (1979): 149-152.

60. J. Garbarino, "Defining Emotional Maltreatment: The Message Is the Meaning," *Journal of Psychiatric Treatment and Evaluation* 2 (1980): 105-110; J. Garbarino, and D. Sherman, "High-risk Neighborhoods and High-risk Families: The Human Ecology of Child Maltreatment," *Child Development* 5 1 (1980): 188-198.

61. Fisher, Berdie, Cook, Radford-Barker, and Day, *Adolescent Abuse and Neglect*; Garbarino and Carson "Mistreated Youth;" P. Libbey, and R. Bybee, "The Physical Abuse of Adolescents," *Journal of Social Issues* 35 (1979): 101-126; I. Lourie, "The Phenomenon of the Abused Adolescent: A Clinical Study," *Victimology* 2 (1977): 268-276.

62. J. Manis, "Assessing the Seriousness of Social Problems," *Social Problems* 22 (1974): 1-15.

63. T. Gregory, personal communication.

64. Education Commission of the States, *Education Policies and Practices Regarding Child Abuse and Neglect: 1978* (Denver, Colo.: Education Commission of the States, 1978).

65. Ibid.

66. E. Polin, chairman, Education Commission, National Parent-Teacher Association, personal communication, January 15, 1980.

67. U. Bronfenbrenner, "Who Needs Parent Education?" *Teachers College Record* 79 (1978): 767-787.

68. Helfer, "Report."

69. Children's Defense Fund, Washington Research Project, *Children out of School in America: A Report* (Washington, D.C.: Children's Defense Fund, 1974).

70. Garbarino and Jacobson, "Youth Helping Youth."

71. P. Giannini, *Juvenile Court Demonstration Project: Improved Court Handling of Child Protective Cases* (HEW grant, awarded 1978).

72. Ibid.

73. T.P. Gullotta, "Runaway: Reality or Myth," *Adolescence* 13 (1978): 843-849.

74. J. Corrigan, "Institutional Abuse and Neglect: An Update," *Child Abuse and Neglect Reports*, June 1979, n.p.

75. G. Albee. "Politics, Power, Prevention and Social Change" (Paper

presented at the Vermont Conference on the Primary Prevention of Psychopathology, June 1979).

76. J. Garbarino, "Investigating Child Abuse," *Investigative Reporters and Editor's Forum*, Spring, 1979.

77. M. Patton, *Utilitzation-focused Evaluation* (Beverly Hills, Calif.: Sage Publications, 1978).

78. J.L. Jenkins, R.A. MacDicken, and N.J. Armsby, *A Community Approach: The Child Protection Coordinating Committee* (U.S. Department of Health, Education and Welfare, 1979).

79. P. Kotler, *Marketing for Nonprofit Organizations* (Englewood Cliffs, N.J.: Prentice-Hall, 1975).

80. Patton, *Utilization-focused Evaluation*.

81. Jenkins, MacDicken, and Armsby, *A Community Approach*.

82. D.L. Pancoast, "Helping Networks and Natural Neighbors: Finding Allies for Families," and A.H. Collins, "The Consultation Model Applied to Child Maltreatment Cases," in *Protecting Children from Abuse and Neglect*, ed. J.Garbarino and S.H. Stocking.

83. Garbarino and Jacobson, "Youth Helping Youth."

Appendix A:
Sources for Materials on
Child and Adolescent
Maltreatment

American Humane Association
Children's Division
P.O. Box 1266
Denver, Colorado   80201
(303)779-1400

Child Welfare League of America, Inc.
67 Irving Place
New York, New York   10003

Children's Defense Fund
1520 New Hampshire Ave., N.W.
Washington, D.C.   20036

Clearinghouse
National Youth Work Alliance
1346 Connecticut Ave., N.W.
Washington, D.C.   20036

National Center for the Prevention
   and Treatment of Child Abuse and Neglect
1205 Oenida Street
Denver, Colorado   80220
(303)321-3963

National Center on Child Abuse and Neglect
Children's Bureau
Office of Child Development, DHEW
P.O. Box 1182
Washington, D.C.   20013
(202)755-7762

National Committee for Prevention of Child Abuse
332 S. Michigan Ave.
Suite 1250
Chicago, Illinois   60604

National Network of Runaway and Youth Services
1705 DeSales St., N.W., 8th Floor
Washington, D.C.   20036

Parents Anonymous
National Office
22330 Hawthorne Blvd. Rm. 209
Torrance, California   90505
(213) 371-3501

Appendix B:
Maltreatment of Youth
Project Materials

Available from the Boys Town Center for the Study of Youth Development.
For detailed information write to:

> The Maltreatment of Youth Project
> Research Use and Public Service Division
> Boys Town Center for the Study of Youth Development
> Boys Town, Nebraska 68010
> (402)498-1580

Youth self-help group materials
> *A Guide to Creating and Maintaining a Youth Self-help Group.*

Awareness materials
> Pamphlet, "Youth Can Help"
> Essay contest guidelines
> Poster: "Little Kids Aren't the Only Ones Who Are Abused"
> "Walking on Thin Ice: Abused Adolescents Speak Out" (a 20-minute film on adolescent abuse featuring interviews with victims)
> Television News Feature on Adolescent Abuse (four 2-minute television reports on adolescent abuse)

Index

Index

Abuse: child-rearing practices and, 10–13; community standards concerning, 6; contributions of science to defining, 7; cultural support for, 6–7, 28; culture of violence hypothesis of, 10–11; definitions of, 5–15, 7; developmental damage resulting from, 7, 8, 9–10; individual differences in experience of, 125; issues in defining, 5; predicting effects of, 7; processes involved in, 28; relationship to neglect, 88; as a result of deviant parent-child relations, 20. *See also* Child abuse; Child maltreatment

Abused adolescents: and anxiety, 175; and blaming the victim, 193; and county jail, 205; different treatment needs of, 233; emancipation of, 198, 239–240; empathy with and foster care for 197–198, 233–234, 236; and homicide, 183–184; and institutionalization, 203–206; as people-in-need-of-supervision, 202; and juvenile delinquency, 180–183; low self-esteem, 173; and physical injury, 173; and pornography, 201; as runaways, 198–200; and self-esteem 173–175; and self-reporting by victim, 168; services to, 224; sex differences in effects of, 182; and social class, 169; as a social problem, 184; and social relationships, 176–177; and special protective service needs, 224–225; and status offenses, 202; and suicide, 179; as throwaways, 200; as victims, 191–194

Abuse-prone families, 31

Abusive families, 19, 25, 115–122; adolescence, and 133, 147; characteristics of, 4, 30, 34, 46, 73, 127–130; childbirth in, 51; emotional abuse in, 68; rejection of

children by, 72; and social isolation, 34; stresses on, 104; success rates in treating, 126

Abusive parents: background of, 111; mothers versus fathers, 130–131; as victims of circumstances, 114

Adolescence: American culture and, 135, 137, 138, 140, 145–146, 147; dependency of, 146; developmental changes in, 135–141, 144, 145; and family economic pressures, 145; parental adaptation to, 141–143, 144, 145, 147; and parental midlife changes, 143–145, 147

Adolescent abuse and neglect: lack of public and professional awareness of, 4

Adolescent maltreatment: adolescent assault as origin of, 114; authoritarian parenting and, 126, 141, 142, 147; autonomy as an issue in, 125; concept of inappropriateness and, 8, 10, 11–12, 13, 131; cultural basis for, 135; data, 116–122; as different from child maltreatment, 115–122, 132; emotional, 11–12; intervention in, 127; neglect, 14; physical, 11; and psychological abuse, 121; remedies for, 132; roots of, 135; sexual, 115, 147–148; short-term versus long-term, 127–130, 132; sources of reports of, 119–120; types of, 125–132

Adolescents: differences between children and, 112, 113; frustration in the schools of, 146

Albee, G., 26, 32, 237

Altemeir, W., 59

Aggression, 176

Alternative youth agencies, 227

America: and child maltreatment, 6, 9, 31, 32; justified violence in, 32; military service in, as setting for

child maltreatment, 80; suburban-
ization of, 26
American Civil Liberty's Union, 206
American Humane Association; National Study of Child Abuse and
Neglect Reporting, 9, 116, 236
American Medical Association, 60–61
Applied behavioral analysis, 219
Archimedes, 68
Asynchrony: as a factor in child
maltreatment, 28, 30
Attachment: contrasted to bonding,
58; discouragement of, as emotional abuse, 74; and humane
development, 60; in infancy,
56–59; and normal child development, 58
Authoritarian style of child rearing,
169, 178
Authoritative style of child rearing,
169

Behaviorist approach, 170
Big-Brother, 231
Billingsley, A., 34
Binet, A., 70
Blackstone, Judge, 195
Bowlby, John, 56
Brassard, J., 33
Brazelton, Berry, 51, 54, 59
Bronfenbrenner, Urie, 23, 24, 25, 27,
42, 67, 82, 92, 222
Burgess, Robert L., 72–73, 75
Burr, W., 29
Butterfield, Joseph, 61

Caldwell, B., 70
Campbell, A., 45
Caplan, Gerald, 33
Caregiver: adequate information for,
41; characteristics of, leading to
child maltreatment, 46; child's
rightful claims on, 73; contributors
to child abuse by, 28, 29; incompetence of, 29, 30, 103; factors
influencing effectiveness in role of,
29; abuse-prone, 31; information
necessary for, 73–74

Carnegie Foundation, 21
Charleston: survey of youth services
in, 229
Chicago, runaways in, 200
Child abuse: community awareness of,
224; cross-cultural review of, 55;
early explanations of, 69; as violation of child-care norms, 70–71.
See also Child maltreatment
Child abuse and neglect: hospital
shopping, 225; intervention in,
216; joint occurrence, 219; lack
of public awareness of, 4; research
needs, 235–236. See also Child
maltreatment
Child advocacy: and schools, 104, 227
Childbirth: American patterns of, 52,
53, 60; by Caesarean section, 52,
53; effects of modifying, 56–57;
and expansion of family social
integration, 61; effects of family-
centered, 59; 61; family-centered,
as an intervention strategy, 57, 61,
62; family-centered, and the
medical establishment, 54, 57,
58–59, 60–61; role of family-
centered, in family development,
52–54, 56, 57–58, 60, 62; impact
of, on human development, 54;
involving fathers in, 52–53; and
parent-infant bonding, 53; prenatal
period, 51; preparation for, 52; as
a psychological event, 53–56; as a
social event, 51–53, 55, 59–62, 60;
Western attitudes toward, 59
Child care: minimal standards, 220–
221
Child development: environmental
factors affecting, 23–27
Child maltreatment: antecedents of,
in infancy, 55; American military
as context for, 80; authoritarian
parenting and, 126, 141, 142, 147;
bias of source in reporting, 84–86;
China as cultural context for, 80;
class differences in, 131–132; collusion of spouse in, 89; compared to
wife abuse, 113, 115; conditions

producing, 31; coping with sufficient conditions for, 103; cultural relativism and, 69; data,
116-122; developmental differences in victims of, 111-115; as a
developmental and social problem,
69; as different from adolescent
maltreatment, 115-122, 132; early
parent-child contact and, 54;
ecological perspective on, 20, 21,
23, 82; elements of, 19; enhanced
parent-infant bonding as an intervention into, 60; factors placing
families at risk for, 20, 46, 54-55,
242; and family isolation, 34, 35;
history of the field, 19-20; importance of early attention to, 84;
as an indicator of quality of life for
families, 20, 83, 104; intergenerational transmission of, 111-112;
and kin networks, 43, 44; mapping
cases of, 83-84; mapping sources of
reports of, 85; medical model of,
20; necessary conditions for, 46,
100, 103, 105; neighborhoods, 44,
242; and parent-infant attachment,
61; predicting rates of, 84, 87-88;
prevention of, 35, 47, 241; and
privacy, 43, 45; rates of, 84; rates
of, related to socioeconomic factors, 84-89; relation to social indicators, 80, 83; remedies for,
132; reporting of, by schools, 99;
and schools, 97-105; social and
economic impoverishment and, 93;
and social isolation, 44; socioeconomic bias in reporting of, 84-
86; sources of reports of, 119-120;
studying human ecology of, 83; sufficient conditions, 45, 46, 100, 103,
104; third-party complicity in, 28;
underlying ethical issues in, 32;
underlying ethical issues in, 32;
underlying problem, 103; understanding of, 92-93. See also Child
abuse; Abused adolescents
Child pornography: 216. See also
Sexual abuse

Child protection, 217
Child rearing: value of socially-competent friend to, 91
Child sexual-abuse treatment program
in Santa Clara, California, 161
Children's Defense Fund, 102, 220,
238
Cleft palate: geographical mapping of,
82
Cochran, M., 33
Cognitive-developmentalist approach,
170
Collins, Alice, 232
Community organizing: and child
protection, 91, 241
Community standards: on child mal-
treatment, socioeconomic differ-
ences in, 85; concerning child mal-
treatment, and schools, 99
Competence: components of, 70;
relationship of emotional abuse to,
as developmental task, 70, 72;
factors affecting development of,
73
Condon, W., 54
Conger, Rand, 72-73, 75
Connecticut: abuse reports in, 114
Cook, JoAnn, 233
Coopersmith, Stanley, 73, 173-174
Cottrell, L., 29
Crisis intervention, 217
Crisis hot lines, 223
Cultural differences: in reporting child
maltreatment, 84-85
Cutler, C., 102

Dearborn's Dictum, 92, 215
Delaware: Developmental Disabilities
Program in, 240
Denmark: child-rearing practices in,
compared to United States, 142
Dependency: positive concept of, 48
Developmental Disabilities Program,
240-241
Dickens, Charles, 51
Domestic violence: independence as
an issue in, 114; power as an issue
in, 113-114; responsibility of

victim for, 114, 115. *See also*
  Abused adolescents; Child abuse;
  Child maltreatment
Downing, D., 14
Duncan, D.F., 30, 104
Door, The, 224
DuPont, Gloria, 197

Ecological approach: to helping low-
  income families, 89
Ecological perspective: on human
  development, 20, 21, 23-27, 28-
  30, 79, 234; on high-risk environments, 81
Ecology: of adolescence, 135
Economic deprivation: effects of, on
  families, 21-23; effects of, on individuals, 24, 81; and social impoverishment, 80
Economic impoverishment: and
  adolescent abuse, 121; and child
  maltreatment, 93
Economic policy: and sociocultural
  risk, 27
Education: life-course perspective for,
  103
Education, American: reformist
  critique of, 98, 102
Education Commission, States' Child
  Abuse and Neglect Project, 101,
  103
El Paso: military child and family
  demonstration project in, 80
Elder, Glen, 22-23, 29, 43, 45, 157
Elmer, E., 34, 168
Emotional abuse, 11-13, 67-75; actionable evidence of, 71, 74-75;
  of adolescents in short-term versus
  long-term abuse, 127; aspects of,
  74-75; behavior associated with,
  68, 73; definition of, 67, 68, 70,
  72, 73, 74; developmental and
  social aspects of, 69, 70; diagnosis
  of, 71-72; and parental rejection,
  72; by schools, 99; theoretical perspective on, 69; transcultural perspective on, 69

Empathy, 175-176
Empowering, 237
Endogamic incest, 155-156
Environment: relationship to growth
  and adaptation, 79
Erikson, Erik, 136, 143
Extended family: in foster care, 234

Face-to-Face, 224
Family: as changing microsystem, 27;
  as child's first microsystem, 24;
  conditions producing vulnerability
  to maltreatment in, 31; as context
  for child development, 54; dysfunction, 135; effects of economic
  deprivation on, 21-23; influence of
  ecological niche on, 93; in mesosystem relationships, 25; relationships with kin and neighborhood,
  42, 43; and school, 105; significance
  of childbirth to, 61; and social networks, 91; as source of sufficient
  conditions for child maltreatment,
  28; strengthening, 230
Family sexual abuse, 152
Family Teaching Model, 235
Family-centered childbirth, 231
Finkelhor, D., 151
Fischer, R., 46
Fontana, Vincent J., 5
Foster care, 226: in America, 103; as
  response to abuse, 121; therapeutic,
  234
Freud, S., 24, 159
Friedman, Robert, 28, 198, 234

Garmezy, N., 9
Gastil, R., 101
Gelles, R.J., 12, 101, 114, 218
Germain, C., 79
Giarretto, Henry, 161
Gil, David, 6, 9, 20, 28, 31, 81, 84-85
Giovannoni, J.M., 34
Goldwater, Barry, 219
Golembiewski, M., 200
Gordon, H., 68
Gray, J., 31, 61, 102

Great Depression, 21–23, 45, 147, 157
Green, A., 29
Group homes, 197
Guardian *ad litem,* 239

Hales, B., 56
Hall, G. Stanley, 136
Harborview Sexual Assault Center, 161
Harlow, Harry, 56
Hawaiian mothers: views of American
    child-care practices, 6
Health visitor, 231
Helfer, R., 19, 196, 236
High-risk families, 20: effects of
    birth-related interventions on, 57,
    58, 61; in high-risk neighborhoods
    81, 82, 89; in low-risk environ-
    ments, 91; and social isolation, 44;
    susceptibility to neighborhood in-
    fluence, 89
History of childhood, 216
Hobbes, Thomas, 194
Homebuilders, 203, 232
Hopkins, J., 59
Houston; runaways, 201
Houten, T., 200
Howard, Jane, 80, 91
Human ecology, 79; of child mal-
    treatment, 235–236. *See also*
    Ecological perspective
Hunt, M., 144

Identification, 171
Illinois: Developmental Disabilities
    Program in, 240
Illusion Theater, 157
Imitation, 170
Incest, 152; and age of victim, 154;
    necessary ingredients, 153–154.
    See also Sexual abuse
Incest taboo, 151, 219
Indiana: Developmental Disabilities
    Program in, 240
Infants, newborn: characteristics and
    capabilities, 53–54
Informal support system, 222
Inkeles, A., 70

Institutional abuse, 241
Intervention: agenda for action, 217–
    218; government, 216
Invulnerable children, 5, 44, 72, 172
Iranian revolution, 26
Italy: childbirth in community in, 60

Justice, B., 30, 104
Juvenile delinquency: and abuse, 168

Kandel, D., 142
Kempe, C. Henry, 19, 41, 102, 103
Kempe, R.S., 103
Kennell, John, 53, 54, 56
Kin networks: and child maltreatment,
    44; cultural patterns that weaken,
    44–45; and domestic violence, 43;
    effects of mobility on, 44; as social
    supports, 47; and families, 42;
    professional views of, 45
Klaus, Marshall, 53, 54, 56
Kohn, Melvin, 26
Korbin, Jill, 55
Kotler, Philip, 241
Kromkowski, J., 80
Kuhn, Thomas, 20

Lamaze method, 231. *See also* Child-
    birth
Latchkey children, 102
Law: family in, 194–196
Leichter, H.J., 45
Lenoski, E.F., 34, 46
Lesser, G., 142
Lewin's Law, 215
Lewis, M., 89
Locke, John, 194
Los Angeles mothers: spanking by,
    32
Lourie, Ira, 144
Lozoff, B., 58

McClelland, D., 70, 71
McEvoy, J., 32
MacFarlane, A., 54
McMorrow, Fred, 143
McQuarrie, Howard, 61

Macrosystem, 215, 234. *See also* Ecological perspective

Mahoney, M, 82

Maltreatment: characteristics of, 24; consequences of, 8; cultural support for, 32; definition of, 5–16; developmental issues, 4, 121; ecological issues, 4; as an indicator of problems in family, 8; necessary conditions, 31, 32; as personality malfunction, 20, 28, 29, 30; physical damage from, 8–9; as product of multiple factors, 28; as role problem, 29, 30–31; sufficient conditions, 28, 31, 34. *See also* Abuse; Abused adolescents; Child abuse; Child maltreatment

Maltreatment of adolescents: compared to wife abuse, 113–115; concept of inappropriateness, 112–113. *See also* Abused adolescents

Manis, J., 237

Manson, Charles, 184

Maternal and Child Health Committee, American Medical Association, 61

Materialism, 234–235

Maze of maltreatment, 214

Medical model, 223

Meltzoff, A.N., 54

Meiselman, K.C., 155

Michigan: Developmental Disabilities Program in, 240

Microsystem, 206, 215. *See also* Ecological perspective

Midolescence, 143–144

Milgram, S., 46, 193

Mitchell, W.E., 45

Moore, M.K., 54

Motherhood: effects of social change on, 55–56

Mulford, R., 70

National Academy of Sciences, 21

National Center on Child Abuse and Neglect, 19, 20, 151

National Committee for the Prevention of Child Abuse, 229

National Neighborhood Commission, 91

Natural helping networks, 231

Nebraska: court order for counselling, 198; parental consent for teenager counselling, 240

Neglect, 13–14. *See also* Abused adolescents; Child maltreatment

Neighborhoods: attitude of professionals toward, 89; character of; determinants of character of, 81; relationship to child maltreatment rates, 84; and child maltreatment, 44; consequences for families of, 42, 81; as context of abuse and neglect, 79–93; defining, 80–81; as ecological niche for families, 80; evaluating quality of, 80–81; "free from drain," 82, 86; goals for, 92; high-risk, 81, 83, 89, 91, 104; importance of, for poor families, 81, 89; contributions to child maltreatment, 82; mapping of child maltreatment cases, 83; measuring economic and social character of, 86; as social supports, 47, 88–89; as surrogates for kin networks, 44

New Jersey: Developmental Disabilities Program in, 240

New York (state): geographical mapping of cleft palate in, 82; investigation of abuse reports in, 197; status offense, 202; institutional abuse, 205; survey of youth services, 229; Developmental Disabilities Program in, 240

New York City: runaways, 199, The Door, 224

North Carolina: law against abandonment, 195

Nurturant touching, 157

O'Connor, S., 59

Osterrieth, Paul, 138–140

Pahl, J.M., 30
Pahl, R.E., 30
Pancoast, Diane, 232
Parent battering, 191. *See also* Abused
    adolescents
Parent-child relations: early parent-
    infant contact and, 53–54; and
    family-centered childbirth, 61;
    limitations of neonatal interven-
    tions in, 57; prenatal influences
    on, 51–52; social support for,
    55–56
Parent education: role of schools in,
    103–104
Parent Effectiveness Training, 146
Parent-Teachers Association, 238
Parental rejection: behavior associated
    with, 73; as central to emotional
    abuse, 72; effects on children of,
    69–70; relationship of, to abuse,
    72. *See also* Emotional abuse
Parental rights: termination of, 103
Parents: lack of cultural support for,
    141, 142, 146; midlife changes in,
    143–145. *See also* Abused ad-
    olescents
Parents Anonymous, 161, 222, 232
Patton, Michael, 241
Paykel, E., 30
Pelton, Leroy, 131
Pennsylvania: investigation of abuse
    reports in, 197
People's Republic of China; rélation-
    ship of economic deprivation and
    social impoverishment in, 80; social
    control in, 48
Permissive style of child rearing, 169
Physical abuse, 10. *See also* Abuse;
    Abused adolescents; Child abuse;
    Child maltreatment
Physical punishment: connection with
    psychological development and
    social competence, 7; cultural
    norm of, 147
Piaget, Jean, 70
Plansky, N., 34, 72
Poverty: and abuse, 131, 132; and

need for social resources, 81; as
    social concept, 81
Privacy: and child maltreatment, 43,
    45; costs of, 48; cultural support
    for, 47; as necessary conditions for
    child maltreatment, 46; social cost
    of, 41–42; and social isolation, 44;
    as threat to information exchange,
    41–42; value of, 41, 45
Protective services, 225–226; burnout,
    227–228; multidisciplinary team,
    226
Psychodynamic approach, 170
Psychological abuse: relation of, to
    becoming an abusive parent, 111.
    See also Emotional abuse
Psychopathic incest, 156. *See also*
    Sexual abuse
Psychotic incest, 156. *See also* Sexual
    abuse

Rejection, 172, 177–178; psycho-
    logical effects, 178. *See also* Emo-
    tional abuse
Rheingold, Harriet, 56
Riesman, David, 42
Risk: age-related, 126–127; develop-
    mental, 24; economic, 21–23;
    exosystem, 26; macrosystem, 27;
    mesosystem, 25; microsystem, 24,
    27; of maltreatment, 8; nature ver-
    sus nurture in producing, 20–21;
    relative and variable nature of, 23;
    sociocultural, 23, 24, 25, 26, 27
Rockwell, R., 157
Rohner, Ronald, 55, 69, 73
Rossi, A., 55, 60
Rotenberg, M., 42
Runaways, 196, 240

St. Paul, Minnesota: *See* The Door;
    Face-to-Face
Sander, L., 54
San Francisco: survey of services avail-
    able, 229
Santa Clara County: active service
    program in, 152

Schneider, C., 31
Schools: as accessories to child maltreatment, 99; adolescent culture
and, 139; adolescent frustration
with, 146; American, and local
values, 101; American culture
definition of, 102; and child
advocacy, 104, 105; and child maltreatment, 97–105; as child's link
to community, 102–103; as component of efforts against maltreatment, 101; culpability of, for child
maltreatment, 99; as focal point for
efforts to support families, 93; as
initiator of efforts against maltreatment, 100; issues concerning
role of, in child maltreatment, 98,
99–101; mesosystem relationship
of family and, 25, 105; as microsystem, 27; as models for child
care, 101–102; and necessary conditions of child maltreatment, 105;
neglect of deviant children by, 102;
and parent education, 103–104;
passivity toward child care standards, 99–100; as positive models,
224; potential for effect on conditions supporting maltreatment,
100; preventive role, 236, 237–238;
as replacements for work, 146;
reporting of abuse cases by, 99,
119–120; role of, in addressing
conditions for maltreatment, 103;
and social isolation, 102; and sufficient causes of child maltreatment, 104; as support systems, 102,
103
Schreiber, 60
Self-help groups, 196, 232
Sexual abuse: of adolescents, 115,
147–148; challenges to professionals, 162; data, 120–121; definition of, 151; effects of, 159–160;
and family dysfunction, 155; and
father-daughter dyad, 154; incidence of, 152; and physical force,
153; and poor marital relationship,
157; problem of, 9, 13; reasons for

termination, 158; and reconstituted
families, 155; role of mother, 156;
socioeconomic character of perpetrators, 153; and stepfather-
daughter relationship, 155; and
strength of incest taboo, 154;
symptomatic effects, 159; and
threat or use of force, 157–158;
treatment, 160–161. See also Incest
Shakespeare, W., 27
Simon, T., 70
Slater, Philip, 42, 43
Social conscience, 215–216
Social impoverishment: and child
maltreatment, 82, 93; defined, 80
Social integration: and family-centered
childbirth, 61; and quality of life,
43; and role management, 30; significance of childbirth to, 61; and
stress, 44; and work life, 30
Social isolation: in America, consequences of, 47; in American
society, 41–42; causes of, 34–35;
and child-rearing, 177; dangers of,
46; and family response to stress,
147; fault for, 34; implications for
intervention, 35; importance of,
in child maltreatment; intervention
into, 47; as key to child maltreatment, 31; preventing identification
of abuse, 75; and privacy, 44; as
result of privacy, 41–42, 43; and
schools, 102; and sexual abuse, 159
Social networks: and families, 91; and
human development, 33; role of
schools in building, 105; of school-
age children, 112. See also Social
supports
Social supports: as focus of family-en-
vironment analysis, 80; isolation of
new mothers from, 55; lack of, in
teenage pregnancy, 52; and stress,
42–44; and suicide and depression,
43
Socioeconomic segregation: and family
well-being, 82; and social impoverishment, 91. See also Social Networks

Society: role of, in supporting child-
care norms, 71
Spock, Dr. Benjamin, 146
Stack, Carol, 44, 45, 89
Stark, R., 32
State: relationship of, to American
child, 102; role of, in protecting
children, 8
Status offenders, 240
Steinmetz, S., 12, 101, 114, 218
Straus, Murray, 12, 32, 43, 101, 114,
218, 235
Stress: as contributor to problems,
42–43
Stresses: of social impoverishment, 82
Support systems: and the family, 47,
61–62, 230–232; functions for
individuals, 33, importance of, to
family, 33; loss of, in childbirth
process, 54; schools as, 102, 103.
See also Social supports
Sweden: legislation, 219, 240

Tacoma; Homebuilders, 229 232
Teaching Family Model, 146
Teenagers: public image, 192. See also
Adolescence
Texas: law on physical force and chil-
dren, 32, 195
Thomas, W.I., 27
Totalitarianism, 216
Trause, M., 56–57
Tronick, E., 73
Types of adolescent abuse, 167–168.

See also Abused adolescents

U.S. Supreme Court: approval of corporal punishment by schools, 99
Uviller, Rena, 206

Valusek, John, 218
Viano, E.C., 32
Vietze, P., 59
Violence: cultural acceptance of, 101,
114; in the family, 218–219, 235.
See also Domestic violence
Voos, D., 54
Vulnerability: increased by low in-
come, 81

Warren, Donald, 81
Webb, W., 42
Weeping in the Playtime of Others,
204
Weissman, M., 30
Wife abuse, 113–115. See also Vio-
lence; Domestic violence
Wilde, Justice, 195
Wilensky, H., 30
Wooden, Kenneth, 204
Work place: parents', effect on chil-
dren, 25, 26
Wynne, Edward, 42

Young, L., 30, 34
Youth Self-Help Groups, 161

Zigler, E., 101

About the Contributors

Michael Cohen, M.D., is a director of Adolescent Medicine at Montefiore Hospital in New York.

Bruce Fisher is project director for the study of abused adolescents, by the Urban and Rural Systems Associates, based in San Francisco.

Mary Fran Flood is a graduate student in the School of Social Work at the University of Nebraska.

Robert Friedman is director of Adolescent Programs for the Florida Mental Health Institute in Tampa, Florida.

Peter Giannini is supervising judge for the Dependency Section of the Los Angeles Juvenile Court.

Ira Lourie is director of Child Abuse and Neglect Projects at the National Institute of Mental Health in Rockville, Maryland.

Norman Polansky is Regents Professor of Social Work with the University of Georgia in Athens, Georgia.

About the Authors

James Garbarino is associate professor of human development at The Pennsylvania State University and was a Fellow and director of the Maltreatment of Youth Project at the Center for the Study of Youth Development at Boys Town. He received the Ph.D. in human development and family studies from Cornell University in 1973. Dr. Garbarino's research includes the study of the human ecology of abusive families. He is the author of numerous articles and one other book, *Protecting Children From Abuse and Neglect: Creating and Maintaining Family Support Systems.* In 1975 he was named a Spencer Fellow by the National Academy of Education, and in 1979 he won a Mitchell Prize from the Woodlands Conference on Growth Policy for his paper, "The Issue is Human Quality: In Praise of Children."

Gwen Gilliam is a science writer for the Boys Town Center for the Study of Youth Development. She has written in the behavioral sciences for *Human Behavior* and *Pacific News Service* and in other areas for *Omaha,* the *Sun, Fever,* and *Alternative Media.* Ms. Gilliam currently copublishes *beef* tabloid. In 1978 she was graduated from the University of Nebraska at Omaha, where she was named Outstanding Journalism Student for that year.